C000233182

First published in the UK in 2010 by Circle Books
Circle Publishing,
One Victoria Villas,
Richmond, Surrey
TW9 2GW
Phone: 020 8332 8400

Telford's Quay, South Pier Road
Ellesmere Port
Cheshire CH65 4FL
Phone: 0151 350 6200

Authors
Geoff Hide and Andy Hunt

Editor
Kristina Pedder

Design
Ian Legge

Illustrations: Ian Legge
Photographs: Charles Hood

Printed in Slovenia on behalf of Latitude Press Ltd

ISBN: 978-0-9564813-0-6

The Expedition Manual

Taking your diving further

Foreword

For more than 50 years the British Sub-Aqua Club has been at the forefront of the exploration of our undersea world. Diving expeditions have played a central part in this discovery process. The enthusiasm nurtured by the BSAC for expedition diving is demonstrated by the unexpectedly wide range of expeditions supported, from the discovery of unknown local dive sites through conservation projects to underwater explorations of international importance. My own distant training with the BSAC has led me in the past to experience a small part of expeditionary diving, including my involvement with the Mary Rose project in the Solent and a brief opportunity to discover the wonderful world beneath the Arctic ice.

I am delighted, therefore, to introduce this new manual, which I feel sure will generate enthusiasm for diving expeditions and provide the tools to conduct them safely. I am also certain that this book will make diving expeditions accessible to many more people and will stimulate the thrill of discovery for future generations of divers.

Table of contents

Chapter 1

What is an expedition?

For most people, the word 'expedition' conjures up images of famous explorers battling against the elements to conquer mountains, cross deserts, explore rainforests to find long lost cities, or endure the cold of the polar regions to reach the poles. History is littered with tales of expeditions and many of the names associated with them are familiar – for example, Livingstone, Scott, Shackleton, and more recently Fiennes.

You may think this is an odd way to start a book focusing on diving expeditions – recalling memories of famous land-based expeditions – but as we shall see there are many parallels and lessons we can learn from the great explorers. After all, to carry out the dive you have to get to the site and you will normally have some sort of base, whether it is floating or on land.

YAMAHA
115

Expedition leaders

Expeditions and leaders

Sport diving has its share of underwater explorers. Those first taking up the sport in the 1950s were probably inspired by the black-and-white films of Hans and Lotte Hass. After the Second World War the name of Jacques Cousteau above all became, and remains, synonymous with the sport. The films of his adventurous expeditions exploring diving locations all around the world, carrying out diving research and promoting his diving equipment have undoubtedly inspired many people.

However, diving expeditions are not just organised by the famous. There are thousands of unsung expedition leaders in all the diver-training organisations in the UK, and throughout the world. These are the divers in diving clubs who organise regular diving expeditions throughout the year.

Expedition leaders may also earn a living in the sport diving industry, offering expeditions through the dive schools and the other commercial organisations in which they work.

So, what is the role of the expedition leader? An expedition leader is the person who is appointed to control and supervise the activities of a diving expedition. The leader should be a willing volunteer, and needs to have an appropriate level of training and experience for the expedition they wish to organise. No manual is a substitute for proper training and experience, but in these pages you will find a wealth of ideas to help you understand how an expedition works from start to finish.

Expeditions for all

The dictionary definition of an expedition is 'a journey with a purpose'. A diving expedition is simply a 'group of divers going diving for a purpose'. By this definition, technically any dive is an expedition. However, most divers would probably agree that diving expeditions are usually a bit more than just another packaged diving holiday; and in practice include diving that extends their personal diving experience, takes more effort to organise, and ventures somewhere they haven't been before.

Expeditions need to be led, but if you do not want to lead, you may want to participate in the team carrying out the expedition. Expeditions can be suitable for all levels of divers, including inexperienced divers with few dives. For example, the Gun Rocks Project organised by Tyneside 114 Aqua Club in the 1970s pioneered archaeological diving, and a number of divers experienced their first dives in open water on that expedition. This was possible because the diving took place at an ancient cannon site in 6 to 15m of water, which at slack water was safe enough for these inexperienced divers.

CASE STUDY 1.1

A one-day club expedition

The wreck of the Chris Christenson is one of the most famous dive sites in the Farne Islands, off the north-east coast of England. It lies in a strong tidal stream just off Longstone island. Nearby there are many other excellent sites, which can be dived at varying states of the tide for second dives.

A total of six divers want to dive this site, using one of their diving club's own boats. The expedition leader is an experienced diver who has dived these sites a number of times before.

The story

A few days before the trip, at a club meeting, the expedition leader checks that the divers' qualifications and experience are matched to the dive, agrees who is to tow the boat and to help keep costs down makes arrangements for car sharing. Slack water, as calculated from the tide tables, will be at 11.00am, so a timetable is agreed to make sure that the first wave of divers enter the water just before slack and the second wave on slack water.

The expedition leader also checks that he has at least two people qualified, competent and confident enough to handle the boat on their own, and also that the boat is in full working order.

The long-range weather forecast looks good, and all the divers agree to call the expedition leader at a set time the night before the dive to check that the dive is still likely to proceed or whether they need to resort to a back-up plan.

On the day of the dive, the expedition leader obtains an up-to-date forecast as a final check. The team set off from home at 7.00am, collect the boat and by 9.30am they have arrived at Seahouses harbour, parked the cars, checked the boat and equipment, checked the first-aid equipment including the oxygen kit, paid harbour dues and launched the boat. They contact the coastguard to check their radio and advise their intentions, and then head out to the site.

Having dived the site many times before, it is easily located with both the GPS and transits. By 10.30am the first two pairs of divers have entered the water with instructions to return up the shot line and be on the surface after 30 minutes.

The boat team recover the divers of the first wave and with their assistance kit up quickly. After a quick check to ensure the tide is still slack enough, they enter the water with instructions to ascend up the cliff face and surface under a delayed surface marker buoy after 40 minutes.

At the end of the dive the divers are recovered and the boat heads off to anchor for lunch. This allows for an adequate surface interval before the second, scenic dive, when divers enter the water in the same pairs and the same order with instructions for a maximum dive time of 60 minutes.

After recovery of the last divers from their second dive, the expedition team head back to Seahouses harbour.

By 5.00pm the boats are retrieved and the coastguard advised of their safe return. The team members retire to a nearby pub to complete log sheets, settle dive costs and exaggerate the size of the seals they saw on the dive.

How they did it

This trip is typical of many well-executed club expeditions.

- The purpose is simply to dive a particular site safely.
- The expedition leader puts together an initial plan a few days before the dive, checking that he has the team to carry out the diving (two boat cox'n, someone to tow the boat and divers capable of the diving).
- Checks on the tides to determine slack water and ensure the timetable is realistic.
- Checks on the weather to assess whether the dive site will be diveable that day.
- On arrival at the launch site, the expedition leader delegates various tasks to ensure they are completed efficiently and on time.
- There is a clear dive plan to ensure that all divers are able to dive the wreck, have a sensible surface interval and a good second dive.
- The day ends at a reasonable time and the necessary administration and dive finances are completed in a sociable atmosphere.

What this summary does not reveal is the full extent of the effort that has gone on in the background to make the expedition run efficiently.

- Boats and safety equipment have been maintained so they work as expected.
- The team has learnt how to operate efficiently by diving regularly together.
- Members of the team have trained to obtain specialist skills such as boat handling, chart work and position fixing, radio operation, GPS operation and oxygen administration.
- Common sense logistics (such as sharing cars) ensure that the expedition is completed within a reasonable budget.

Diving with a purpose

Expeditions are organised for a wide variety of purposes. Quite often an expedition may achieve a number of different things. The primary purpose of a wreck diving expedition, for example, may be to dive a new wreck, but with secondary or supporting purposes to survey the wreck and conduct a basic marine life survey. An expedition leader, however, needs to take care not to lose track of the main purpose of the expedition.

Location of previously undived sites: wrecks or reefs

The discovery of a new, undived wreck is something that excites most divers. The UK in particular has a very rich underwater heritage with an estimated 100,000 wrecks in UK waters. Even after 50 years or so of sport diving, many are still to be found and dived. Continued advances in underwater sonar equipment can only increase the knowledge of wreck locations. New dive sites are not just limited to wrecks: underwater pinnacles, reef systems, walls, caves and tunnels are nature's own attractions and are a lure to divers.

CASE STUDY 1.2

A boat charter to a remote coast

A diver is interested in diving a remote part of Scotland with the idea of locating and diving some offshore pinnacles, diving some known but less accessible dive sites and looking for some new wreck sites.

The story

Twelve months before the proposed expedition, the potential expedition leader contacts divers who might be interested in the plan. A suitable dive platform has been found: a hard boat booked for four days but at the end of the quiet season to take advantage of off-peak charter rates. A core group of divers, known to the expedition leader, confirm their interest and pay a deposit. A deposit is paid to secure the boat.

Over the next 11 months, the expedition leader has a number of things to do, particularly to fill the remaining places on the expedition. A minimum level of experience is set. All divers must have completed a minimum of 100 UK dives and have the ability to launch a delayed surface marker buoy from mid-water unaided. A written expedition plan is produced containing all the necessary information to attract divers to the expedition and ensure they have all the relevant details.

With nine months to go, the expedition team is complete and all deposits have been paid. Completed application forms have been received by the expedition leader and contain important contact details, relevant medical information (for example, about allergies) and details of next of kin for use in an emergency. The diving platform is a liveaboard boat and so accommodation and food are not major issues for the expedition leader. At one stage there is concern that the ratio of male/female divers would make cabin-sharing arrangements awkward, but this is soon resolved.

Research is conducted into the wrecks in the vicinity, particularly those of the SS Cathcart Park and the SS Nyland, using the BSAC wreck registers and the UK Hydrographic Office. Some intelligence is gleaned from local skippers and divers who claim to have dived the wrecks.

Two of the expedition team travel to a library in Edinburgh, but turn up very little apart from a small paragraph on the back pages of a newspaper (the front pages covering the Titanic disaster, which by coincidence was at the same time). A shipping company involved in the rescue of crew from one of the ships is also contacted. The search area is narrowed for one of the wrecks – the Cathcart Park – but there is not much information on the Nyland.

It is clear that some specialised wreck-finding equipment is going to be required. A team member manages to borrow a side-scan sonar from colleagues for a small fee. A berth on the boat is reserved for a trained operator and the expedition members agree to cover the operator's expenses.

Advice on magnetometers, and prices for equipment hire, are sought from a professional survey company. It turns out that the local geology with its magnetic anomalies would not make a magnetometer search easy.

The expedition leader decides that focusing on finding the unknown wrecks for the duration of the expedition would probably mean missing some of the other expedition purposes and would also raise the cost considerably. A decision is taken to concentrate on using the side-scan sonar only.

In order to be environmentally sound and keep costs down the expedition leader plans car-sharing arrangements. One of the members has a four-wheel drive vehicle and offers it for transporting most of the heavy equipment, leaving space for passengers in smaller vehicles. Car parking arrangements are confirmed.

Another team member is delegated to be the official expedition photographer.

Others are asked to manage the expedition accounts, obtain two-way hand-held radios and ensure diving equipment spares are available.

Six weeks before departure, the remaining charter boat fees are paid and the expedition is ready to go.

Two weeks before the expedition, the team undertake some shake-down dives of their own to check that all their equipment works. The expedition leader dives with new members of the team to check their skills and attitude.

Day one: the team gather on the quayside in Oban to meet the skipper and load equipment onto the boat. Everything has gone according to plan, except that the operator who was expected to come with the side-scan equipment is not available – the team will have to learn to use it themselves.

The original aim of the first day is to carry out a check-out dive and then dive one of the known sites on route to the south-west tip of Mull. Time now also needs to be spent learning how to use the side-scan sonar.

The side-scan sonar is set up and the team carry out the different roles that are necessary; some launching and deploying the towfish at the rear of the boat, others operating the processor on the bridge and others operating the hand-held radios communicating between the two. The expedition leader liaises with the skipper to determine an appropriate course and speed for towing the fish.

Practise with the side-scan sonar threatens to put the first day behind schedule, so a shakedown dive is carried out on a different site to that planned. The dive proves to be mediocre, but does satisfy the requirement for a check to make sure divers and kit are working.

More practise with the sonar is carried out on the way to the second dive site, the SS Meldon. As the operators try to detect a known wreck, it becomes apparent more practice is required interpreting the output from the sonar.

Day two: the boat weighs anchor early and departs for the Torran Rocks. Today's aim is to attempt to locate the Cathcart Park.

After some hours of searching with the sonar, nothing other than some interesting rock formations are identified. Falling back on the research, divers are deployed into a small bay next to one of the rocks with a plan to search the 15m contour for signs of wreckage. They return to report a strengthening tide and much kelp hindering the location of wreckage.

The skipper reveals he has information from a local salvage diver about a wreck that is possibly the Nyland. It lies in deep water and is completely upside down nearby. To maintain team morale and seize an opportunity to dive a nearby virgin wreck, plans are changed and preparations are made to dive the reported wreck. A shot is deployed and the echo sounder shows a wreck-like trace. There appears to be very little tide at the surface. A trapeze and spare decompression gas are deployed on the shot line by the first wave of divers, before the second wave enter the water. The wreck is located in 50m, upside down as expected, but the currents at depth are stronger than expected and make the descent difficult causing some buddy pairs to terminate the dive early.

During the surface interval the opportunity is taken to use the side-scan sonar to search for the SS Cathcart Park again. A possible interesting target is identified and located. The echo-sounder trace also suggests a wreck-like object. Unfortunately there is quite a strong tide running on the site, but two experienced divers kit up to investigate the site. Some time later they surface having had a fantastic dive on an uncharted underwater pinnacle, and as predicted by tidal information, in an increasingly strong tide.

The boat proceeds to the site of a known wreck of the ammunition ship SS Ostende, where the final dive of the day takes place.

Day three: the weather forecast is not favourable and a strengthening southerly breeze prevents diving on the Torran Rocks area. A couple of dives are conducted on sheltered back-up wall dive site, which turns out to be a site of large underwater basaltic rock columns with many crawfish.

Day four: the weather has improved but the side-scan sonar is broken; a fault has occurred on the cable somewhere between the towfish and the processor unit. A 6–60m wall is identified on the chart instead and chosen as the first dive site. Then the boat steams back to Oban with dives conducted on a couple of shallow 6m sites on the way back.

Back in Oban, the kit is offloaded. The skipper and the team are thanked before everyone heads home.

Over the next couple of weeks, an expedition report is written up, slideshows and presentations given and an article submitted for publication in the diving press.

How they did it

- This expedition needed considerable effort in advance to make it happen.
- The expedition leader formed a core team and got sufficient interest and enough deposits to confirm the boat booking. It is not uncommon for boats to be booked a year or more in advance, so this is a crucial

- Booking a liveaboard boat helps to simplify some key aspects of the expedition such as accommodation, food and gas supplies.
- Good food on an expedition is important for nutrition and maintaining the team's physical strength, but also in boosting morale and maintaining their mental strength.
- There is the initial problem of filling spaces on the expedition to make it affordable to all. Divers from other clubs are actively sought. The required diving standard is not lowered, however, and the expedition leader focuses on the number of dives applicants have done and checks a key skill to measure their experience.
- What appear to be mundane details are sorted out quite early on. One consideration was cabin allocation. As well as the male/female ratio, which influences cabin allocation, there will inevitably be someone who snores.
- Specialised wreck-finding equipment is required and fortunately one team member is able to use their contacts to obtain it for the expedition at minimal cost.
- The expedition leader manages the team to make the best of the skills and resources they offer. Although not necessarily as glamorous as providing the high-tech kit, there are still necessary jobs to make the expedition go smoothly, for example organising the transport, sourcing hand-held radios, doing the accounts, and keeping the photographic record.
- Research into the dive sites is extremely valuable and the better the research the more likely you are to find the dive site. Although the internet makes some research easier, not all information is on the web and there is no substitute for contacting and possibly visiting libraries, archives, the coastguard, the RNLI and other sources to get the information.
- As with all expeditions, there will be problems to solve. The sonar operator cannot come at the last minute, and the weather and on-site conditions force changes in plans.
- Not all changes to plan occur as a result of problems, any change can introduce unexpected challenges. The skipper of the boat had found details of the Nyland, which was one of the targets so the group dived one of the expedition targets, but conditions were not ideal.
- Overall this was an expedition with a definite purpose, an expedition leader supported by a competent dive team and a co-operative skipper. The result, despite the problems, is an enjoyable and productive expedition with a follow-up article in a leading diving magazine.

CASE STUDY 1.3

Environmentally aware

Well-known scientist David Bellamy, himself a member of the BSAC, organised two marine life surveys in the 1960s and 1970s, which in turn became benchmarks in their fields.

The stories

Operation Kelp was a massive environmental science project, involving 25 BSAC branches and 262 members from all over the UK, who took kelp samples from the North Sea as a method of checking pollution. Bellamy and the divers won the British Sub Aqua Jubilee Trust's Duke of Edinburgh prize in 1969 for their hard work.

Project Starfish collected kelp, mussels and starfish for research on pollution in the food chain. The project has gone down in history as one of the largest single undersea biological investigations ever undertaken.

The results

Today, many UK clubs and individuals are involved in marine life projects in support of the work of the UK's Marine Conservation Society.

Club divers can produce valuable data to support the work of professional marine scientists.

A wreck survey

The production of a wreck site map is becoming more popular as divers becoming increasingly aware of our rich wreck heritage. Sometimes the challenge of properly mapping a wreck may provide additional stimulus on its own, or it may be the desire to produce a map for the benefit of other divers through the publication of a wreck guide or for an underwater archaeological project. BSAC runs a wreck appreciation course, which covers basic survey techniques. The Nautical Archaeological Society, in the UK, is a good source of information for such projects and provides more advanced courses.

Commemoration

In recent years there have been a number of expeditions to investigate wrecks at the request of families of former crew, who may have been lost during the sinking. Members of the British Sub Aqua Club have been involved in some very high-profile expeditions. For example, in 2002 a joint military and civilian expedition to the South China Sea successfully recovered the bell of the battleship HMS Prince of Wales, with the authorisation of the Royal Navy, to prevent it being looted by less respectful divers and to return it to its rightful owners.

Deep wreck exploration

Gas mixtures containing helium and advances in rebreather technology have opened up deeper wrecks for exploration. However, these sites bring additional demands for meticulous expedition planning particularly in the underwater teamwork aspects required to undertake such dives safely.

Reef and wildlife surveys

We all have a role to play in the stewardship of our planet. There are many examples of ongoing scientific expeditions to monitor reef systems and other habitats across the world to assess the impact of human activity on underwater ecological systems. For example, in 2006, *Exercise Jurassic Shark* was carried out by members of the Joint Services branch of BSAC. This major scientific expedition worked with a local university to tag sharks off the Cocos Islands and to draw attention to the plight of the sharks (see *Science in warm waters*, page 155).

Training expeditions

The purpose of an expedition may just be to extend a diver's own range of diving skills. The wreck and the scenery underwater may provide a stunning backdrop or a vehicle to complete the training, but the primary purpose is the training itself.

It is usually best to keep the number of aims of an expedition low and therefore complete each one well. This is particularly important for training expeditions where the focus should be on the development of the diver rather than other purposes, which may distract and even become a safety issue.

For example, suppose you have a team of divers wishing to gain the skills to dive a particularly deep wreck by doing a trimix course and you also wish to survey the wreck itself. It would be best to organise a separate training expedition to complete the course and become competent and confident in the deep-diving skills and then head off to survey the wreck rather than trying to complete both simultaneously.

Chapter 2

Researching dive sites

The oceans are vast places, and the distance between the site of a good and a bad dive may be only tens of metres, so getting it right can be difficult; more so if you are diving a previously unexplored site. It makes sense to research dive sites in advance and there are many good sources of the necessary information. An expedition to a known site may need much less research than one to an unknown site but, nevertheless, background information can lead to more interesting and safer diving. This can make all the difference to the divers' enjoyment and to whether the expedition fulfils its objectives. Diving on an intact wreck is great: missing it and hitting the muddy bottom beside it is disappointing.

The importance of information

Visiting a favourite wreck can be made much more interesting if you have photographs of the ship before it was wrecked. The story behind the wreck can bring it alive for the expedition members. Photographs, plans and other information also make the diving safer by helping divers to orientate themselves and recognise features for pilotage underwater. Pictures can help at briefing sessions as visual cues, for example, to show the location of possible dangers such as snagged netting.

Sometimes information about familiar sites can raise some interesting questions. The case study of the motor yacht Alastor, later in this chapter, gives details of an example where a very familiar wreck in Northern Ireland, which had been dived for more than 50 years, turned out to be a different wreck altogether.

It is even more important on expeditions to unknown or unfamiliar sites to have as much information as possible. Knowledge of tides, quality of the seabed, what to expect and exact positions are essential for safe and interesting diving. The type of information and the precision of that information will depend on the type of diving you wish to do. A wreck dive or wreck search will demand an accurate position while for a drift dive, tidal stream information may be more important than exact position.

POP ART
SURREAL THINGS
LEONARDO DA VINCI
SHIPWRECK
WGS 84 POSITIONS
777

Charts

Using charts

Where better to start than with a map? A chart is a map that gives more information about the sea and seabed that it does about the land. Charts tell us about: the coastline, the topography (both above and below water), buoyage, lights, dangers, depths of water, quality of the seabed, the tides and currents and some limited information about wrecks. They are a valuable resource for dive planning.

The UK Hydrographic Office (UKHO) is the UK's main provider of navigational charts of all areas of the world in the form of its Admiralty range of products. Charts come in both paper and electronic form. Paper charts can be obtained from most chandlers and specialist suppliers. Sources near you are easily found on the internet.

Electronic charts, of various types and brands, can be viewed at home on a computer to plan your expeditions. Many can be used with Global Position-fixing System (GPS) units onboard a dive boat, not only to view the chart but also to plot the boat's position on it. With the correct compatibility, voyage-planning and position-fixing data generated on your PC can be transferred to the chart plotter onboard and can be used to translate your plan into action.

There are two types of electronic chart. A raster chart is an image of a traditional chart stored electronically and essentially it looks like the paper chart and has the same detail. A vector chart is produced by storing the basic information from a chart in such a way that each time the chart is viewed, it is generated from the original data. Vector charts are much more flexible and additional features (such as more detail) can be added and integrated into them. Generally, vector charts use less computer memory and can therefore be recalled more quickly.

Other publications are available in the Admiralty series, such as tidal stream atlases and pilots. These give information on tidal streams and passage planning, harbours and moorings. Other organisations, such as

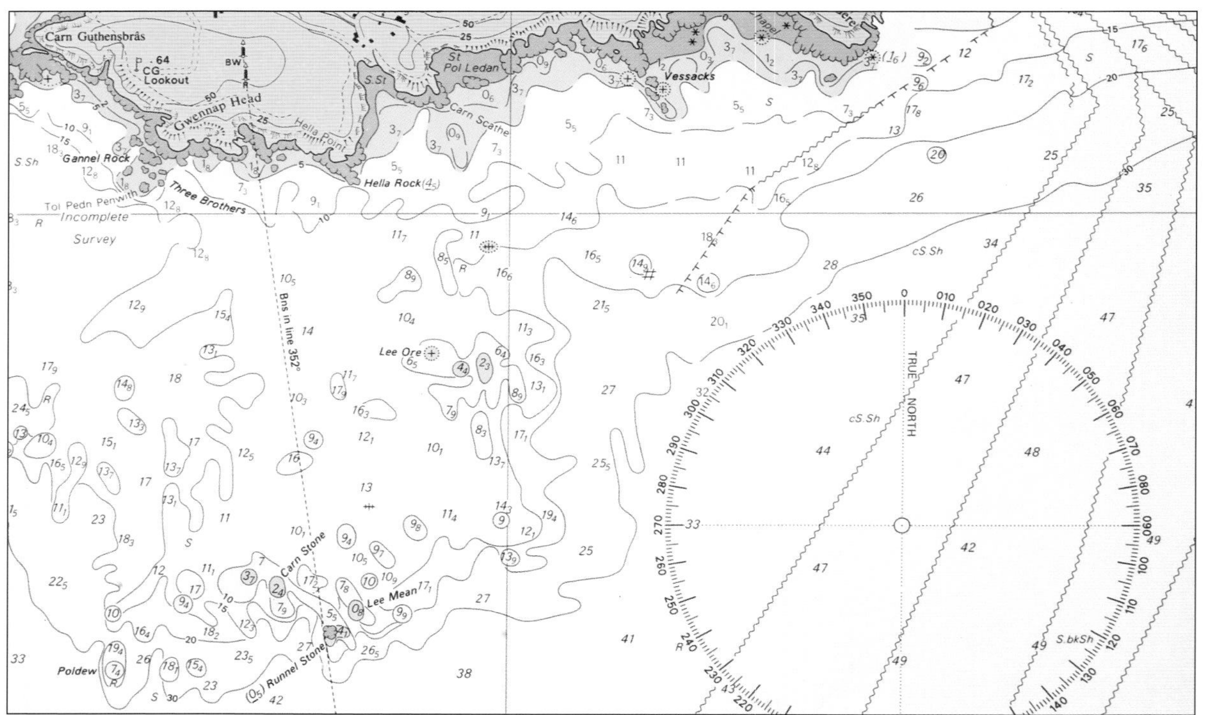

Admiralty charts contain detailed infomation about the seabed and features on land that are useful for navigation

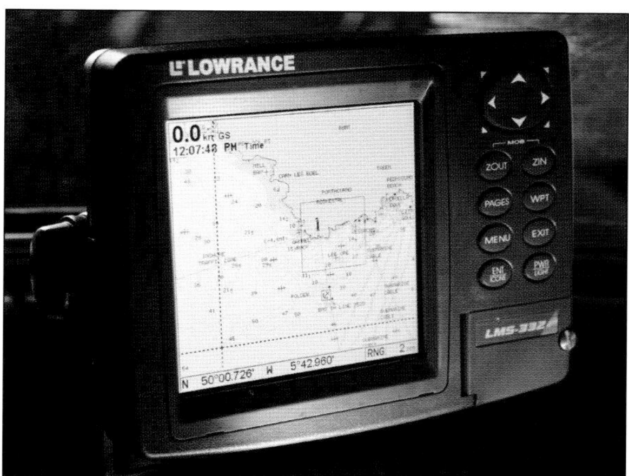

An electronic chart can be viewed on a chart plotter

yachting organisations, also produce charts and associated material.

As most data is collected by the UKHO, most chart and tidal information is ultimately based on their surveys. In this section, we will concentrate on their Admiralty charts. Plenty of information can be found in Admiralty charts about dive sites if they are used carefully. For example, information on position, depths, tidal streams, quality of the bottom, important landmarks, and navigational hazards is there among much more.

The key to using Admiralty charts is *chart 5011*, actually a booklet, which contains a description of the meanings of the symbols and conventions used on the charts.

It is important to remember that charts are primarily used by commercial shipping around the world and therefore the information shown is designed to help shipping to avoid hazards such as rocks, reefs and wrecks. These hazards are the very things that divers are interested in, however, you always need to think carefully about the information presented on the chart. Depths, for example, may be shown as the depth of clear water and not as the depth to the hazard.

Wreck information

Chart 5011 shows a number of different symbols for wrecks, which can be used to gain information about a wreck of interest or alert you to prohibited historic wreck sites that you may not be allowed to dive on (see *Protecting our underwater heritage*, page 132).

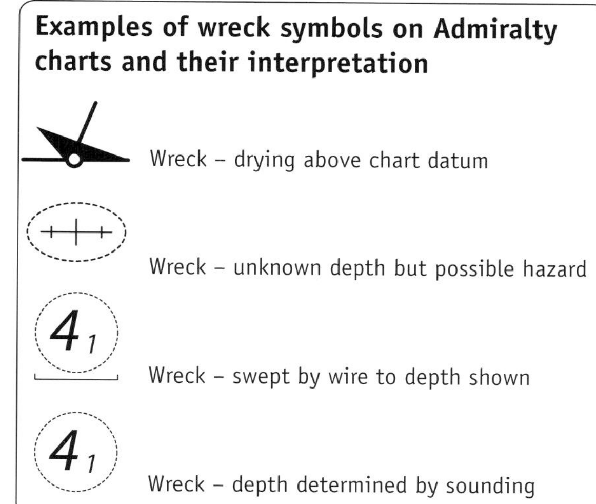

You can find out if the wreck breaks the surface or uncovers at low water - providing you with an easy way of finding the wreck. The type of wreck symbol used tells you the depth of the wreck and how this was measured but beware, the usefulness of this information will depend on the way the depth was measured. For example, a depth obtained by sounding may give a good indication of the overall depth of the top of the wreck but may not identify any particularly shallow parts (such as masts) or deeper parts. A depth obtained by wire sweep may only identify the shallowest part of the wreck, such as a mast, and may not represent the depth of the main part of the wreck. Worse still, a depth obtained by wire sweep may only say that there is clearance above the wreck to the depth shown, which is the information shipping needs to proceed safely. The wreck itself may be much deeper or perhaps completely flattened.

Care needs also to be taken when interpreting the depth information itself as, although a chart may be up to date, the survey may have been conducted many years ago and wrecks deteriorate with age. For example, the wreck of the Nordhuk lies in 30m off the Isle of Skye. The bridge section of the wreck was virtually intact in 1984, but today is flattened on the seabed.

An important depth to note is the charted depth of the seabed surrounding the wreck. You can use this

Wreck symbols

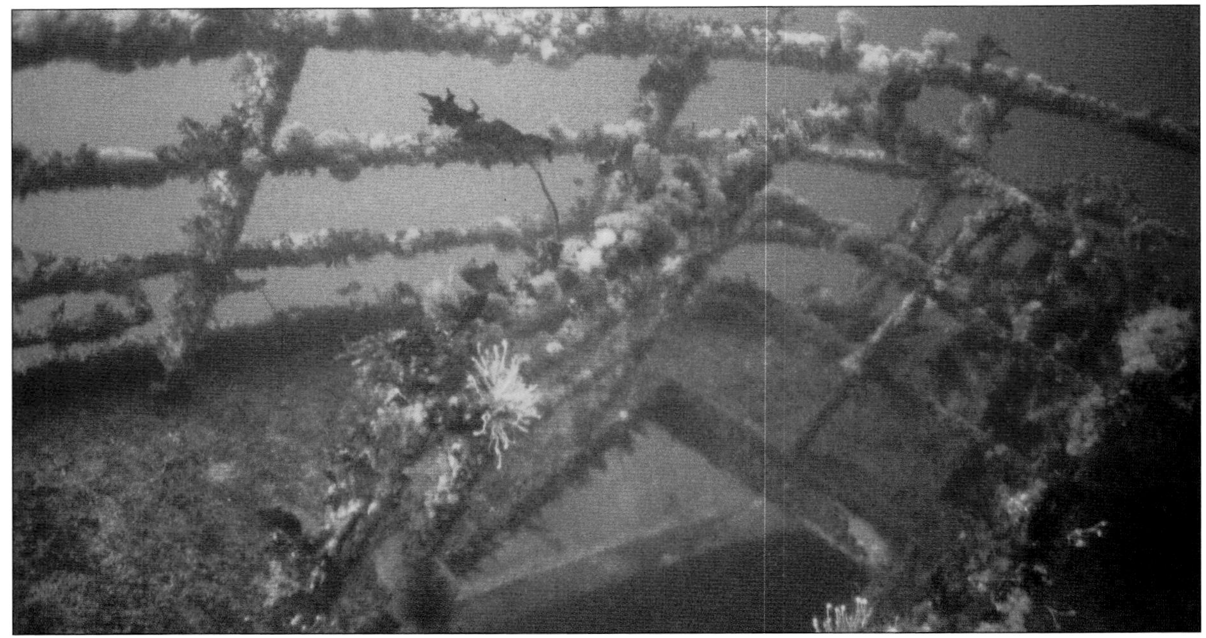

The railings of the Nordhuk were intact in 1984

The Nordhuk's bridge section stood proud of the seabed in 1984

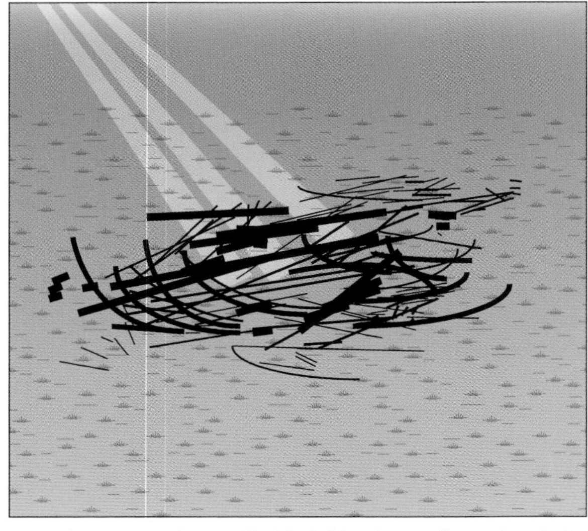

Since 1984 the Nordhuk's bridge has collapsed and the average depth of a dive on the wreck has increased

information to calculate the deepest depth you may encounter (although the current often generates a scour next to large parts of wreckage, which is deeper than the seabed) and your expedition plans should take into account this worst-case scenario.

The charted depth is the depth of water above the seabed at chart datum, which in the UK can be considered to be approximately the depth at the lowest low tide.

To calculate the depth of water on the day you want to dive a site, look up that day's tide height in a tide table for the proposed location. If you add the tide height at high water on the day to the charted depth, you will know the predicted depth of water on site at high tide. The rule of twelfths, or tidal curves, can be used for a more accurate prediction of depth on site at a particular time (for more detail see the BSAC manual *Seamanship: a guide for divers*).

Underwater topography

Charts also contain much relevant information for expeditions based around marine biology, or the exploration of underwater features such as drop-offs, rock formations or caves. The type of seabed can be easily found using *chart 5011*, for example, rock (R), sand (S), or silt (Si). In some cases sufficient information is provided to enable you to determine the rock type or marine life associated with your proposed dive site, for example, chalk (Ck), quartz (Qz), weed (Wd), mussels (Ms), and oysters (Oy). This information might direct you to appropriate sites if, for example, the purpose of your expedition was to record marine life or geology. Perhaps knowledge of the rock types might help you to find specific underwater features – for example, limestone is often associated with cave formation.

Often it is the changes in depths that are of most interest to divers. Underwater contours join areas of equal depth and these can be used to predict how steep or shallow a slope is. In general, the closer together the contours are the steeper the slope. But beware, close contours don't always mean a drop off – especially if you are looking at a small scale chart, that is one that shows a large area in less detail. Often these can turn out to be a muddy slope.

A good indicator of a drop off is when the contours merge together – although again, this may not always be the case. Sometimes, you need to take several pieces of information together. Even where contours merge, the seabed is unlikely to drop away steeply if it is sandy. Close contours may be more interesting on a rocky seabed.

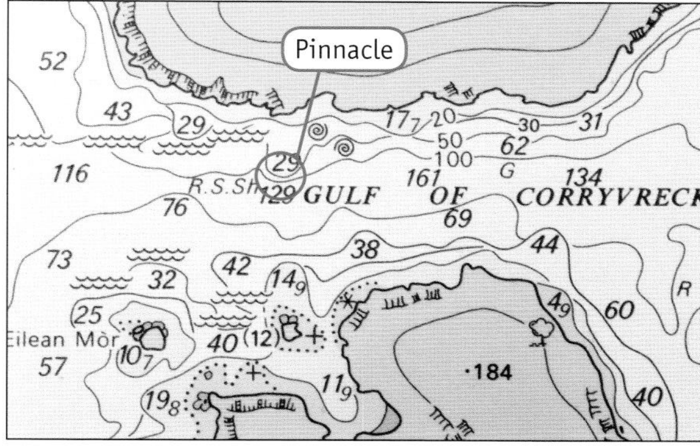

Close contours on a chart can indicate a drop off as shown here around the Corryvreckan pinnacle

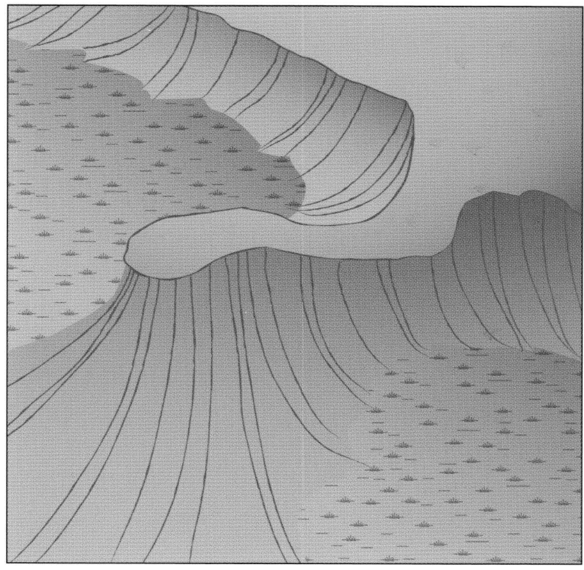

Looking at the chart we see that the Corryvreckan pinnacle is, in fact, an underwater promontory

Sometimes, it is helpful to try to relate the underwater contours to surface features. For example, guarding the entrance to Lochmaddy (Loch nam Madadh) harbour, in the Outer Hebrides, there are two prominent, sheer sided, rocks known as the Madadhs - (Madadh is the gaelic word for dog). Marked on the chart is an underwater feature, showing drop offs, of similar size and in line with the Madadhs. When you dive this feature, it is an underwater replica of the Madadhs.

Madadh Mor and Madadh Gruamach, looking south west

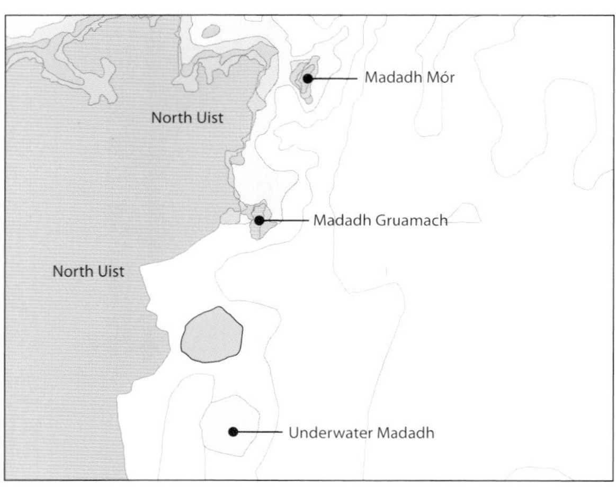

Contours on the chart suggest that the underwater pinnacle will be a third Madadh

Other sources of information

There are many sources of information about dive sites, some in print, some out of print and increasingly a repository of information on the internet. The quality of information in dive guides can vary from accurate positions and detailed information to some inaccurate and misleading information. If possible, you should check your information against different sources and cross check with information from charts.

Diving magazines can provide more up-to-date articles, which introduce new sites or update information on known sites. Also out-of-print books and magazines, found in second-hand bookshops, can often reveal information that has been lost - dive sites tend to be found and then forgotten as time passes. What may have been known and dived as a site in the past, may be new and interesting to you. Alternatively, it may be interesting to use past information to develop an expedition to record the deterioration of wrecks or changes in marine life.

Your expedition may be going to sites unknown to you, but others may have dived or researched them. Many diving clubs post their own information on dive sites on their websites.

Before planning your expedition, you should try to find out what is already known about your proposed sites and try to identify if there is anything new to discover. Are the positions of wrecks already known, are there descriptions of the dive sites, have any marine surveys been carried out, do the dive guides mention any sites that are un-dived but may be worthy of diving?

Detailed information about wrecks can be found from a number of sources. The main one in the UK is the Wrecks Section of the UKHO (see the UKHO website). Their booklet, *NP96*, gives details of the services they offer. In general, you will have to pay for the information in advance. It is not necessarily expensive but you need to be specific about the information you want - either by naming the wreck or giving an exact location. If you choose to search a large area, you should obtain a quote first. The wrecks section has information on more than 50,000 wrecks.

Another comprehensive source of information in the UK is a series of books - *Shipwrecks of the British Isles* - by Richard and Bridget Larn. These are organised regionally and each lists every known shipping casualty covered (at least accurate at the date of publication) in order of date of casualty. Some diving information is given.

Off Scotland by Ian Whittaker is a comprehensive list of losses around the Scottish coasts. Arranged by position, this gives brief details of each ship/aircraft and its loss. Some positions seem accurate: others are estimates. Another classic book is Charles Hocking's *Dictionary of Disasters in the Age of Steam 1824-1962* and the more recent *Modern Shipping Disasters 1963-1987*.

Newspapers can be a useful source of reference for wreck stories, pictures and other interesting information but may not be useful for detailed positions. It may be necessary to trawl through them with great detail to establish the full story. For example, in January 1900, the papers report a ship running aground at Dunbar, a popular diving location in Scotland - a wreck hunters dream? Unfortunately, if you follow through the reports over the next month, you find that much effort (including the use of explosives) was put into clearing away rocks and refloating her. Newspapers can be a great source of pictures but you need to respect copyright. Generally, photographs older than 50 years are not subject to copyright, but on the other hand originals held by newspaper archives are of much superior quality and permission to use should be sought from the publisher.

Archaeological and marine biological academic journals can be good sources of information on specific sites for marine organisms or for sites of archaeological interest. These will probably not be available in your local library, but may be found in university libraries, although access can be a problem. If you have access to the four main UK copyright libraries - British Library (London); National Libraries of Scotland (Edinburgh) and Wales (Aberystwyth); Boddleian Library (Oxford) - you will almost certainly be able to get them there

In your search for new dive sites for your expedition, do not forget the knowledge of boat skippers. They may have taken parties of divers to your site before and may be able to give you information or pass you onto clubs who can.

Looking for new sites

If you are looking for unknown dive sites, this can be much more difficult. For scenic dive sites, using a chart is the best approach. Try to identify sites that have interesting features—drop offs, a rocky or boulder-strewn seabed, underwater pinnacles or perhaps tidal streams for drift diving.

Wrecks can be more difficult to locate. The chart and Admiralty records are probably the best source of information to locate wrecks that are not often dived. Or you can delve into sinkings, using the library, the shipping publication *Lloyds List* and newspapers as sources of information. These rarely have detailed information on positions and a great deal of research may be needed before you can be certain of an exact location. Remember also, to follow the stories to completion. As already mentioned, many ships are recorded as running aground or sinking in shallow water and then a small note in the newspaper several weeks or months later may reveal that the ship has been re-floated or salvaged.

CASE STUDY 2.1

It's all in the name

For over 50 years the Alastair has been a popular wreck for scuba divers in Northern Ireland. She lies in 25m of water in Ringhaddy Sound in Strangford Loch. The identity of the wreck has never been challenged until 2003.

The story

In 2003, a team of divers from Queen's University, Belfast, set out to practise underwater survey techniques on the wreck to develop their skills. The team, led by Thorsten Brabetz, set out to conduct detailed measurements of the wreck, and to assess their techniques they compared these with a photograph and the plans of the Alastair. To their surprise, they found inconsistencies between their survey and the plans - for example, there was no evidence of the big panoramic windows that should have been on the Alastair. When they measured the length of the wreck, they realised that it was longer than it should have been.

Something was wrong. Was this the wreck of the Alastair? The team set about searching the records to try to identify their ship.

The Alastair was launched in 1937 and was always presumed to have been the vessel that caught fire and sank in Ringhaddy Sound in March 1946. However, the team traced the history of the Alastair only to find that she was being used as a floating restaurant in Paris and was afloat until 2002! This clearly was not the vessel that everyone had been diving.

After more than a year they tracked down a vessel that could have been the wreck. The motor yacht Vita was owned by Thomas Sopwith, the builder of the first world war plane the Sopwith Camel, and was launched in 1926. The Vita's dimensions corresponded to those of the wreck. In 1929, the Vita was sold to John Shelley-Rolls, a great nephew of the author Mary Shelley who wrote *Frankenstein*. He renamed the Vita as the Alastor. Ten years later, the ship was requisitioned by the Royal Navy for conversion to an auxiliary vessel for the war effort. The team traced her movements using the Royal Navy's *'Pink List'* and *'Red List'*, dated lists of all Navy vessels and their status. In 1943, she was transferred to Belfast to support the incoming Atlantic convoys. In 1946 she was sold to the Greek government, but was held in Ringhaddy Sound awaiting removal to Greece when she caught fire and sank.

How they did it

- The history of the ship needs to tie in with the wreck location.
- Careful work using a combination of detailed research, detailed measurement of the wreck by manual methods and side-scan sonar can reveal a wreck's true identity.
- The shape and dimensions of the wreck need to match plans and photos of the ship. So the team produced a three-dimensional, computer-generated picture of the wreck, based on the surveys conducted.
- An essentially amateur group can carry out and document this type of project, with the right support.
- This project was supported by the Nautical Archaeological Society 'Adopt a Wreck' scheme and the team received considerable help from the society.

This project shows how easy it is to dive on a familiar wreck without knowing its real identity.

Three-dimensional computer graphic of the Alastor generated from survey data

The Alastor

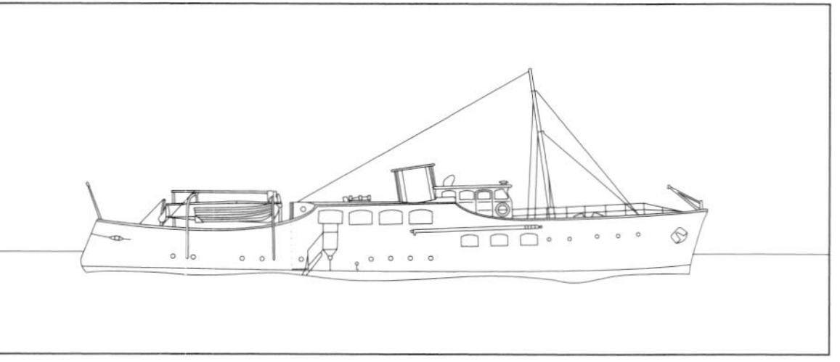

The Alistair

(All images of the Alastor are reproduced with permission from Thorsten Brabetz, Queen's University Belfast Sub Aqua Club)

The Alastor

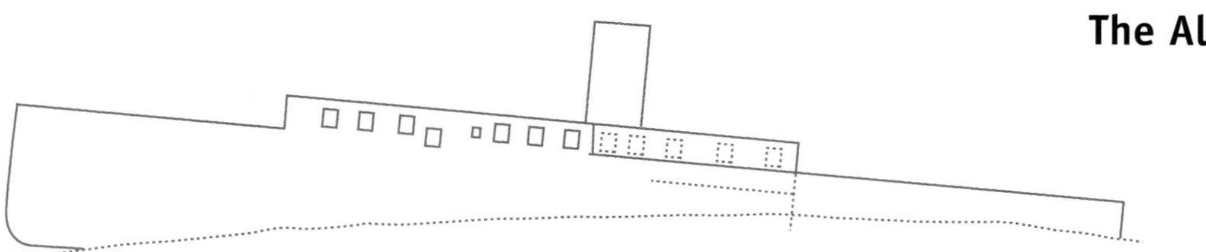

Port-side elevation drawing of the Alastor based on the survey measurements.

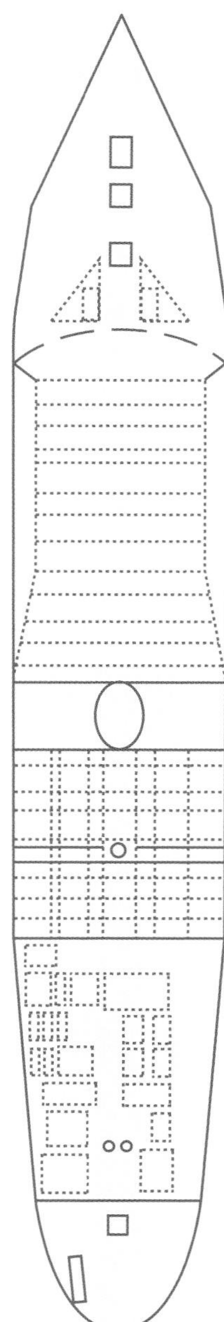

Results of the survey of the Alastor

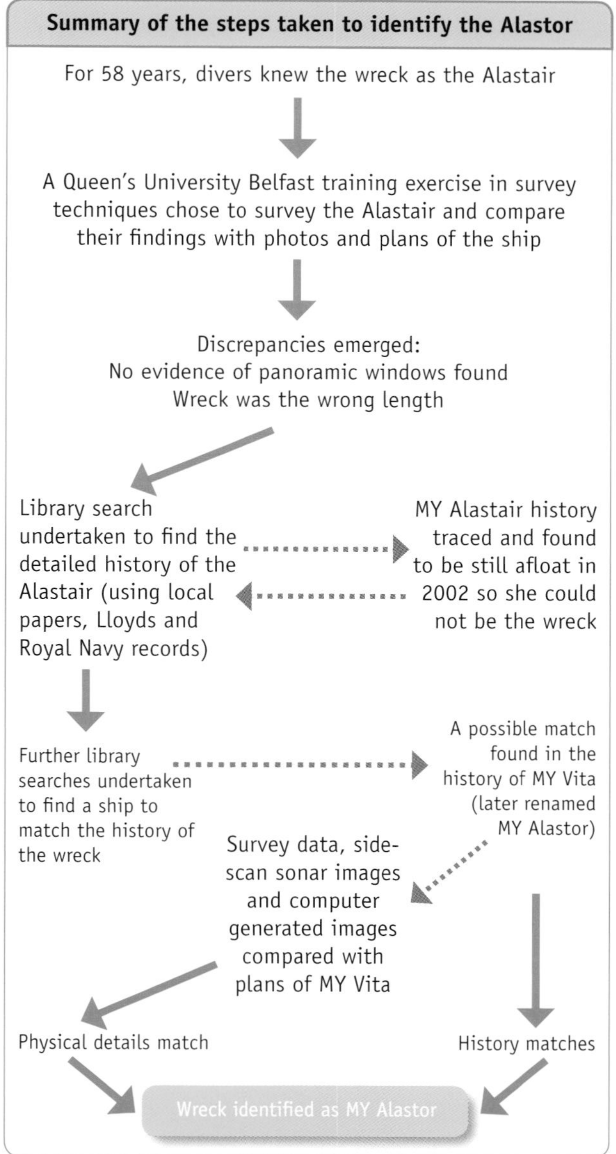

Chapter 3

Planning and organisation

Proper planning and preparation greatly increase the chances of success for a diving expedition. For major expeditions, this can mean starting to plan a year or more in advance of the diving itself. Once an expedition leader has a clear idea of the purpose of an expedition, the what, where, when, who and hows become important.

When an expedition plan is finally put into practice the team should develop a daily routine quite quickly so that everyone on the expedition team knows what they need to do and when. This, of course, does not happen by accident. For the expedition to be a success, the expedition leader will need to do most of the following.

- Put together and manage an expedition team.
- Thoroughly plan and prepare in advance of the expedition, including backup dive plans and emergency evacuation plans.
- Liaise with the boat skipper and provide advice on dive planning and managing during the expedition.
- Provide organisation and direction as required and continually drive the expedition forward.
- Ensure all diving is carried out within safe diving practices. The British Sub Aqua Club publishes its recommendations on safe practice in *Safe Diving*, which is freely available on the internet.
- Set a good example to the team.
- Take on the role of diving officer for the team members during the expedition.

Planning for, and dealing with, emergencies is a particularly important area and is dealt with elsewhere. Chapter 4 is dedicated to risk assessment and Chapter 8 is about dealing with emergencies.

DUI
DUI
Breathing

Outline plan

Initial investigation

Once the purpose of the diving expedition has been defined, some initial investigation work is required to assess its feasibility. It is useful to put together a brochure with some basic information on the expedition, to inform potential team members and attract divers to join the team.

Purpose

What type of diving is involved in the expedition? Is it simply an expedition to explore some wrecks that you haven't visited before, or is it to complete a detailed marine life survey of an offshore reef. Chapter 1 gives many examples of expedition purposes.

Location and dive sites

What are the planned dives and where geographically are they? The location and the likely water temperature will help some divers make up their minds whether they wish to participate.

Details of the planned diving, particularly depth and times and also the nature of the dive sites, may also determine the qualifications required of the expedition members. It is necessary to specify any special diving experience required for the proposed dive sites. This may be defined just in terms of paper qualifications plus a minimum number of dives, such as sports diver plus 30 dives since qualification. Or you may have more demanding requirements for a deep technical-diving expedition.

Timing

When will the expedition take place? For many diving expeditions the best timing coincides with neap tides and a high likelihood of good weather conditions, particularly in the UK. Some sites can only be safely dived a few times a year on the best neap tides. However, these may not coincide with the best time for the availability of expedition members. The timing may require some thought, even at this early stage, to ensure the best chances of building a good team.

Transport

How are you going to get to the expedition base, and to the dive sites? What diving platform will you need? Many club expeditions in the UK rely on using divers' own vehicles to transport people and kit, so some assessment of capacity may be needed early on. You may need to carry personnel and equipment, and tow boats.

Some initial consideration and research into planes, trains, car routes, ferries and boats is necessary. Check that the services you are interested in are operating when you would like to go, and find out whether there are any restrictions, particularly on transport of weights or gas cylinders.

Confirm that the dive boat you prefer is definitely available and try to provisionally book a slot. It is not uncommon for boats to be booked up at least 12 months in advance.

Accommodation

Accommodation will have to be chosen early on in the planning stage, to ensure suitability and availability. More thought about allocating rooms, provisioning, and cooking will be required later.

Costs

At this stage the why, what, where, who and how questions should have been answered in the broadest terms and this should be sufficient to give a good estimate of the cost. Many expeditions are self-financing, so the total cost is a critical piece of information. Whatever is stated at this time sets the expectations of potential expedition members, so it is usually best to opt for a value from the upper end of your estimates. If the cost actually comes in below this, then it will be a welcome refund.

Make sure you are really clear about what is included and what isn't. For example, nitrox is usually available on liveaboard boats, but may not be included in the price. Also, highlight any external funding that you are seeking and make it clear the implications of getting the funding (or not) to the overall cost.

Outline expedition plan

It is best to summarise all of the above into an outline expedition plan. This does not have to be too long: it may often fit onto a single sheet of A4 paper. Writing it down will not only help consolidate the ideas, but it forms the basis of a brochure to help attract participants or funding.

Forming the expedition team

An expedition leader with a team who can work together well stands a much better chance of running a safe and successful expedition.

Building the team, then, is a crucial part of the early expedition organisation. The expedition leader needs to know about the team's diving qualifications and experience to make sure that they meet the requirements of the expedition. Everyone must be comfortable with the purpose of the expedition, how it will be run and in particular the nature of the diving. It is important to set the correct expectations for the team. They need to be fully aware of what the expedition goals are and how the team will achieve them, so that they will not be disappointed.

Selecting the team

Start with the personalities of the team, not their diving qualifications. Those with a helpful, positive attitude and a willingness to learn may well be better team players than more qualified people without these attributes. For most expeditions there will need to be some compromises and the expedition leader should manage his team to bring out their strengths and resolve any conflicts.

A check of diving qualifications, however, is still extremely important. A diver certification card is not normally enough and the expedition leader should confirm that the diver has the experience to match. For example, a diver with a basic paper qualification but with 600 dives will almost certainly require less attention than someone who on paper is more advanced but only has 100 dives logged. Someone who has done 300 clear, warm-water dives might require more attention than someone with the same qualification and 150 drysuit dives all carried out in cold water.

A check-out dive in relatively benign conditions is a good way of assessing the diving experience of potential team members for the expedition, once you have checked their paperwork. The state of their equipment and how they put it together, usually give you the first clues as to their experience.

If at any stage the expedition leader needs to decline an applicant a place on the expedition, the reason should be given clearly, tactfully and politely. For example, the expedition may be full, the applicant may have insufficient experience, or the expedition is looking for someone with different skills. Many oversubscribed expeditions will have a reserve list so that if one of the original team drops out someone is available to take their place quickly.

Establishing its core

Building up a core team to share the responsibility of looking after the other members of the team helps to spread the load. The core team will understand how things need to be done, knowing the expedition leader's requirements in advance (for example, the preferred method of deploying the shot line on a wreck or how the gas filling rota works). If they are managed well, the core team can help to reduce the task loading on the expedition leader.

The core team will more than likely consist of people whom the expedition leader knows well and trusts, particularly in terms of their diving abilities and skills.

Recruitment

For most expeditions, building the complete expedition team takes considerable effort and the places on the team will need to be advertised. Many dive clubs have their own procedures for announcing expeditions and this may simply be an informal announcement at a club meeting in the pub or may involve emailing club members with an expedition brochure.

There may not be an immediate response. Very often people will express an initial interest and then need some time to think about it. Other expeditions, sports or family and other personal commitments will more than likely be competing for the time of the potential expedition member. Follow up expressions of interest personally with a phone call or a face-to-face meeting somewhere social. This provides a great opportunity to answer any questions or concerns that the potential expedition member has, or you think has, directly and also allows you to gauge their commitment.

You may need to recruit members from outside your own diving group or club. This may mean a bigger advertising campaign. However, having a network of diving contacts particularly in dive clubs is useful, as if they cannot go themselves they might recommend someone else.

The precise makeup of the team will depend on the

nature of the expedition. Usually you will want a number of people with each important skill, such as an oxygen first-aid qualification, rescue management skills or experience as a diver cox'n, rather than just one. This makes the dive organisation much simpler and means that if an individual drops out or indeed is diving, there are sufficient others with the appropriate skills left on the surface.

The expedition may also require particular non-diving skills. For more extreme diving expeditions, this becomes more likely. The most obvious example of this is trained medical personnel such as paramedics and doctors. However, technicians capable of servicing expedition equipment, qualified marine biologists, archaeologists, sonar operators, and skilled photographers may all be required.

As with diving skills, it may be that you need to have a couple of people with the required skill set: the main skill provider plus a deputy - a spare.

Local contacts

It can be difficult to prepare for an expedition without at least one local contact. Usually this will be the skipper of the charter boat or the owner of the dive centre whose facilities you are using. When a problem does occur, they are usually your first port of call - unless it is a problem that requires the emergency services.

For more remote diving expeditions, contacts may be the owner of the accommodation being used, the harbour master in charge of the slipway you are using or a local boat mechanic. While remote communities do not have the same infrastructure as a larger town, they are often self-sufficient and can usually assist with most problems an expedition might face and so it is vital to maintain good relations.

Good expedition leaders value local contacts as a part of the wider team. Remember, though, that local contacts will not usually be on holiday themselves; they will be earning a living at what they do.

As a part of observing the Divers Code of Conduct (see BSAC website), keep locals informed of your intentions and support local communities where appropriate. Divers are very conspicuous by the nature of the sport. Bad behaviour in the past has resulted in divers being banned from particular sites and will certainly not do you any favours if your expedition runs into problems that need local help to resolve.

Deposits

Once potential expedition members have confirmed an interest in the expedition, it is strongly advisable to get some financial commitment from them. A non-refundable deposit is usually the best way to do this.

For some expeditions the deposit may be 100 per cent of the cost - paid up front. However, for most it will be a percentage of the total costs initially and the remainder to follow later on.

CASE STUDY 3.1

Covering the costs

Costs must be set out and financial contingency plans made, even for a straightforward club expedition.

- A club RIB expedition is estimated to cost £380 per person.
- The accommodation costs and ferry tickets add up to £180 per person.
- A deposit of just over half, about £200, taken in advance is reasonable.

If someone drops out once deposits have been paid, then additional costs should be minimal for the remaining members of the team, as the fixed costs (accommodation and transport) have been covered by the non-refundable deposit.

Logistics

Once the initial planning is complete, time needs to be spent looking at the expedition plan in detail. Logistics, when used in a diving expedition sense, refers to the management of getting divers and their equipment safely from the start point (home) to the end point (the dive) and back again. In practice, this means you need to consider transport to your dive base, the accommodation at the dive base and the nature of the diving platform.

Transport

How to get the team and equipment to the desired location to make the expedition work is an important consideration.

When making the transport arrangements remember to consider the following:

- The location of the expedition and the best route to get there.
- The equipment that needs to be taken.
- Numbers of divers and non-divers to transport.
- The mode of transport itself (trains, planes, ferries, cars, animals).
- Any particular legislation or conditions of carriage that need to be complied with.
- Location of accommodation in relation to the dive sites.
- Organisation of food/meals.
- The supply of breathing gases.
- The supply of fuel.

Travelling by air

The growth in the number of airlines and reduction in prices has undoubtedly opened up diving expedition possibilities that were not previously possible or economical. However, the expedition leader does have some additional considerations when travelling by air.

Weight limits

Before booking with an airline, check the information available about the terms of carriage. Airline baggage policy is continually changing and so make sure you check with the airline before booking tickets.

- At the time of booking, make sure that you tell them you are divers, that you will be taking diving equipment

CASE STUDY 3.2

An island expedition

An expedition is going to Islay, off the west coast of Scotland, and needs to get seven divers and three non-divers, two boats, two compressors, dive and personal equipment and non-perishables over to the island.

The story

The location of the expedition base on the island of Islay has been chosen so that it is only 30 minutes leisurely drive from any of the three main launch areas at Portnahaven in the west, Bunnahabhain in the east and Port Ellen in the south. The nearest fuel station is a mile from the expedition base. Gas supplies will be provided by two portable compressors run at the base.

How they did it

- Research shows that the most cost-effective option is to drive up to Kennecraig in the expedition team's own vehicles to catch the ferry to Port Ellen.
- A four-wheel drive vehicle can tow one boat and take the compressors and most of the diving equipment and food. A large estate car can tow the second boat.
- The remaining six expedition members will travel up in three cars with the remaining equipment.
- To keep the ferry costs down, one of the vehicles will remain on the mainland, as four vehicles will be sufficient to cater for the needs of divers and non-divers. The vehicle ferry can now be booked.
- Given the conspicuous nature of the team, advice is sought immediately on any restrictions on boats and diving cylinders.
- As a result, the appropriate paperwork (a SITPRO form) is completed for each vehicle carrying dangerous goods (compressed gas), identifying the number, size and pressure of every diving cylinder taken with the correct UN identification number for the gas it contains. This is faxed through for the ferry company to check well in advance. Permission is given to transport the cylinders.

Knowing the finer details of the plan allows an economical, environmentally sound travel plan to be put together.

and need extra allowances. Get a signed copy of the allowances that have been agreed.

- If booking online, spell it out in the area for extra information and have a printed copy to show at the airport; e-tickets can be a problem as information and allowances can be left off and you will not know until you collect the ticket at the airport.
- In many instances there will be a dive centre near your destination, so it may be a better option to hire heavy equipment. There is no need to take cylinders and weights by air.

Security and customs issues

Some items are likely to be difficult or impossible to take with you across national borders, or when travelling by air. Remember that airport security staff or customs officials are unlikely to be familiar with dive equipment. There are lists of items that are banned from airplanes. Dive knives, for example, would need to go into your hold luggage.

Where items cannot be taken for whatever reason, you will normally be able to source them locally at your destination, particularly if it is a well-known dive destination.

- Pressurised cylinders and any pyrotechnics will not be allowed.
- Many divers take small emergency cylinders and pony cylinders and these will almost certainly raise suspicion. Even if you can show that they are empty, they may not be allowed.
- Rebreathers use the caustic substance sofnolime and any containers of the substance should be marked as such. To the average security official any container containing a chemical, whether marked or not, will be suspicious. Planning ahead and getting written permission from the airline and relevant customs officials to take the material and taking safety datasheets along with you may help. Sourcing the substance locally at your destination may be a better option.
- It is usually best to pack a rebreather in a protective box rather than a soft bag to help it withstand the rigours of the airline baggage system. Most box lids can be secured with cable ties and it is best to pack some spare ties inside the box in case it is subject to a security search. Check that the box is within the size restrictions of an airline's luggage policy. Packing a sales brochure with the equipment may to help explain to officials what the equipment is.

For more remote destinations, either think of a way of safely removing the need for the equipment or find an alternative means of transporting the items. There are many reputable postal and freight companies who should be able to help and will usually have a better idea of the paperwork required to clear customs at both ends.

Accommodation

Accommodation can range from hotels, bed and breakfasts, self-catering cottages, chalets and caravans, hostels, huts and campsites to a liveaboard boat.

A number of factors should be considered when looking for sleeping and living accommodation for the expedition:

- Roughing it for the sake of it is not generally a good idea, although it may appeal to the more budget conscious and hardy in the expedition team. Usually, the more comfortable the accommodation the happier your team will be. In the UK and other cold-water diving destinations somewhere warm and dry is needed, whereas in hot climates somewhere with air conditioning will almost certainly be appreciated.
- The male/female ratio of the group must also be considered. Whether sleeping accommodation is single sex or mixed will depend on the attitudes and relationships of expedition members and in some cases the policy of the accommodation being used.
- Minors (under 18 years old) in the group require special consideration. Never mix adults with minors (except parents and their own children) or minors of different sexes.
- On diving expeditions there is invariably a need to dry something out or repair/maintain equipment. Repairs to a drysuit puncture, for example, will require the drysuit to be dried thoroughly beforehand. In areas used to divers or those involved in other watersports, accommodation with drying rooms and kit stores are generally readily available.
- Your cooking arrangements may also affect the accommodation you require. A large group, who are

self catering will need a large kitchen. A group staying in bed-and-breakfast accommodation may only require a shop to buy lunch and a pub or restaurant for an evening meal.

Secure car and boat parking is important to ensure the minimum risk from theft. Secure car parking is particularly important if dive equipment has to remain in vehicles because of lack of secure drying or kit storage rooms.

Selecting a dive platform

The choice of dive platform will be driven by many factors including availability, budget and the nature of the expedition. The choices for most diving expeditions are as follows, and each has its advantages and disadvantages from an expedition point of view:

- A liveaboard hard boat
- A day hard boat
- A rigid-hulled inflatable boat
- An inflatable boat
- A shore dive

For example, a technical, trimix expedition to a wreck ten miles offshore would probably opt for a hard boat of some description due the amount of equipment needed and the distances being travelled.

An expedition to St Kilda might select a liveaboard boat or a fast RIBs with a long range. The liveaboard boat would take longer to get to St Kilda and would have a limited time available on the island for diving because of the sailing time to and from the home port. However, it is certainly a more comfortable platform in the potentially rough weather.

Unfortunately, weather windows are quite short and may prevent liveaboard boats from getting to St Kilda at all. A RIB-based expedition can have a distinct advantage. Launching from the Outer Hebrides, a RIB expedition leader can monitor the weather and make a dash to St Kilda and return before the weather conditions deteriorate. However such an expedition would require more planning to ensure safe diving. Factors to take into account would be sufficient fuel; an accurate up-to-date forecast direct from the Met office; excellent communications particularly with the coastguard; adequate boat insurance; that the team were capable of the journey; and that there were permissions and a place to stay on the island.

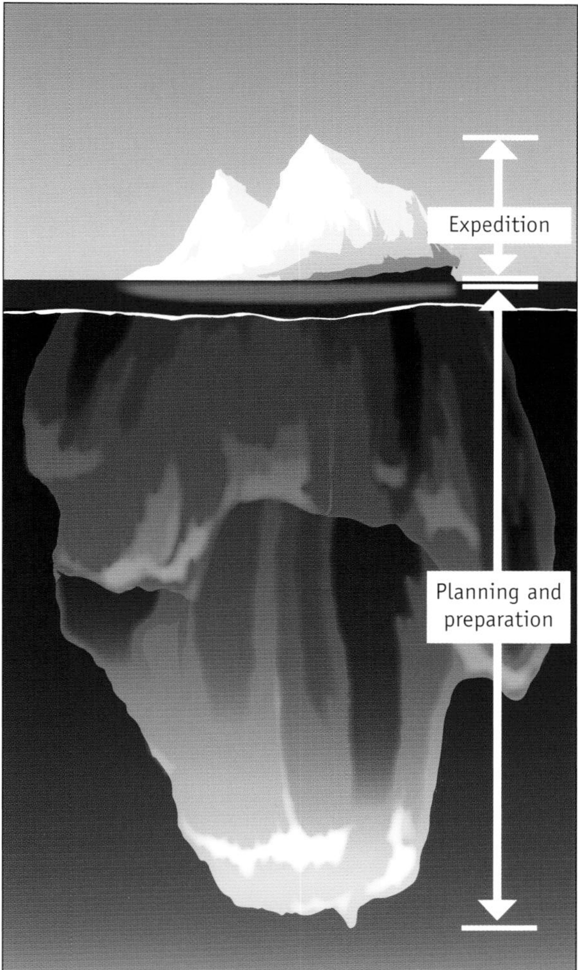

An iceberg is a good representation of the relationship between planning, preparation and delivery of an expedition. The expedition itself only happens because of all the hidden background work (the planning and preparation).

Platform pros and cons

The merits of different dive platforms

Platform	Advantages	Disadvantages
Liveaboard charter boat	✓ Generally very comfortable, minimising diver fatigue ✓ Expedition logistics simplified with accommodation, food and gas supplies all onboard ✓ Large range, with supplies for at least for a week ✓ Power supplies for charging batteries and operating laptops ✓ Large kitting up and equipment storage areas ✓ Large dry areas with suitable areas for planning ✓ Usually have an onboard compressor	✗ Expensive ✗ Slow and not very manoeuverable
A day boat	✓ Reasonable range ✓ More manoeuvrable and generally faster than a liveaboard vessel	✗ Less diver comfort, although most have a cabin area to shelter divers from the elements
Rigid-hulled inflatable boat	✓ Fast allowing for quick transit to and from sites ✓ Highly manoeuvrable and better able to work against the current at tidal sites ✓ Shallow draft permitting access to shallower water and navigation around shallow reefs ✓ Fun to drive	✗ Limited kitting up and storage room ✗ Divers exposed to the elements and wind chill in particular ✗ Launch requires proper slipway especially when towed by a 2WD car ✗ Difficult to launch across beaches unless towed by suitable 4WD or tractor ✗ Need suitably qualified diver cox'ns ✗ Boat must be properly maintained
Inflatable boat	✓ Largely superseded by RIBs, these are often relegated to the role of a small tender to a larger vessel. However, they can offer a very versatile dive platform and should not be overlooked ✓ Usually small enough to be carried by team across a beach to the appropriate launch site to give access to more remote sites ✓ Can be dismantled for transport inside a van or a container	✗ Limited kitting up and storage room ✗ Divers exposed to the elements and wind chill in particular ✗ Uncomfortable ride in waves ✗ Fewer places to fit electronics ✗ Generally limited range (usually 10 miles or less from port depending on configuration, load and surface conditions) ✗ Need suitably qualified diver cox'ns ✗ Boat must be properly maintained
Shore dive	✓ No need to manage boats ✓ Usually cheap ✓ May be the only access available for particular expeditions such as cavern dives, inland dives, river dives	✗ Care required to ensure diver rescue can be carried out without boat cover ✗ Shore access point may require considerable trek across land

Detailed planning

Getting to the dive base is one thing, but you still need to plan to find the dive sites to avoid disappointment.

Dive site information

It is essential to spend some time getting the most accurate details possible for the sites. Many club expeditions may well be aiming to dive locations previously visited by other divers. However, it is well to be wary of information from books and magazines as there are many reasons why the information may not be accurate enough. It is better to try to talk to other divers who have actually carried out diving at the sites.

The basic information needed about a dive site is given the table below. It is handy to have a summary of this key information on a waterproof slate ready for use in the wet areas of the boat during the expedition.

Information needed	Source
Location (latitude and longitude)	Nautical charts, historical records, other divers, dive guide books and magazine articles. Be aware of the use of different GPS datums.
Depth and tidal conditions (particularly the timing of slack water)	Nautical charts and almanacs, dive guide books and magazine articles, other divers.
Expected layout of site	Dive guide books and magazine articles, topography from charts, ship's plans, other divers.
History of site (this background information is very useful to help understand a site)	Dive guide books and magazine articles, newspaper reports.
Transits	Dive guide books and magazine articles. Be aware that it can be quite difficult matching up a sketched transit with the real thing.

A liveaboard boat is self contained

Inflatable boats can launch almost anywhere

A day boat may not have shelter for divers

A RIB launch needs a slipway and often a 4WD

CASE STUDY 3.3

A well-known wreck, but new to us

A club has heard the story of the wreck of the Otranto, off Islay, and wants to dive the site.

The story

There is plenty of material to hand about the wreck, including articles downloaded from the internet, a second-hand copy of the out-of-print dive guide *Dive Islay* written in 1986, a copy of *Argyll Shipwrecks* by Moir and Crawford, the Admiralty chart 2168 Approaches to the Sound of Jura, Imray sailing directions and Reeds Nautical Almanac. The details, shown opposite, are assembled.

How they did it

- Even for this relatively well known wreck there are two distinct recorded positions.
- That they are 0.46 nautical miles apart suggests one of the numbers is probably wrong.
- The other evidence (depth, proximity to reef) suggests the guide book position is probably the most accurate.
- For many locations in coastal waters, tidal streams are quite predictable. Tidal stream information is available on most nautical charts and referenced to a nearby port to give tide times. Tidal stream atlases, nautical almanacs and sailing directions are other useful source of tidal information. It turns out that slack water is not needed to dive this site, but for other sites it is.
- Make the most of the information available to determine the time when divers need to be entering the water and in which direction they will be expected to travel with the tide, particularly with drift dives.
- The time when diving will take place is crucial to the overall timetable. It may well be that the time of slack water doesn't coincide with a sociable time and, unless the dive site is particularly special, the leader may be forced to look for an alternative site on that particular day.
- Many expeditions are planned to coincide with neap tides as the currents are weaker, and slack windows are greater.

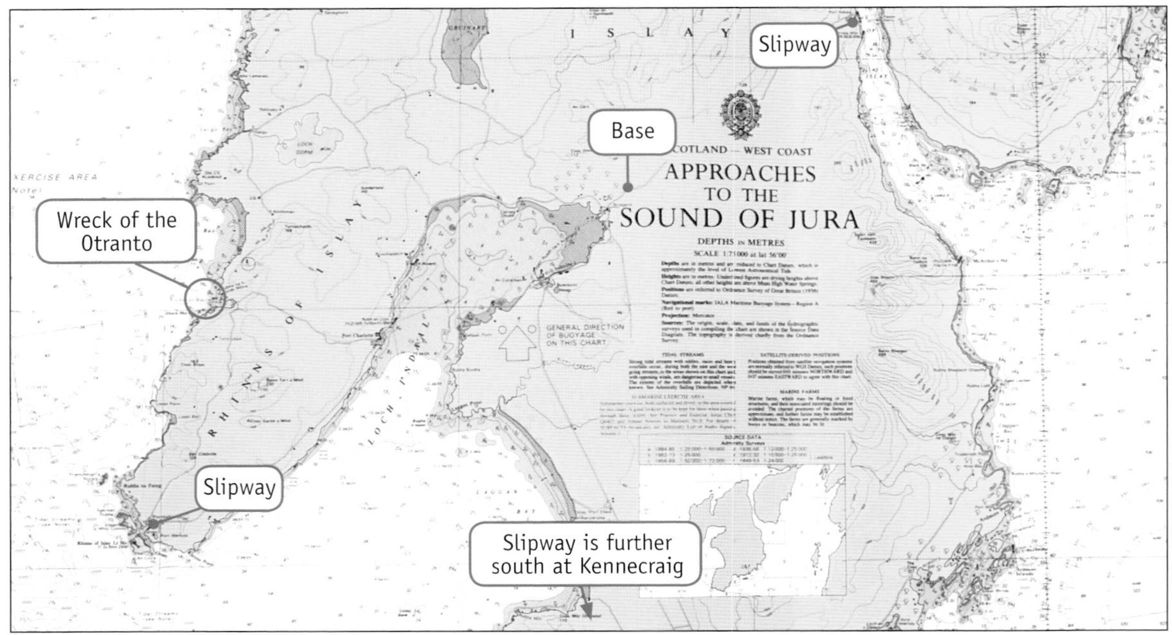

Information needed	Source
Location	Machir Bay Charted position: 55° 45.984′ N 006° 29.326′ W From *Argyll Shipwrecks*: 55° 45.796′N 006° 28.611′W Marks should place you 'in the middle of the engine room area'. But the distance between the two is 0.46 nautical miles
Depth and tide	Wreck is between 7 and 16m deep Atlantic swell can make conditions difficult, otherwise tide on site is slight
Expected layout of site	A heavily salvaged wreck. Six large boilers lie off to the side of the reef. Good sketch based on information in *Dive Islay*. 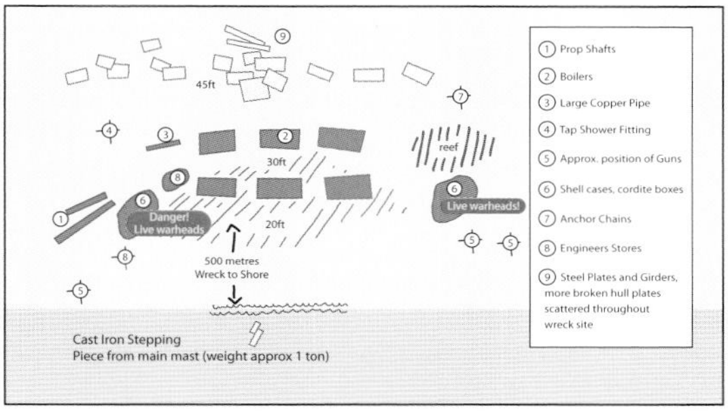
History of site	Worst convoy disaster of the first world war. In collision with SS Kashmir on 24 December 1918, Otranto drifted and sank in heavy seas – 364 men lost their lives, 596 were rescued by HMS Mounsey. Sixteen made it ashore. Quote from *The New York Times* 'All the Americans [survivors] voiced their deep gratitude to the islanders for the tender care they gave the men. The survivors were put to bed in private houses and were so well provided for in every way that no one wanted to leave when the relief ship arrived.'
Transits	From *Argyll Shipwrecks* 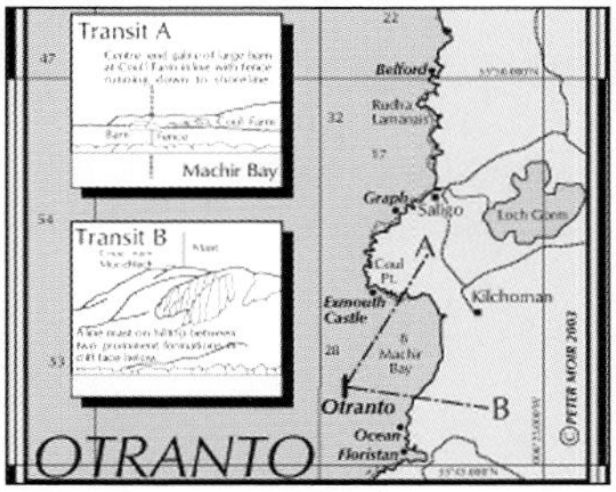
Launch sites	Portnahaven (across beach) launch is 7 nautical miles away Care is required to navigate through the tidal race in Frenchman's Pass. Confused sea likely and some shallow rocks.

CASE STUDY 3.4

Drifting along

A drift dive is planned in the Sound of Islay. The intention is to dive the wall underneath Dunlossit House Pier, and then drift off, with a mixed ability group of divers. The current is likely to be strong and there will be little slack water.

The plan

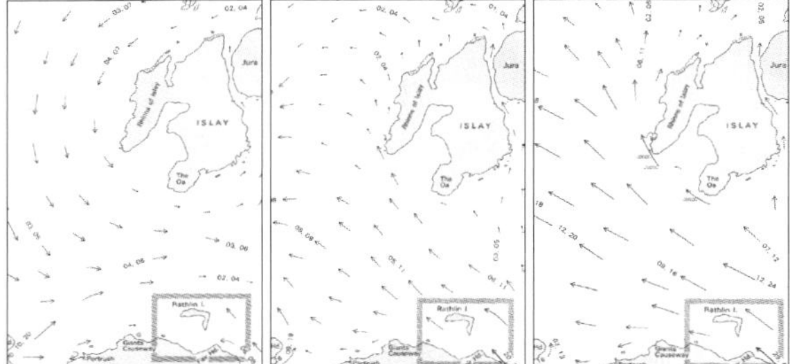

The following sources of information are available to the expedition leader: Admiralty chart 2481 Sound of Islay; tide tables for Dover (from the internet); tide tables for Port Askaig, Islay (from the internet); local knowledge; Admiralty Tidal Stream Atlas of the area, NP222.

From the tidal stream atlas, high water slack is apparently one hour before high water Dover (2h 20min before HW Greenock) and low water slack is five hours after HW Dover (3h 40min after HW Greenock). Although the tidal stream atlas references Dover or Greenock, for the local height of the tide we need to consult the local tide tables.

After HW slack the tide is expected to head south through the sound, and after LW slack it is expected to be heading north. HW slack is predicted to be 9.56am local time (BST) and LW slack 15.56pm. Since the wall drops to 60m and the tidal range is only 0.2m the state of the tide makes little difference to the depth of the dive, so HW slack is preferred and gives plenty of time for a second dive.

We know from the chart that on spring tides the maximum current on the surface is likely to be five knots. But we do not know how much slack water there is or indeed the precise timing or the current on neap tides, as there is no further tidal information on the chart. Comparing the size of the tidal range with the ranges during the rest of the month, we can tell that at the start of the week it will be a spring tide and towards the end of the week it will become a neap tide. Therefore, we would probably want to dive this site at the end of the week. Local advice is that the tides never seem to stop but should be manageable at the site chosen at predicted slack water.

The dive will be planned so that the first pair, of experienced divers, enter the water three-quarters of a hour before slack in order to investigate the site and then surface on slack water. The remainder of the group will enter at slack water and drift at the end of their dive. The divers will assemble on site one hour before the first divers are due in, to locate the entry point and monitor the tide.

What actually happened

The team arrived on site one and a half hours before the intended dive time and on-site tide conditions were assessed. There was little wind and the sea was flat so the boat was drifting with the tide. The GPS indicated a drift of 1.5 knots on the surface, which decreased an hour later. The eddies on the surface also noticeably reduced.

Divers kitted up and entered the water before slack with the current heading north as expected. At 15m the current suddenly changed direction. It seems the tide below 15m had already turned. The tide was manageable and the first pair surfaced on time and informed the second wave of divers and boat cover, who proceeded to manage a drift to the south.

How they did it

The team planned to arrive on site early, to watch the local conditions and react accordingly, as predictions may not necessarily match the actual on site conditions.

- Even for the most predictable of sites, weather patterns can delay or advance the change in tide, sometimes quite significantly.
- Coastal or underwater topography influences the strength and direction of tides, so extrapolation of nearby data is not neccessarily accurate.
- Tidal races are often found near headlands or in between islands, where water is funnelled by the local topography.
- Currents can vary with depth.
- Surface currents (often driven by wind) can be travelling in a completely different direction to the

currents below. This has significant implications for boat cover, which may be going in completely the opposite direction to the divers.

- Sometimes, particularly on spring tides, there may not be a slack water window. The tide may simply change direction.
- Caution should be exercised when diving sites where tidal patterns are not predictable. It may take a number of diving expeditions to a site to build up a more accurate picture of when it is possible to dive.
- Where possible, seek advice from local divers and fishermen and other water users.

Financing the expedition

The expedition leader needs to ensure that there is sufficient income to pay for all the expedition expenditure. Most expeditions are financed by the expedition team, who share the costs.The expedition leader should make it clear what costs are included in the expedition price and what are not. Usually deposits are payable by expedition members to secure places and in turn this money goes to pay deposits to confirm, for example, accommodation and charter boat bookings.

Larger, more ambitious expeditions may require additional financial support from outside the expedition team.

Sources of funding

Companies, local councils, charities, grant-giving bodies - local or national, individuals and the public may all be sources of additional funding for expeditions.

In the UK, the BSAC Expeditionary Grants Scheme (BEGS) and the BSA Jubilee Trust are two examples of sources of funding specifically for diving expeditions.

Obtaining external funding can require a significant amount of work, including writing an expedition plan or brochure, giving presentations on your expedition, attending interviews, making phone calls and at the very least filling in some application forms.

Once funding has been obtained, further paperwork is likely to be needed to comply with any conditions of a grant and to prove appropriate use of the money. Progress reports and formal expedition accounts are likely to be asked for.

Each source of funding will have its own particular requirements and conditions, which will need to be met. The expedition leader should ensure these are thoroughly investigated to assess whether the diving expedition would meet the requirements and whether or not the conditions are too onerous.

Control of costs

The expedition leader is likely to be distracted by many other aspects of the expedition and so it is usually best to appoint an expedition treasurer to keep track of incoming and outgoing money and keep proper accounts.

An initial budget should be put together in order to get a proper understanding of the costs on an expedition.As the expedition plans develop, the budget will, undoubtedly, require adjusting.

Open, transparent and up-to-date accounts are very useful in making sure the expedition does not spend beyond its means and for identifying areas in which savings can be made.

Catering

It is said that an army marches on its stomach.The same can be said of an expedition. Good food and nutrition is vital not only for the physical well-being of the divers but also their mental health and morale.An expedition can be ruined if the food is unrecognisable, too foreign (despite what expedition members may say before leaving!), inedible, in inadequate quantities (particularly for cold-water diving) or leaves the expedition members with a stomach upset.

Many diving expeditions will rely upon the food provided on the liveaboard boat or their accommodation, particularly if diving abroad. Many day boat expeditions, for example, may have breakfast in their accommodation, have a snack or packed lunch on the boat and an evening meal in a restaurant. For the expedition leader the workload is reduced; rather than a massive shopping list, careful selection of accommodation, a restaurant and a shop are probably all that is required. However, the price will be higher.

For more cost-conscious expeditions, self catering is usually preferred. It is a safety issue to ensure that those who are preparing food for the expedition team are competent, willing to do so and that everyone adheres to basic food hygiene procedures. A basic food hygiene course, aimed at people who handle food at work, is a good way of learning about the risks and responsibilities of handling food.

As a part of your planning, make sure you know of any allergies or medical conditions among the team members. Also, find out the team's likes and dislikes. You can then decide what meals are to be prepared (breakfast, lunch, evening, snacks) and plan your shopping list. Quantities can be dealt with by calculating the portions for one person and then simply multiplying by the number of people in the team.

Where you buy the food will depend on where you are going. It is usually best to source perishable foods such as meat and dairy produce locally on arrival, particularly if you have a long journey. If you are going abroad, you will not normally have any choice but to buy locally. You need to make sure that the cooking facilities at your destination are adequate for the group you have.

For more extreme and remote diving expeditions catering arrangements can form a major part of planning the expedition. Ration packs, tinned and dried foods may be required because of storage constraints and drinkable water may also be limited. A full investigation of this aspect of expedition nutrition is beyond the scope of this book. However, some of the principles mentioned earlier still apply.

Equipment required

Apart from personal diving equipment, the main two items required for most diving expeditions are a boat to dive from and gas to breathe. The other equipment required will depend to some degree on the nature of the diving expedition and its location.

The expedition leader needs to ensure that the expedition team are aware of equipment and paperwork they require; not only for diving, but also for getting there and back.

- Along with knowing what equipment your team will need, they also need to know how to use it.
- Consider the implications of equipment failing. Do you really need to take extra equipment? Is it critical to the success of the expedition?
- A detailed checklist is a good way of making sure all equipment is relevant.
- Make it clear what equipment is being provided by the expedition team itself and what equipment individual participants must bring.

If the expedition's area of operation is within the UK Search and Rescue Area, the dive locations are likely to be within VHF range of coastguard stations, and contacting the emergency services will be relatively straightforward.

Special communications equipment (such as satellite phones or MF radios) may be necessary of you are diving further afield.

There is a sample equipment checklist on page 48.

Using club boats

In the UK, the Combined Diving Associations in association with the Maritime and Coastguard Agency have produced the *Guidelines for the Safe Operation of Member Club Dive Boats*. The guidelines are readily available online and outline, in particular, what safety equipment should be carried as a minimum and what UK legislation needs to be complied with by those responsible for operating club boats.

Expedition leaders also need to check the small print of the boat's insurance documents and understand what is and isn't covered by the policy, and in what operating areas. As a minimum, third party insurance for injury to others is recommended. For example, some policies for small boats do not allow overnight mooring or limit area of operation to within coastal waters or place restrictions on who can drive the boats.

Don't forget that if you are using RIBs or other small boats and are towing them to the launch site, whoever is towing them will need to be competent to do so, obey the appropriate highway codes and have suitable insurance cover for the vehicle and the towing activities.

Charter boats

When chartering a dive boat you need to be sure it is fit for purpose. In the UK, all commercially operated boats must comply with coding regulations laid down by the Maritime and Coastguard Agency. A register of vessels complying with these regulations is available on the internet and vessels should display an up-to-date certificate in the cabin. There are different classifications of vessels, which means that a particular vessel will have restrictions on where and when it can operate.

Just because a vessel is on the register does not mean it necessarily suits your needs or whether the skipper is willing and able to meet your expedition requirements.

Gas supplies

In the case study of the Islay expedition, page 31, the expedition is self sufficient for breathing gas as it has access to compressors and oxygen plus portable blending equipment. The penalty for self-sufficiency is that your team will have to spend a considerable amount of time filling cylinders. For a team of ten divers using two 12-litre cylinders each day this could take anything up to five hours on the two small portable compressors.

You also need to make sure you have trained people operating the compressors who can make sure filters are changed regularly, condensate traps are bled, and air intakes are placed correctly.

Blending gases requires additional skills and equipment such as gas analysers and inline filters. Again people doing any blending should be suitably trained.

The alternative to the self-sufficient route is to use a reputable local filling station (for example, in the UK an IDEST approval should be looked for). This will probably be more expensive than being self sufficient, but it should free up a considerable amount of time for the expedition team providing it is close to your base of operations.

Special equipment

There are many examples of special equipment that could be required on an expedition, such as a portable recompression facility, side-scan sonar, laptops and software, photographic equipment, scientific instruments and communications equipment.

Whatever equipment is required, the expedition leader should ensure that whoever is using it can do so safely, effectively and legally.

Risk assessment and emergency planning

We all assess risks all the time in our daily lives. An expedition leader needs to assess risks, plan to avoid them and have contingency plans in case they do happen. Let us be clear that assessing risks is not just about completing a piece of paper. A good expedition leader will be continually thinking and asking the question 'what if this happens' and coming up with a way to deal with the problem. However, formally writing out a risk assessment well in advance of an expedition is a very good way of figuring out how to avoid the risks and knowing how you are going to handle a risk in advance of it happening.

Risk assessment and emergency planning are such important topics that we develop them further in Chapter 4 and Chapter 8.

In the wider context, the risks that need to be assessed for a diving expedition can be broken down into three categories: first and foremost is safety, then financial and finally logistical considerations.

The expedition leader needs to consider all three in order to minimise the chance of the expedition injuring someone, costing more money or failing to achieve its aims.

Safety risks

Assessing safety risks involves assessing the likelihood of diving or other hazards occurring and injuring someone. An expedition is a success if everyone returns to tell the tale in one piece. Meeting the expedition's main aims at the expense of safety is not a successful expedition.

A non-diving expedition perhaps illustrates this the best. Shackleton's famous expedition to the Antarctic failed in its original scientific objectives; the team were trapped on ice for months and their ship crushed and sunk. However, everyone lived to tell the tale. Shackleton put this down to God's providence, but God had also given him the gifts of leadership and meticulous planning skills, which he used to bring everyone back alive.

On diving expeditions, an expedition leader will at some point have to make a call on whether to abandon the dive or proceed with it. Assessing the risks due to the weather, sea conditions, the fitness of divers and capabilities of the least experienced divers will influence that decision.

Financial risks

By financial risks we essentially mean that the cost of the expedition may become prohibitively expensive for those participating in it. For example, if you initially think the expedition will cost £300 and then just before or during the expedition the costs escalate to £600, this will not endear you to your expedition team and may leave you with a very big bill.

It may be that these escalating costs are linked to other risks. For example, if diving abroad and someone is unfortunate enough to become ill evacuation and treatment can cost many thousands of pounds. You need to make sure this can be paid, usually by making sure there is adequate insurance.

An accurate costing with contingency built in helps mitigate the financial risks.

Logistical risks

Logistical risks cover pretty much everything else. For example, one of your cars or boats could break down, bad weather could delay travel or disrupt dive plans, a key member of your team may become ill, or a key item of equipment could fail.

The nature of the expedition will dictate to some degree how much effort goes into reducing the potential effects of these occurrences.

In the UK, for example, if a vehicle breaks down, membership of one of the vehicle recovery services will go some way to resolving the problem. Having an extra vehicle to help the other vehicles get your team to its destination – particularly one capable of towing a boat – should enable the expedition to continue.

However, a vehicle breakdown somewhere remote may mean you have to find a trained mechanic, carry a comprehensive vehicle spares kit and have some reliable emergency communications.

Bad weather can easily put paid to the best plans. Having alternative dive sites and/or having multiple dates or the flexibility to change the planned date of the expedition are probably the only ways to mitigate against this.

Diver preparation

Training to extend diving skills can be the sole purpose of an expedition. For example, many clubs and schools organise week or weekend expeditions with the sole aim of ticking all the boxes in a particular training programme.

However, where training is not the primary focus of the expedition, there will almost certainly be a need for some sort of task-oriented training and this is best completed well in advance of the expedition itself so divers have time to consolidate skills learned during their training course.

For example, a deep diving expedition will require the dive team to practise putting their dive plan into action. Learning how to deploy a trapeze, with spare gas and how to react to an emergency situation, are all best run through in more benign conditions as a training exercise. This way any teething problems with procedures and equipment can be identified and rectified.

Some expeditions can successfully combine a diving purpose with training, but care is required to avoid conflict between the two objectives as you may fail to achieve either.

In a diving expedition to survey a reef, for example, training on marine life identification and survey techniques will probably work quite well together.

On the other hand, trying to complete any training course in the evenings after a day of diving is likely to be hard work because students and instructors are tired.

Of course, training may not be geared to underwater skills at all. It may be that courses are required in driving with four-wheel drive, towing a boat, expedition first aid, navigation, compressor operation, gas blending, radio operation, oxygen administration, archaeological survey skills, marine life identification, and side-scan sonar operation.

So, for most expeditions it is best to identify the skills required for the expedition and make sure training is completed and skills consolidated before the expedition takes place. This way, during the expedition the team can focus on its main aims and objectives.

Build-up dives

There may be particular equipment or procedures that expedition members need to become familiar with. This may require a series of build-up dives before the expedition to ensure that the divers are dive fit, fully acquainted with the equipment and procedures, and working as a team.

Other expeditions may not require such rigorous preparation, but it is recommended to carry out a relatively easy shakedown dive on the first day of the expedition or immediately prior to the expedition to check that the equipment is working and to provide an opportunity to resolve problems.

The timetable

Following the flowchart below you should know from your initial planning, where you want to go, what you will be doing, who (or at least the number of divers) is going, when you are going and how you are going.

It now needs joining together into a clear and concise timetable so that everyone knows what is happening when. As you start to plan, you should be able to see any problems.

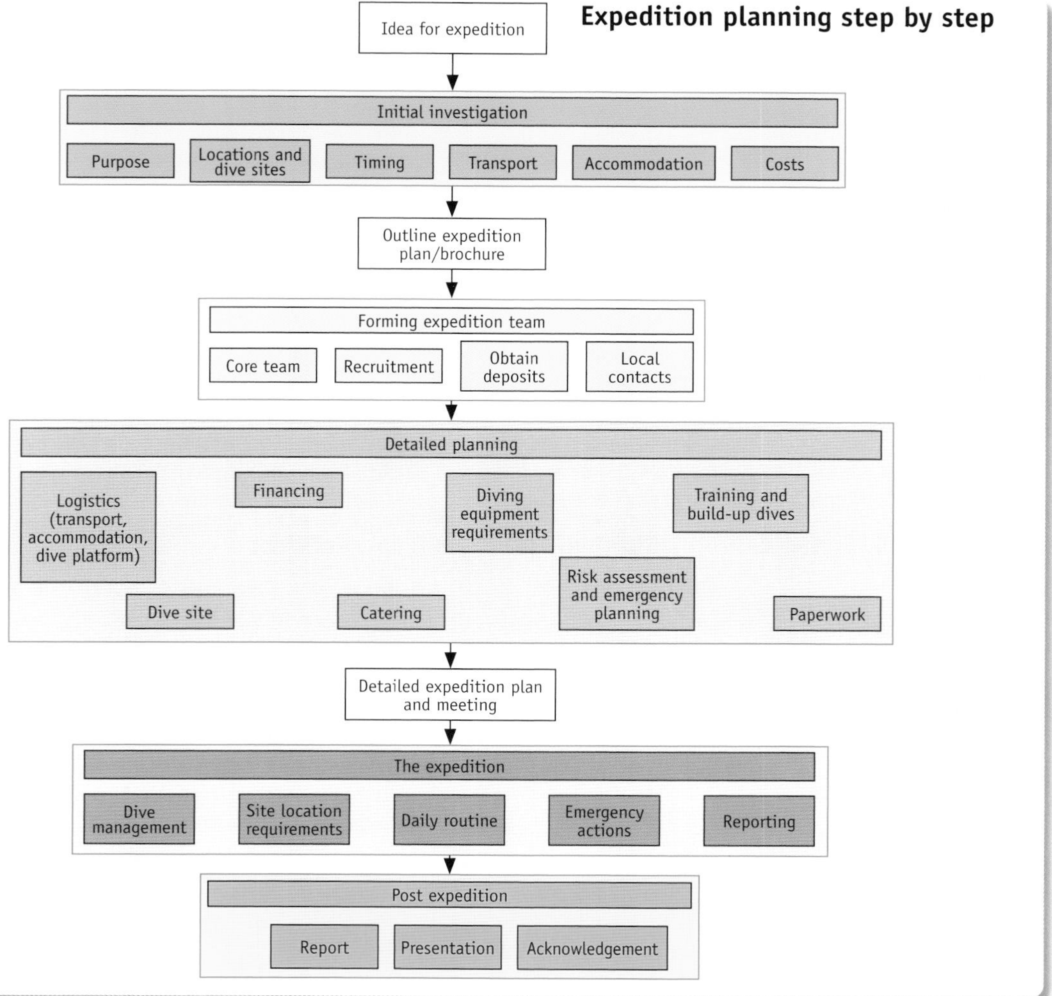

CASE STUDY 3.5

Thinking logistically

A mixed group of divers and a couple of non-divers are heading to dive in Islay, where there are no longer any commercial sports diving operators.

The story

The initial plan is to drive and catch the ferry from Kennecraig. All the diving equipment is to be loaded into a 4WD vehicle, which is also towing a RIB. Cars will be shared as far as possible to minimise costs. A farmhouse has been booked in the centre of Islay about 30 minutes drive from the ferry slip. Non-perishable food will be purchased in advance, perishables on demand.

How they did it

Six months before the expedition an initial timetable is distributed to the group:

Friday: meet in Newcastle to load vehicles after work.

Saturday: set off early from Newcastle, pick up the boats en route, drive to Kennecraig for the afternoon ferry. Settle into accommodation and go shopping.

Sunday: begin diving.

Very soon some problems become apparent.

- The 4WD weight limit is likely to be exceeded and the equipment is too bulky to fit inside.
- The time taken (calculated using an online route planner) to collect the boats from storage and tow them would mean a very early start (3am) in order to arrive at the ferry for 11.00am (with some time in hand for emergencies).
- Not everyone can drop equipment off on the Friday because of work.
- There is some difficulty in getting the commitment to go shopping for the non-perishables.

However, these problems have been identified well in advance of the expedition and there is time to resolve them. Two weeks later after discussions with the team the plan is essentially the same but the detail has changed.

- The 4WD will take the compressors and the majority of the cylinders.
- Only two passengers will travel in the 4WD.
- Kit and passengers will be shared with other vehicles.
- One car will now be left on the mainland at the ferry terminal.
- Sharing cars will leave one vehicle free for the non-diver in the group to get around the island.
- The two vehicles towing the boats will travel up after work on Friday departing at 5.00pm and arriving about 11.00pm.
- A B&B has been identified near the ferry terminal with plenty of space for two boats and able to cope with late arrivals.
- A date is re-arranged earlier in the week for a kit dump, in the expedition leader's garage.
- Shopping will be ordered on-line and delivered to the same address the day before the expedition to provide ingredients for a pre-agreed menu for the week.

We can see that arriving at these decisions has taken some time and effort with the expedition leader receiving feedback from the team on various aspects of the initial plan. Potential problems have been identified and resolved using email and telephone calls between the expedition team.

Accommodation deposits have already been paid and the ferry places for the group now need to be booked to guarantee a sailing.

Contact is made with the ferry company, who provide advice on the paperwork required to transport pressurised cylinders on their ferry. Places are booked for all the vehicles and the boats. The paperwork is not difficult but does involve collating vehicle registration details and an inventory of dangerous substances they are carrying with reference to UN identification codes.

Now that it is clear how the team and equipment are going to get to the island, some thought is required on the local logistics on the island.

The rendezvous point on arrival on the island is the farmhouse accommodation. Rooms have been allocated in advance. Fortunately with six rooms and with many of the dive group travelling with partners, the allocations will not be a problem. The accommodation also has a wet kit area for the dive equipment and a large car parking area for the RIBs and vehicles. It is also relatively isolated and on a hill top, making it easy to use the portable petrol compressor. Once on the island a group will need to do the shopping for perishable provisions, having checked out the available fridge space.

The accommodation is in a central location roughly 20 to 30 minutes' leisurely drive to slipways on three sides of the island. A petrol station is two minutes' drive away and it has a convenience store.

So far the logistical planning in this example has been fairly straightforward. Not much thought has been given yet to the diving itself, but rather to the structure to support the diving; the accommodation, transport and feeding the team.

Paperwork, permissions and permits

Most diving expeditions require a minimal amount of administration paperwork. While this sounds tedious it can be absolutely vital to the outcome of the expedition.

To assist the planning of the expedition, some internal paperwork will probably have to be generated such as an expedition brochure, an expedition plan, various check-lists and application forms as already described.

Individuals in the dive team will usually have to provide written proof of qualifications, experience, current membership of diving organisations, medical certificates (some countries do not accept self-declaration forms) and third party and medical insurance.

In the UK, and at most locations around the world, land and resources are owned, either by the state or individuals. External paperwork may be required in order to gain permission/permits to dive a particular site.

Allow plenty of time to get the necessary paperwork. Do not leave it to the last minute. This may include, but is not limited to:

- Access to wrecks: some sites are protected and will require written permission from the owner or the local government (or both) before being allowed to dive. In the UK, the Ministry of Defence produces lists of wrecks that are strictly off limits to divers unless written permission is obtained. Sites are usually identified as protected on charts but it is always best to check with the appropriate authorities (see *Protecting our underwater heritage*, page 132).
- Access to sea areas: some areas of sea are protected and may require written permission and permits to dive.
- Launch permits: at most harbours there will be some sort of permit required to launch and recover boats. Make sure you understand the local bye-laws, which are usually a condition of the permit.

Failure to obtain the necessary permissions or not having the correct documents can result in at best not being able to dive the desired site or at worst legal action, which can lead to hefty fines, confiscation of equipment or imprisonment depending on the offence.

Before the expedition

The detailed plan and meeting

It is useful to collate the output of all the planning into a detailed written plan that can be issued to all the participants before the expedition. Allow participants as much time as possible to read and understand the plan, put together their equipment and make comments.

The actual level of detail needed will depend on the nature of the expedition. For most weekend expeditions with a dive-fit dive team, a single page of A4 may be sufficient. However, a complicated scientific project may require many pages detailing the scientific work in addition to the logistics and other arrangements.

Typically, a very detailed plan for an expedition might run to about 15 to 20 pages in total, but bear in mind the longer it is, the less likely it is to be read thoroughly.

The expedition leader should arrange for a meeting of the entire expedition team. This will give the team the opportunity to meet each other, run through the plans and sort out the equipment and any issues arising.

If this is not possible, it is advisable for the expedition leader to make contact with each member of the expedition team. A quick phone call is sometimes more effective than a blanket email in making sure that the participant is fully aware of the plans and if they have any issues that need attention.

Encourage everyone to take an active part in 'making it happen' and check that everyone is aware of their duties on a daily basis. It is important that everyone shares duties and responsibilities for the duration of the expedition, in accordance with their training and abilities.

Where an expedition team has not had the opportunity to meet face to face beforehand, an initial introductory meeting at the dive base is vital.

The expedition leader should introduce themselves at the start of the expedition, reminding the expedition team that they are the first point of contact for any issues that arise during the expedition.

It is a good idea where divers may not know each other for them to introduce themselves, informing the rest of the expedition team about their diving experience, why they are on the expedition, their specific role and what they are hoping to get from the expedition.

The expedition leader should encourage a culture of 'helping each other' as this will make for a successful and enjoyable expedition.

Ensure the domestic arrangements are understood by everyone, covering such things as:

- The accommodation arrangements and house rules.
- The daily rota, checking that everyone understands their roles.
- The sleeping arrangements, ensuring that everyone is happy with whom they are sharing a room. (People who snore may be an issue.)
- The dive planning and management arrangements.
- How the catering will work.

A written daily rota is a good way of clarifying who is responsible for what. There is an example of an expedition rota at the end of the chapter (*see page 49*).

During the expedition

Dive management

Expedition leaders must give some thought to how they manage the dives. Most expedition leaders will want to dive themselves and will need to leave someone else in charge on the surface at some point.

Dive management is far more than just completing a dive log sheet. It is the bringing to bear of all the expedition resources to achieve the diving aims in a safe manner.

When it comes to the day's diving programme, someone needs to be in charge. This person is the dive manager and there also should be an assistant dive manager. The expedition leader may sometimes be the dive manager but must also be able to delegate these roles to the more experienced divers in their team.

The dive manager's job typically starts with checking that weather conditions, equipment and the dive team are all ready for the day's planned activities. Should any major problems be identified then a new plan may have to be considered and discussed with the expedition leader. As soon as a plan is decided upon, it is wise to brief your dive team of the plan.

Site location techniques

This is an important aspect of planning and can sometimes be lost in among all the other planning. Knowing exactly where you are intending to dive and how you are going to find it and when you can dive it can take a considerable amount of time even if the sites are relatively well known. Even the best guide books have errors in position details and rarely state the timing of slack water. Position errors are covered in more detail in Chapter 6.

Daily routine

Most expeditions will start with a slightly chaotic first day regardless of how well they were planned. The team will then usually settle into daily routine fairly soon without much input from the expedition leader.

Diving, after all, usually involves getting up, travel to the site, eating, going diving, eating, going diving, travel back from the site, preparing for the next days diving, eating and relaxing.

However, the expedition leader should make sure a clear and concise daily brief is given so that the expedition team is fully aware of the plans for the day and the routine stays efficient and enjoyable rather than becoming a test of endurance.

There are many things that could be included in a brief, but remember that it generally needs to be 'brief'.

- It could start with a weather forecast and quick read through of the main points from a written timetable of the day's activities. Timetables are a simple but very effective tool for helping keeping the days activities running on time (see sample timetable, page 49).
- Ensure diving buddies are suitably paired in terms of qualifications and experience for the dive and interests. Check with everyone that this diving is within their experience and is also within safe diving guidelines.

- Liaise with the boat skipper on behalf of the expedition team to ensure that the skipper knows who in the team decides what, to avoid the skipper receiving contradictory information.

Run through the details of the dive plan to be followed and remind the team of any specific risks identified and who to keep the risks to a minimum. On arrival at the dive site, check that the dive plan is still workable. Be prepared to change your plans should conditions on site dictate.

Make sure the team have fully understood the plan, and clarify any issues they raise.

Emergency actions

At any stage of the expedition there may be an emergency that needs to be dealt with. Diving operations will, in general, have to be halted until the emergency is over. Plans to deal with common diving emergencies are discussed in Chapter 8.

Reporting

For well-organised scientific expeditions, reporting is usually built into the expedition itself. For other expeditions the reporting may simply be a case of completing log sheets and logbooks.

Most expedition leaders do not really enjoy report writing, particularly at the end of the expedition. One way to minimise the burden is keep a diary throughout the expedition, perhaps delegating someone different each day to write a paragraph on how the day went. For most expeditions, a diary will form most of the report content.

Wherever possible make sure the necessary paperwork is completed on the day, otherwise the burden becomes too much at the end of the expedition.

After the expedition

Although the diving may be complete the expedition may not be completely finished. Acknowledgements, presentations and reports will follow on from most expeditions.

Acknowledgements

It is important to thank all those who contributed towards making the expedition happen. This may be the hard boat skipper, a local dive facility, local people who have assisted, sponsors and even those on the expedition itself. Sometimes this may require more than just a quick phone call or email; a formal letter may be more appropriate.

Make sure that you leave your expedition base as you found it, so that no one has cause to complain. After all, you may wish to return and should do your utmost to get along with all those whom you come into contact with, taking away and leaving good memories of your expedition.

Presentations

Presentations are a way of sharing your expedition experiences with others and follow on from many expeditions. For some expeditions these may even be a means of funding the expedition or building support for future expeditions, financial or otherwise. If you plan to give a presentation, it is important to remember who your audience are and to tailor the presentation accordingly. If you are presenting to a group of non-divers, for example, take care to avoid too much jargon and consider omitting details that only divers find interesting.

Reports

There may be a certain amount of administration still to do, particularly if grants or sponsorship are involved. This may well involve writing an expedition report and providing dive log sheets and a financial statement.

A good report will also include notes so that expedition can be improved next time. Feedback from those participating in the expedition is valuable in this respect and it may be appropriate to provide everyone with a form to complete.

Checklist

Expedition checklist

Personal kit		Personal diving kit	
Passport and visas		Hood	
Joining instructions and contact details		Drysuit	
Diving qualifications		Gloves	
Boat-handling qualifications		Cylinders for two dives	
Travel documents		Pony cylinder	
Diving emergency insurance documents		Regulators	
Travel insurance documents		Stab jacket/wing	
Medication (and any supporting paperwork)		Weight belt	
Mobile phone		Fins	
Money		Woolly bear	
Sleeping mat		Computer	
Sleeping bag		Net cutter/knife	
Towel and tea towel		Torch (chargeable/bring batteries)	
Toiletries		Talcum powder, wax or zip lube	
Waterproof coat		Spare kit	
Hat and gloves		Boat coat, hat and gloves	
Warm clothing			
Suitable stout walking footwear		**Personal location aids**	
Sun block		Collapsible hi-visibility flag	
Dry bag		Delayed SMB and reel	
Thermos flask		Spare SMB	
Drinks container		Reserve torch	
Lights/torches and batteries		Whistle	
Plastic plate, plastic cup, knife, fork, spoon		Personal flares	

Boat equipment		First aid equipment	
Boats (fully operational)		Expedition member details (sealed)	
Spare fuel tanks		Oxygen first aid kits	
Engine oil for 2 stroke engines		First aid equipment	
Trailers (fully operational)		Advanced medical equipment	
Third party boat insurance		Satellite phone	
VHF radio			

Gas blending equipment		Diving planning	
Oxygen/helium bottles		Charts and nautical almanacs	
Decanting equipment		Tide tables	
Oxygen analyser		Decompression tables	
Helium analyser		Laptop with deco software	
Laptop with blending software		Laminator	
Blending tables		Extension leads and plug adaptors	

Site location and marking		Transport	
Laminated GPS co-ordinates		Driving license	
Magnetometer		Breakdown insurance (inc. trailers)	
GPS and echo-sounder		Maps	
Side-scan sonar		List of alternative slipways	
Shot lines and buoys		Self-help vehicle manuals	
Decompression trapeze			

Sample expedition day rota and sample timetable

Name	Dive manager	Deputy dive manager	Cox'n/Navigator	Boat crew	Wake up call	Prepare breakfast	Prepare packed lunch	Prepare dinner (if you don't cook you wash up!)	Gas filling
1 Geoff	Mon	Tue			Sat	Fri	Thu	Thu	Mon
2 Andy	Tue	Wed			Mon	Sat	Fri	Wed	Mon
3 Fiona	Wed	Thu			Tue	Mon	Sat		Wed
4 Kath	Thu	Fri			Wed	Tue	Mon	Sat	Thu
5 Gordon	Fri	Sat			Thu	Wed	Tue	Mon	Fri
6 Clare	Sat	Mon			Thu	Wed	Tue	Mon	Fri
7 Graeme			Mon	Tue		Fri			Mon
8 George			Tue	Wed	Mon	Sat	Fri	Wed	Tue
9 Max			Wed	Thu	Tue	Mon	Sat		Wed
10 Colin			Thu	Fri	Wed	Tue	Mon	Sat	Thu
11 Jeff			Fri	Sat	Thu	Wed	Tue	Mon	Fri
12 Paul			Mon	Tue		Fri			Mon

	Saturday
Breakfast and make packed lunch	6.30am
Briefing and depart for slipway	7.00am
Load and launch boats	7.30am
Depart for and location of dive site 1	8.00am
Arrive at dive site 1: Dunlossit Pier	8.30am
Dive 1 (two waves)	10.00am
Lunch, transit and locate 2nd site: Drift near Wye Regis Wk	12.00pm
Dive 2 (two waves)	13.00pm
Set off for slipway	15.00pm
Arrival at slipway and recover boats	15.30pm
Return to accommodation	16.00pm
Charge tanks, prepare evening meal	17.00pm
Evening meal	19.30pm

Application form

Sample expedition application form

Title: Mr/Miss/Mrs/other: .... (male/female) ......

Name: ....

Permanent address ....

.... **Postcode:** ....

Telephone number (home): ....

Telephone number (mob): ....

E-mail address: ....

BSAC membership no: .... **No of UK dives:** ....

Diving qualifications

....

What skills or resources can you bring to the expedition?

- ☐ Oxygen administrator
- ☐ First aider
- ☐ Underwater photographer
- ☐ Underwater videographer
- ☐ Marine biologist
- ☐ Wreck research
- ☐ Side-scan sonar operator
- ☐ Can draw wreck layouts
- ☐ Prepared to help write report
- ☐ Diver cox'n
- ☐ Access to 4WD
- ☐ Access to RIB

Other

....

Your equipment configuration (e.g. single 12-litre + pony, rebreather, twin 10-litre etc)

....

Next of kin (and relationship e.g. wife, husband, father, mother):

Name: .... **Relationship:** ....

Telephone number (home): ....

Telephone number (mob): ....

**THIS APPLICATION FORM IS SEALED IN AN ENVELOPE
AND TAKEN ON THE EXPEDITION FOR OPENING IN CASE OF EMERGENCY.**

I confirm that the information given in this application form is correct, to the best of my knowledge, that I am fit to dive and that I will dive in accordance with BSAC safe diving practice.

Signature: .... Date: ....

Sample expedition feedback form

Name

1) How did you rate the dives we completed (5 – excellent, 1 - poor)?

1	Dive site 1		5	Dive site 5		9	Dive site 9	
2	Dive site 2		6	Dive site 6		10	Dive site 10	
3	Dive site 3		7	Dive site 7		11	Dive site 11	
4	Dive site 4		8	Dive site 8		12	Dive site 12	

2) Which ones of these did you think were challenging and adventurous?

3) Did you think the briefings for the dives were adequate? (yes/no, and comments)

4) How did you rate the skipper? (5 – excellent, 1 – poor and comments)

5) Are there any aspects of the expedition that you thought were unsafe?

6) How do you rate the accommodation? (5 – excellent, 1 – poor and comments)?

7) Were the arrangements for food adequate (yes/no, and comments)

8) Do you think the expedition was well organised? (yes/no, and comments)

9) Did you enjoy the expedition and what did you learn?

10) Would you recommend a similar expedition to others?

Chapter 4

Risk assessment

What is risk assessment? Risk assessment is commonplace in daily life. At its simplest, it is a process for identifying possible hazards, understanding the level of risk associated with the hazard, deciding on the severity of the hazard and then planning how to minimise the risk.

In diving expeditions, risk assessment can become a more complex process – the risks can be more varied, less predictable and potentially more serious if they occur. A growing culture of litigation means that we not only need to think and act on risk assessment, but we may be asked to demonstrate that we have done this. In this chapter we will look at the broad scope of diving incidents that could be encountered on expeditions and then look at the process of conducting risk assessments.

The British Sub Aqua Club has been analysing sport diving incidents that occur both above and below the water since 1964. Details of overall trends and individual diving incidents are published in BSAC's annual *NDC Diving Incidents Report*, which can be found on the BSAC website.

Types of incidents

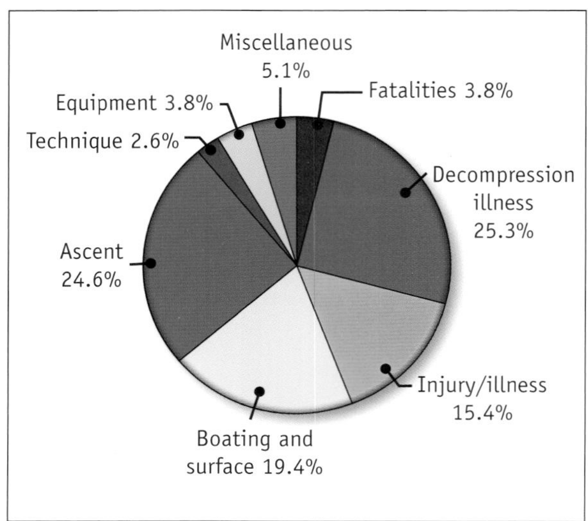

Proportion of diving incidents by type (2005-07 averages)

The BSAC diving incident report form assists data capture

Reporting diving incidents

The BSAC incident report categorises incidents into standard groups (see chart, above). The number and nature of the incidents varies from year to year, but you can see the average occurrences of each type over the last few years in the chart above.

Meaningful analysis of diving incidents relies on good data capture. BSAC works collaboratively with the Maritime and Coastguard Agency, the Royal National Lifeboat Institution and the rescue services to get information. However, the best quality information comes from divers themselves. They are able to provide detailed information to enable the BSAC Incidents Adviser to draw the best conclusions from the data.

It is important, therefore, for divers to report incidents. The process is confidential and is based on the Incident Report Form available on the BSAC website, which will guide you through the information required.

Learning from diving incidents

Collation of detailed diving incident statistics allows us to better understand some of the factors that cause them. This knowledge is reflected in the *Safe Diving* guidelines published by BSAC (see the BSAC website), which are updated regularly in the light of incident data.

This publication provides details of all recommended procedures for safe diving and should be part of the toolkit of all expedition leaders.

Apart from detailed procedures listed in *Safe Diving*, there are some general considerations that come out of the incident reports. There are three basic principles that could reduce diving incidents if followed by all divers:

- Dive within your personal limits. Too many diving incidents are caused by people diving too deep, or at sites that they are not prepared for.
- Plan and prepare your dives in advance. For example, planning slack water times will reduce the effects of strong tidal streams on your divers.
- Being dive fit and skilled enough for your planned dive. This is especially important early in the season and shake-down dives are always a good time to review fitness and to practise techniques. As can be seen from the incident reports, ascents are a particular source of problems – being properly prepared and having the appropriate skills for the proposed dive can significantly reduce the likelihood of an incident.

Risk assessment within diving

In diving, risk assessment usually operates in an informal manner and often uses terminology particular to divers, rather than phrases that might be used more formally by organisations such as the UK's Health and Safety Executive. As long as we are sport diving and have no financial gain, we are not at work (see *Diving at work regulations,* page 131) and we are not obliged to produce a written risk assessment. Although, as we shall see shortly, there may be very good reasons why we should.

On a normal day dive, risk assessment is carried out informally. For example, a weather report is obtained and decisions on safety of dive sites are made. Tides are looked at, to determine safe entry points to the water and slack water times, to improve the safety on the dive. Divers are paired up according to suitability of experience levels for the dives to be conducted. Appropriate equipment is prepared and checked. All of these assessed risks are communicated to the diving group by means of a brief by the dive manager and, finally, the dive buddies communicate with each other through a pre-dive brief. These briefings are constructed using the SEEDS principle: dividing the brief into sections on Safety, Exercise, Equipment, Discipline and Signals.

Ongoing risk assessment is carried out based on feedback from post-dive debriefs and by update briefs from the dive manager. Our risk assessment, then, is the SEEDS brief (and the planning and preparation behind it). Organisations such as BSAC build in this level of risk assessment within their training programmes, and adherence to those training programmes will ensure an appropriate level of informal risk assessment.

An expedition leader needs a greater understanding of the risk assessment process and to be able to develop a more formal process to help with risk assessment in more complex situations, such as occur on diving expeditions. Also, we need to explore how we can formalise the process so that you can show that an appropriate risk assessment was carried out, if needed.

We need to have an understanding of useful risk assessment terminology for diving in relation to that used by the HSE.

BSAC has developed a process of risk assessment to achieve these aims. The overall objectives of risk assessment for diving as defined by the BSAC are:

- To place the emphasis on the prevention of incidents rather than on the actions needed to resolve them.
- To reduce the number and seriousness of diving incidents.
- To continue to promote safe diving practices to all divers.
- To ensure that divers can enjoy their sport safely.

A structured approach to risk assessment

Risk assessment is a common sense process and can be used informally, however, for those unfamiliar with the process a structured approach can be useful.

There are five simple steps to this structured approach.

1. Decide what the potential and significant risks are.
2. Decide who or what is at risk during the activity.
3. Decide how dangerous the risks are by using a system of evaluation.
4. Decide what controls could be put into place to help minimise the risks.
5. Record the actions and decisions taken by putting the plan onto paper for further use, updating and filing as a permanent record.

Many of these stages are inherently built into the BSAC training programme.

Who carries out risk assessment?

Risk assessment is usually conducted by a number of people involved in a diving expedition. The expedition leader will plan the whole expedition, taking into consideration as many aspects as possible, and will produce an expedition plan that will record decisions on aspects such as dive sites, dive types as well as domestic activities. These decisions will help to formulate the overall expedition and to take into account the broader risks. The type of expedition and the decisions made will, of course, depend on the experience of the expedition leader. The expedition leader will provide an overall briefing to the expedition team.

The appointed dive manager for the day will lead the expedition plan for the day or they may have created their own plan for the duration of the day's diving. The dive manager has to carefully consider the overall activities of the day, such as assessing the limitations of the divers, personal experience and diving grades of those attending. From this they will put together a plan that can be communicated to the divers through a brief. It is the knowledge and experience of the dive manager that will ensure all significant risks have been covered and controls put in place to minimise the risks.

A dive leader will be appointed within each dive pair, and it is the responsibility of the dive leader to ensure that the pair conduct a safe dive within the structure provided by the dive manager and the limitations of the least experienced of the pair.

The dive buddy has the responsibility for their own conduct, for self-help when needed and looking after their buddy. So, in expeditionary diving, risk assessment is carried out by everyone at all levels.

Conducting a risk assessment

There are four main terms that are used in discussions of risk assessment:

- Hazard – the aspect of the activity that is likely to cause harm.
- Risk – the likelihood that harm will actually occur.
- Generic – general risks likely to occur on any dive.
- Specific – risks specific to particular activities.

Step one is to decide what are the more significant hazards that your divers will be exposed to. These can range from the generic diving hazards, such as mask squeeze and pressure effects on ears or lungs, to specific hazards associated with the type of diving, such as snagging on fishing line while wreck diving. You will also need to consider the specific dive site. If you know the site, a generic assessment can be done prior to visiting the site. These risks will be ones that are clearly associated with the type of site being used, such as rocky shore or known tidal streams. When you arrive at the site, the specific hazards of the day can be addressed, for example, the visibility and current weather conditions.

Step two is to decide who is at risk from each of the significant hazards you have identified. For example, some hazards may apply to all of your divers (such as tidal streams), while others might be specific to certain groups such as trainees (for example, mask squeeze).

Having listed both the generic and specific hazards, step three is the evaluation of the risk of these potential hazards occurring. This can be done using a risk matrix (see the Risk Evaluation Matrix opposite).

Once the risk level has been identified, step four determines how to control each risk. This is not the action needed if the hazard has occurred, but what procedure or action must exist to limit or control the risk of the hazard occurring. These can be simple generic controls, for example, reminding divers to breathe normally on ascents, or by specific procedures such as diving on slack water to reduce the likelihood of divers being carried away by the tide.

In the event of a hazard occurring, it must be dealt with effectively. Step five is to plan and record what actions will be taken to deal with the hazard. For example, this could involve a description of the procedures planned to evacuate a diver suffering from decompression illness from the dive site.

Evaluating the risk

Evaluating the risk for each hazard, in step three, can be carried out using the matrix shown opposite. The principle behind this evaluation is that it gives an assessment of the importance of the risk based on the severity of the risk and the likelihood of it happening. A certain amount of experience is required to use this risk matrix to evaluate whether a particular hazard occurs frequently or rarely. In addition to our own experience, the diving incident statistics can help to inform us. It is also going to be rather a subjective decision as to the likely severity of a hazard. By cross-referencing the likelihood and severity a decision can be reached as to the level of risk.

For example, a heart attack while diving is a possible hazard. The diving statistics show us that this is a rare occurrence but it can, of course, be fatal in its worse case. By using the matrix, shown opposite, this will give a level of risk of medium.

Excess pressure on eardrums can occur occasionally such as in divers under training or with a cold. The results might be considered as a major injury in its worse case – a burst eardrum and possible permanent loss of hearing. By using the matrix this gives a level of risk as medium.

RISK EVALUATION MATRIX					
Frequency of occurrence / Severity	Fatal	Major injury	Moderate injury	Minor injury	Trivial injury
Very common	High	High	High	Medium	Low
Frequent	High	High	Medium	Medium	Low
Occasional	High	Medium	Medium	Low	Low
Rare	Medium	Medium	Low	Low	Low

Risk evaluation matrix (Source: BSAC)

Producing a written risk assessment

Step five is to record the risk assessment. The BSAC risk assessment sheet is just one example of a layout for a written risk assessment, but it is one that has been adopted by many diving agencies. The example shown here evaluates the risks of generic diving hazards. The grey shaded columns show the frequency and severity values used to obtain the risk evaluation from the risk evaluation matrix, above. The table on page 58 shows the information that needs to be included in a risk assessment planning sheet.

It can be seen that the five features of a risk assessment are all present: a brief description of the hazard, an identification of who is at risk, the level of risk based on the matrix, a description of the controls to limit the risk and finally a description of the measures to take in the event that the controls are insufficient.

A risk assessment sheet will form part of the dive plan for the day or for the expedition.

The form is available from the BSAC website.

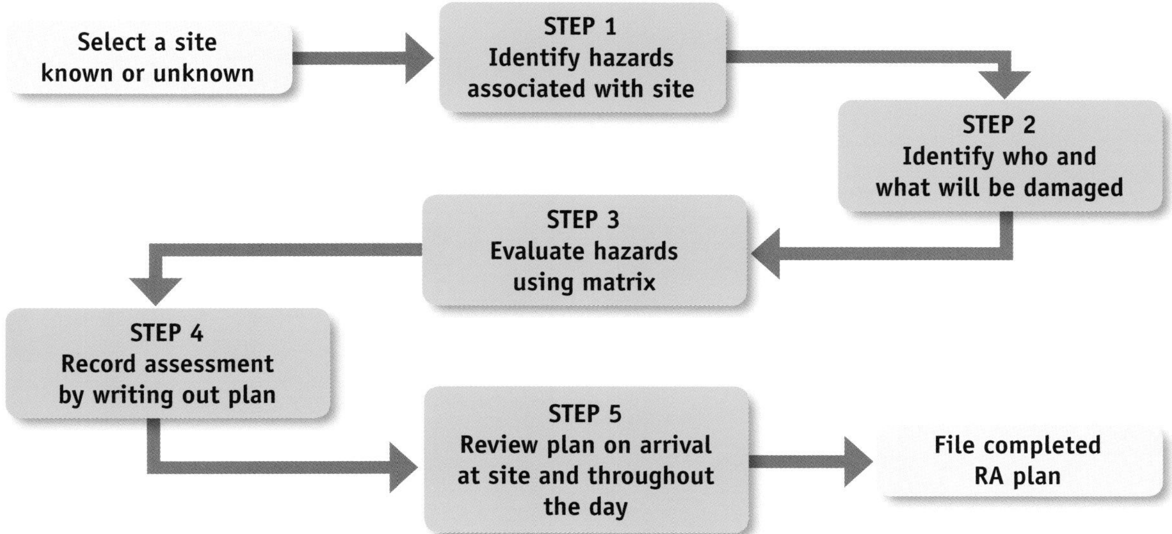

Five steps to completion of a risk assessment: this can be used as a reminder of how to conduct a risk assessment for an expedition. An example of a risk assessment carried out for a day's diving expedition is shown in case study 4.1, page 61

Generic hazards

Hazard	Who	Frequency	Severity	Risk evaluation	Controls	Immediate measures to deal with consequences if risk does occur
Heart attack	All	Rare	Fatal	Medium	Medical self-declaration/ referral to medical referee	Basic Life Support (CPR) by instructor Emergency services activation plan
Ear damage	All	Occasional	Moderate injury	Medium	Trainees receive specific instruction in ear clearing Divers or snorkellers do not dive when suffering from a cold	Assistance from instructor or buddy
Mask squeeze	Trainees	Rare	Minor injury	Low	Only mask which encloses both eyes and nose in the same airspace used. Trainees receive specific instruction in mask equalisation	Assistance from instructor or buddy
Running out of gas	All divers	Occasional	Fatal	High	All scuba sets fitted with cylinder pressure gauges Monitoring by instructor Instructor/trainee ratios in accordance with BSAC recommendations	All divers carry alternate source

A risk assessment of some generic diving hazards using a format adopted by BSAC,

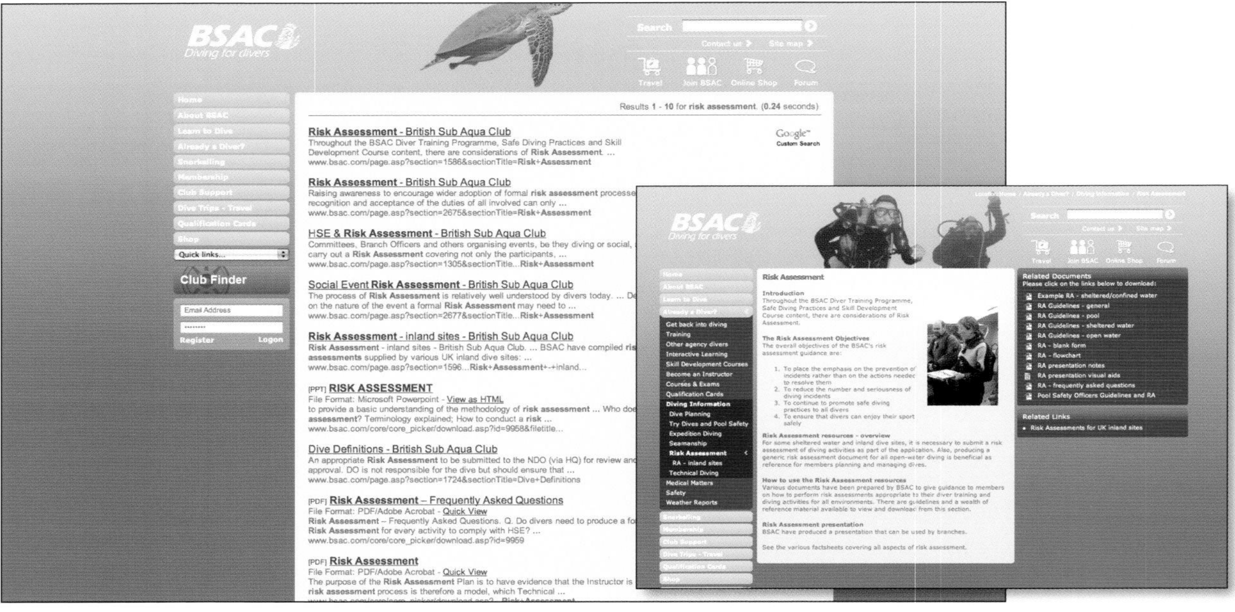

A comprehensive database of risk assessment and health and safety issues can be found on the BSAC website

Risk assessment should place the emphasis on the prevention of incidents through safe diving practice

Legal responsibility for risk management

In diving, there is sometimes confusion as to who takes responsibility for diving activities. For example, in BSAC branches it is usually the diving officer who is responsible for overall safety of diving activities. However, what if that person is not present at the dive site or perhaps doesn't even know the diving is taking place? In such a situation they cannot be expected to take responsibility for actions taken by divers. How do we clarify the responsibilities for safe actions for various types of dives – especially any dives that do not conform to what we would normally associate with safe practices. BSAC provides advice on what it considers to be safe diving practices in the booklet *Safe Diving*, available on its website. This is an A–Z reference guide on procedures that should be followed to minimise risk in diving. BSAC categorises dives as those that conform with *Safe Diving* and those that do not. Furthermore, they have defined the responsibilities of divers in relation to these types of dives. These responsibilities are shown overleaf.

Responsibilities

Authority and responsibilities within the BSAC

Dive definition	DO's responsibility	Member's responsibility	Example
Diving within current 'Safe Diving'	If the dive is conducted with diving officer's (DO) approval, the DO accepts full responsibility for the dive. The DO is accountable to ensure that the person appointed as the dive manager is properly qualified and experienced for the task and will manage operations so as to be within current 'Safe Diving'.	To comply with 'Safe Diving' and with the instructions given by the appointed dive manager. To report to the dive manager any departures from 'Safe Diving' whether planned or unplanned. To be aware that 'Safe Diving' and DO or dive manager's instructions are designed to minimise risk and maximise safety of the diver and others. Deliberate contravention may result in the DO taking action to protect BSAC members and other divers. DOs may refer to the document *'BSAC Volunteers—Procedure for change of status'* in the event of required action.	Any DO authorised dive. DO may sanction all dive leaders (and above) in the club to organise and run branch dives to known locations without notification unless training is to be conducted or inexperienced members (eg ocean divers) are in attendance. DO may sanction all advanced divers (and above) in the club to organise and run branch dives to unknown locations without notification, unless training is to be conducted or inexperienced members are in attendance.
	If the dive is conducted without DO approval, the DO is not responsible for the dive but is still responsible for the conduct of branch training and previously awarded qualifications.	To comply with 'Safe Diving'. Deliberate contravention may result in the DO taking action to protect BSAC members and other divers. Warning: the dive manager, the most experienced diver and/or the member may be held responsible for any adverse consequences of the dive.	A BSAC member diving on holiday. A BSAC member diving on a shuttle boat. A BSAC diver attending a BSAC course (and therefore not requiring the approval of the branch DO).
	Technical dive planned to depths below 80m within 'Safe Diving'. An appropriate risk assessment to be submitted to the National DO (via BSAC HQ) for review and approval. DO is not responsible for the dive but should ensure that approval from NDO has been sought.	To comply with 'Safe Diving' – members should only dive to the depths that they are qualified to dive to and must submit an appropriate risk assessment to the NDO via HQ for review and approval. To comply with the procedures listed within the approved risk assessment.	A deep dive conducted by an experienced team of divers who are qualified to dive to the planned depths and who have received approval from the NDO based on an appropriate risk assessment. A team of BSAC divers developing new diving techniques at depth who have received NDO approval based on an appropriate Risk Assessment.
Diving outside current 'Safe Diving'	A DO must not permit or sanction plans to dive outside current 'Safe Diving' and they should warn the members accordingly. Although they are not accountable for the dive, the DO would still be accountable for previous BSAC training and qualifications awarded.	Member is not able to dispense with legal responsibility of 'duty of care'. Members must recognise that the further away they stray from recommended guidelines ('Safe Diving'), they expose themselves to a greater risk of incidents and a greater risk of litigation. To be aware that 'Safe Diving' is designed to minimise risk and maximise safety of the diver and others. Deliberate contravention may result in the DO taking action to protect BSAC members and other divers. DOs may refer to the document *'BSAC Volunteers—Procedure for change of status'* in the event of required action. Note: disclaimers accepting personal responsibility or absolving others of responsibility for personal injury or death have no validity in UK law. It is not possible to avoid responsibility for negligence through disclaimers.	A diver exceeding the depth to which they are qualified to dive. Solo diving

CASE STUDY 4.1

Remote risks

This partial risk assessment for a drift dive, formed part of a risk assessment for the RIB expedition to Islay that was considered in the case studies in Chapter 3.

The story

The intention is to dive the wall underneath Dunlossit House Pier with a mixed ability group of divers. The current is likely to be strong and there will be little slack water.

How they did it

- The expedition leader has to be careful not to get bogged down in trivia. For example, experienced divers know that not clearing your ears on descent can cause major problems. Clearly for an in-experienced diver in the team it would be relevant to cover this.
- Appropriate risks must be identified. In this example, they are the issues of adventurous drift diving -getting separated, being located on the surface, and the risks associated with equipment have been identified as particular risks.
- A great deal of thought has gone into controlling these risks. The site will be assessed to check likely depths to be encountered, direction in which current is running and at what strength (is it too strong?). Divers will have to plan to end their dive at a certain time and then launch a delayed SMB at the end. They need to have a sufficient, separate air supply and be dive fit and experienced to undertake this dive.
- Use of an SMB from the start of the dive can increase the risk of separation as divers try to respond to any eddy currents they encounter on more adventurous dives. The surface current is also usually faster than the current the diver is travelling in causing the diver to be dragged upwards by the line. Therefore DSMBs are used at an agreed time, deployed from mid-water, towards the end of the dive.

Hazard	Who	Frequency	Severity	Risk evaluation	Controls	Immediate measures to deal with consequences if risk does occur
Loss of control in up and down currents	All divers	Occasional	Major injury	Medium	Correctly weighted for dive. Experienced and dive fit divers only (150+ UK dives including experience of fast dives). MUST have sufficient, separate air supply and MUST be capable of launching a DSMB unaided midwater.	Launch DSMB midwater to anchor diver on surface. Swim in direction of line.
Diver separation particularly on the adventurous drift dives	All divers	Occasional	Major injury	Medium	Divers to dive in buddy pairs at all times. Contact to be maintained throughout the dive. MUST have sufficient, separate air supply. Surface detection aids (DSMB, spare, flag, whistle) to be carried by all divers	Divers to surface immediately. Re-establish contact. Contact the coastguard immediately if diver overdue. Commence search.
Fast ascents, entanglement and task loading due to use of a SMB on an adventurous drift dive	All divers	Rare	Fatal	Medium	Experienced divers only. Check topography and conditions on site. Deploy DSMB at given time towards end of the dive from midwater.	See diver separation procedure.
Divers run over by ferry	All divers	Rare	Fatal	Medium	Divers to deploy DSMB and surface if drifting too far north. Careful timing of diver entry to water to avoid ferry crossing	Divers to surface immediately. Re-establish contact. Contact the coastguard immediately if diver overdue. Commence search. Rescue and first aid as appropriate.

Chapter 5

Management and leadership

Every diving expedition needs a leader, as we have seen, the expedition leader has overall responsibility for the expedition and plays a key role in its planning and organisation.

However the day-to-day management of the expedition, by a dive manager, is just as important. There are various levels of responsibility associated with this management during the expedition. The dive manager may be the expedition leader or someone else in the team.

Dive managing is an essential task: a successfully managed expedition runs smoothly and is more enjoyable for the whole team.

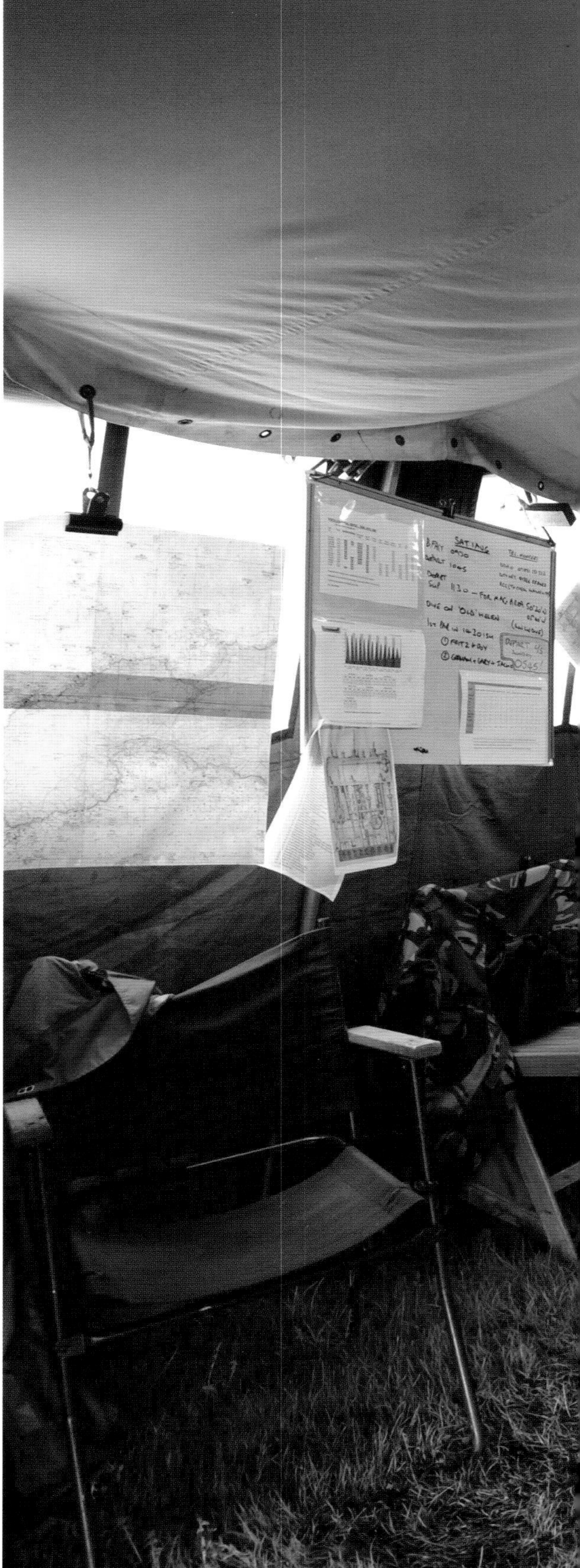

DIVE LOG

Dive manager's role

Roles and responsibilities

It is common practice on single day expeditions for the expedition leader to take on the day-to-day management of the dives - acting as the dive manager.

For longer expeditions, the expedition leader may appoint a series of dive managers to run the diving activities. This delegation has several advantages. It allows the expedition leader the time to consider overall aspects of the expedition while allowing the dive managers to specialise or concentrate on organising their specific activities. It also enables the dive team to develop their dive management skills - initially by carrying out a supporting role in the dive management team and then by gaining more experience within the role of dive manager itself.

For a more complex series of dives, deputy dive managers can also be nominated to assist the dive manager and to cover the times when the dive manager is below water, or indeed for specific tasks. The role of deputy dive manager provides an opportunity for the training and development of dive managers.

Aboard a boat, the responsibility for the boat lies with the skipper of a larger liveaboard boat or the diver-coxswain of a smaller boat. In both cases, they will have specific roles concerning the safety and operation of the boats. In some cases, for example the large boat skipper, they may have ultimate authority as to whether the boat sails or not. The skipper or cox'n may also have assistants.

When complex levels of responsibility exist in such situations, communication is extremely important. It is one of the roles of the expedition leader to ensure that this communication takes place.

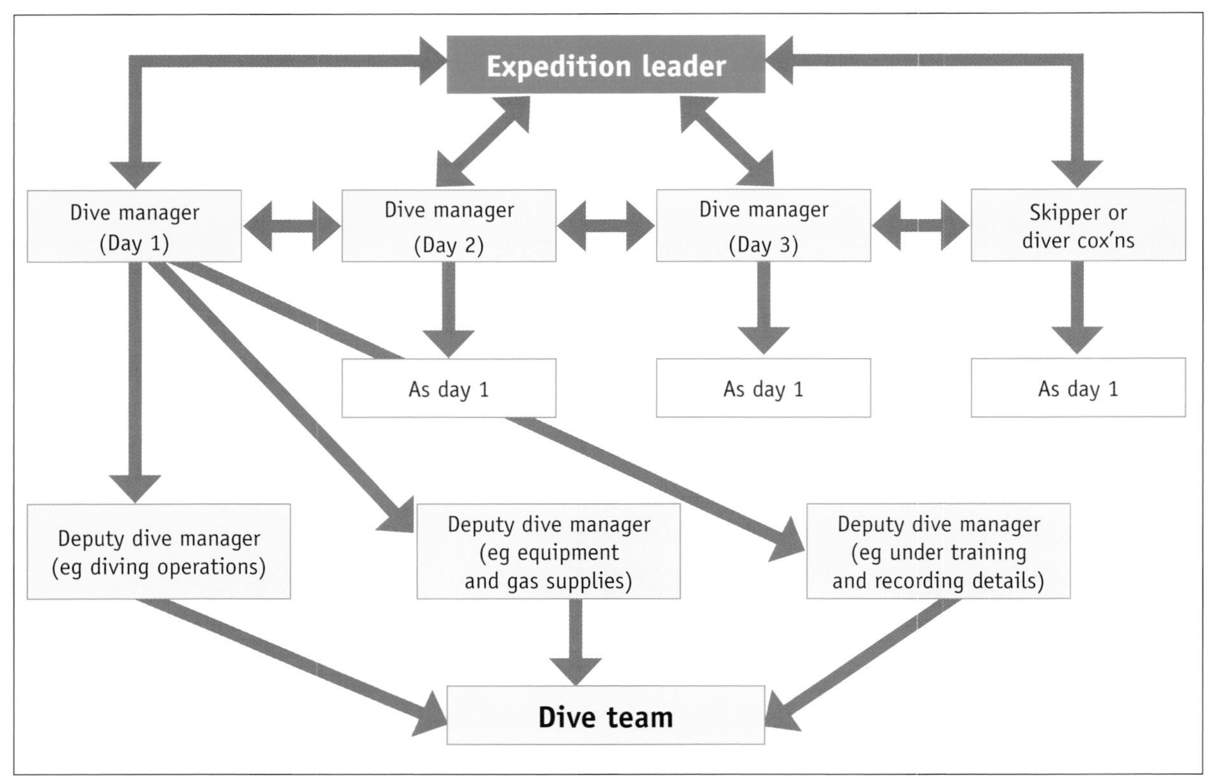

Roles and responsibilities of expedition personnel and how they interact

The dive manager runs the day's diving activity

Dive management

The dive manager is in overall control of all of the day's activities and personnel. Clearly this person needs the ability to organise diving or diving-related activities, and also the leadership skills to enable effective management of the team.

The dive manager for an expedition will normally be an experienced diver, such as a BSAC First Class Diver or Advanced Diver (or equivalent). They could, perhaps, also be someone being coached under the supervision of an experienced diver.

The dive manager has a role in the planning of the day's diving, in conjunction with the expedition leader, and has to be prepared for the dive day in advance. The dive manager needs all the background information to support any risk assessments, decision making about, or adaptations to, the plan.

The role of the dive manager on the day becomes that of an overall manager. So, although the dive manager is responsible for the diving activity for the day, they are not expected to do everything. A good dive manager will delegate. There are certain essential roles and the rotation of these duties on a day-to-day basis can help to build up the experience of the expedition team.

The essential roles are as follows.

- **Deputy dive manager** – to give backup support to the dive manager for specific tasks and when the dive manager is diving.
- **Boat officer** – to organise boat-related tasks on larger boats with a skipper, such as loading and stowing kit.
- **Cox'n** – to drive the boats, where the expedition includes the use of small boats.
- **Equipment officer** – to take charge of equipment, particularly if the expedition requires the use of extra expedition-specific kit.
- **Safety officer** – to check and look after the use, and stowage, of safety equipment.
- **Navigator** – to pay specialist attention to site location or passage planning.
- **First aider** – to deal with any minor medical matters.

Before diving

Boats

Ensure that small boats, if being used, are prepared and all their safety equipment is ready, checked and sufficient fuel is available, as recommended in the Combined Diving Associations manual *Guidelines for the Safe Operation of Member Club Boats*, available on the BSAC website.

If using a large boat, ensure that liaison with the skipper is effective and that both dive manager and skipper are aware of each other's needs.

Divers

An essential part of the expedition paperwork is a list of divers, qualifications and next of kin. This list should be available throughout the day. The dive manager will, in liaison with the expedition leader, allocate buddy pairs that are suitable for the day's diving objectives. The choices may be based on feedback from diving on previous days or based on information supplied before the expedition.

If a major expedition involves divers from different backgrounds, it may be necessary to have a check-out dive to enable the dive manager and expedition leader to gain robust knowledge of the experience and capabilities of the team members. The buddy pairs for the dive objectives may require specific training or need to accommodate special interests within the group.

Briefing

Delegation

The day's plan should include adequate arrangements to fulfil all the important roles when specialist members of the team (such as the cox'n, dive manager) are diving.

Briefing

A meeting point and time for an expedition briefing for the day needs to be arranged.This briefing may be led by the expedition leader, with the dive manager covering the specifics for that day. The dive manager needs to ensure that sufficient time is allowed for boat loading, equipment preparation and checks to be carried out before heading off for the dive.This is especially the case if the dive is planned for slack water.

The dive manager should be prepared with all equipment and details they need.A mobile phone is a good idea as are copies of the day's plan, itinerary, site location information, risk assessments and any other details appropriate to the day. This may include local site safety information and telephone numbers of local and emergency contacts such as the harbour master and coastguard.

To aid in the management process, a checklist is helpful. At the end of this chapter there is an example of a dive manager's checklist.

Final checks

The decision to go, change plans, or cancel a dive, depends how the weather affects the site and the journey to the site. So a final weather check, from the latest forecasts or from the coastguard, is essential.

On a large boat, the skipper may be able to provide information on the likely effects of weather on the dive site and offer alternative sites.

Running through the checklist a final time and making any necessary adjustments ensures the dive manager has everything necessary to carry out and manage the dive.

Before leaving, advise the coastguard that diving is taking place, and give details of the site's location and the number of divers involved. Should any problems arise, the coastguard can liaise with the emergency services and pass on any relevant information.

At the start of the day

The first job of the dive manager, at the start of the day's diving, is to organise the briefings that are needed for that day's diving.

The boat brief

The dive manager should first introduce the skipper or cox'n and ask for a boat briefing. This will cover any important points on boat safety, loading and housekeeping arrangements. On a charter boat, the skipper is required to do this as part of their working practices. This may need to happen before you are allowed onboard.

The skipper's safety brief should include:

- Description and location of all emergency equipment and safety procedures.
- Introduction of the crew and explanation of their role during the dive day.
- Designation of dry and wet, and possible no-go areas, on the boat. The skipper may also ask that when locating the dive site, all divers keep out of the wheelhouse so they can concentrate on the job in hand.
- Entry and exit procedures – the skipper should explain the best method of entry into the water and the procedure for getting back onboard using the ladder/diver lifts.
- The skipper should confirm the surface markers that they want divers to use on the site or whether they want all divers to use the shot line. Also, if other dive boats are on the dive site, they may request an additional signal from surfacing divers to identify them as belonging to their boat for pick up.

The dive manager's brief

The dive manager's brief is important because it enables information covered in the risk assessment to be communicated to the expedition team, as well as management information on how the day will proceed. This brief could take place before, during or after departing depending on the circumstances.

There is a dive manager's briefing checklist at the end of the chapter, beginning on page 72.

The dive manager keeps everyone informed with a thorough briefing

The dive manager's brief should cover:

- The dive objectives – the reason for the dive and what outcome is expected.
- A description of the site – a drawing or diagram may help if the site is known.
- Points of interest – this may include compass bearings or pilotage information on how to locate points of interest.
- Hazards – to take account of or avoid.
- Depth, visibility and currents – including a reminder to all divers to return to the shot or a recommendation to use distance lines in poor visibility. If the site is tidal, the dive manager should inform the group of any anticipated currents and their direction relative to the dive site.
- Anticipated surface conditions.
- Buddy pairs and the order of diving.
- Maximum dive times.
- Anticipated surface interval and a reminder of the effect of the first dive on subsequent dives.
- Separation and diver recall procedures.
- Out of gas procedures, if appropriate, including agreed signals.
- Roles of other personnel during the diving (such as who is the deputy dive manager and when they will take over).
- Reporting procedures for the dive log (gas, dive details).
- First-aid equipment location.
- Any specialist equipment required.
- Dive task or organisation. In the case of a complex task such as a multi-dive survey, a more detailed brief may be required to outline the roles of each of the divers in the team activity. This may also involve the use of dry runs of complex activities.
- General conduct – interaction with other water users, protection of the marine environment, particularly with regard to marine conservation and wreck protection.
- Reiterate any points arising from the risk assessment that have not been covered elsewhere
- Finally, give an opportunity for the buddy pairs to talk to each other and clarify any details if necessary.

During the day

The job of the dive manager is to 'make it all happen!' That job is not over once the brief is complete. The dive manager's role is to direct operations during the day to ensure that activities are carried out at the correct times, to monitor progress and compare it with the day's schedule.

A good dive manager will have delegated key tasks to others so that their main role is co-ordination of the plan. Timing is often crucial, especially when slack water is important, and adjustments to the plan may be needed during the day to keep things on track.

The dive manager will need to give the divers adequate notice to be ready to dive and to ensure that they have time to kit up, carry out a buddy check and be ready to dive.

A key role of the dive manager is to be aware of developing situations around them. Keeping up-to-date log sheet information throughout diving activities is important. Safety is the prime purpose of maintaining all dive details and information on each buddy pair. Knowing when divers are expected to surface is important in identifying any potential incidents. The dive manager needs know that the divers are monitored at all times. At all times during the diving, someone needs to be appointed to watch out for divers surfacing or any other signs of potential trouble.

The dive manager needs to be aware of developing situations that may affect the diving day. These could be

Reacting to change

changes in weather conditions that may force a change to the dive plan. A partnership between the boat skipper or cox'n and the dive manager is important. Ideally, the earlier the dive manager becomes aware of a change in circumstances, the easier it is to make changes to the plan.

Sometimes other factors influence a developing situation. For example, a late departure or poor weather slowing the passage can affect the timing of arrival for slack water leading to difficulty diving the site. Delay with any activity (such as taking too long to find and shot a wreck, diver equipment problems or boat problems) can often disrupt the plan. A good dive manager will have planned for these eventualities, pick up the developing situation early and will be able to take account of these in the running of the day.

Working with the skipper

The dive manager should establish a good working relationship with the skipper to achieve the dive objectives. Remember that the skipper or cox'n is responsible for the safety of the boat and those onboard. This includes the safe dropping off and picking up of divers. The skipper, or cox'n, will have the final say about whether it is safe to dive at that site with the current weather conditions.

Some hard boat skippers may not be sufficiently experienced for your expedition team's needs or may because of commercial pressures be inclined to proceed in marginal conditions. In which case the expedition leader or dive manager should advise accordingly.

The dive manager should organise the divers to ensure they are ready to dive when requested by the skipper. The dive manager should ensure that the skipper gets any assistance required, particularly when recovering divers

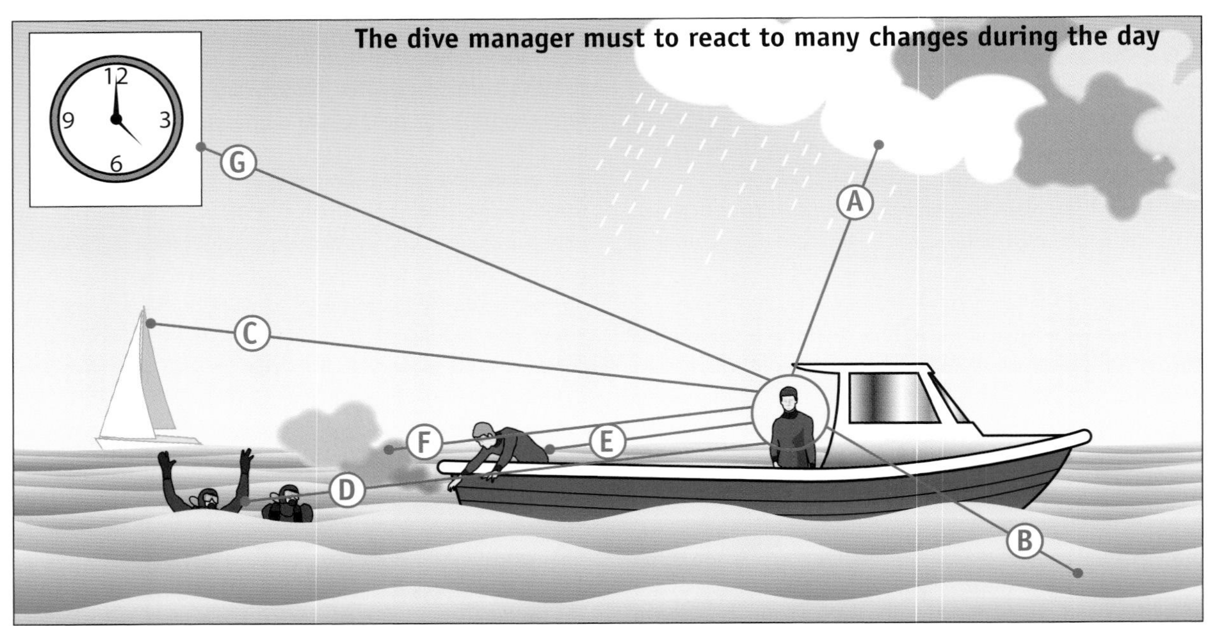

A Changes to the weather
B Changing conditions at sea –wind, waves and tide
C Potential hazards at sea or hazards to divers
D Developing situations with divers in the water
E Developing situations affecting divers in the boat
F Problems with the boat
G Awareness of timing and causes of delay (such as boat or diver problems that may affect diving at slack water, late return to shore, unexpected darkness)

The dive manager and the boat's skipper need to work together

or berthing. The deputy dive managers need to work with the skipper to ensure a smooth operation when the dive manager is diving.

It is the dive manager's responsibility to manage the diving activity and the dive log sheets – do not expect the skipper to do this. However, some skippers may wish to keep their own records. Even though the skipper and crew will probably monitor the divers' position on the dive site, it is also important for the dive manager to do the same. The dive manager may consider staggering the waves of divers to ensure adequate surface cover is available.

After the diving

When all diving is completed, it is the dive manager's job to ask if everyone is feeling OK, that they are content with the diving/expeditionary activities and that there are no major problems that have not already been highlighted to the expedition leader or dive manager. These should be sorted out before continuing with a debrief.

The dive manager's debrief

The debrief is to review the day's activities, encourage the expedition team, assess the success of the day (including the completion of any tasks) and preview the activities of the following day. This gives us the handy memory aid to structure a debrief around: REAP.

Review

- Planned timeline of the day and expedition activities and compare with the actual timeline.
- Number and types of dives planned and the actual dives carried out.
- Comment on the planned depths and times of dives in relation to what actually happened.
- List any unplanned occurrences during the day/expedition that may have affected the timeline/success of objectives.
- List any unplanned factors that may have affected the divers wellbeing.
- Compare planned use of resources (such as breathing gas, food, boat fuel) with what was actually used.

Encourage

- Highlight the successful completion of objectives, success in adhering to planned timelines and activities.
- Provide preliminary results obtained from the objectives.
- Outline any individual highlights of dives that have been reported to the dive manager or expedition leader.

Assess

- Consider any unplanned factors that have contributed to an altered timeline, altered plan, incomplete objectives or have affected the divers' wellbeing.
- Suggest solutions to be considered to recover the situation or prevent similar situations in the future.
- Consider the effect of unplanned factors on expedition/diving resources.

Progress

- Consider future improvements to deal with unplanned factors, in detail.
- Consider the expedition/day's diving overall – how might it be improved for the future.
- Reiterate the successes of the expedition and results obtained.
- Look forward to what could be achieved in the future.

The dive manager should also collate dive log information and ensure that appropriate dive times and depths have been adhered to. They may request feedback on the day from the team.

- Were the dive objectives achieved?
- Did the divers enjoy the dives?
- Did any problems develop that require attention?

Thanks can be given to the expedition team, any assistants and the skipper for making the day happen in their respective roles.

The coastguard must be notified of the boat's safe return. All tasks need to be completed before departing or finishing for the day. Any accounting matters need to be recorded and any faulty equipment logged.

The dive manager should also ensure that any data collected on the dives are adequately stored for later reporting and that the day's activities are reported to the expedition leader.

Leadership

Both the expedition leader and the dive manager are required to lead and manage a team of divers. In some cases, this may involve divers from different places. They may have different ways of doing things, different techniques, different abilities, different backgrounds and different attitudes. Sometimes it can be a challenge to meld such a group into a functioning team.

Interpersonal skills

The dive manager's role in the group may vary. Some days leadership is required, other days support for the team. We may need to vary how we behave in these roles so as not to generate conflict. Conflicts are most likely in times of stress – these occur mostly during developing situations when difficulties are encountered.

Conflicts usually arise out of poor communication, lack of clear plans, an inability to make effective decisions and the threat of failure to achieve set objectives. A good dive manager will see these situations developing and plan to deal with them.

A sensible, well thought out, clearly communicated plan will often prevent conflicts before they develop. Different people have different styles of leadership but confidence in leaders is underpinned by clarity of decisions and ability to deal quickly with developing situations.

Personal style

There are two styles of leadership: some lead from the front and are always clearly visible giving instructions and some lead from the back and are always guiding, persuading, coaching and directing the activities of the team by working among them. Both methods of leadership work well: the best approach is to try to use each technique when appropriate.

It is effective to stand out and direct the team at certain times, such as during a pre-dive briefing or when taking control during an emergency. At other times, such as during normal diving activities, it is more appropriate to take a more relaxed approach by co-ordinating, guiding and supporting individuals to make things happen.

The personality of the dive manager may drive them toward one type of leadership approach or the other, but it is better to try to be flexible and use both approaches. Sometimes these roles are not very easy to adopt and potential leaders may need to learn to project themselves more, even if it is against their natural instincts. Some leadership skills can be learned by watching others lead. A good approach is to try to spot the two types of leadership.

A good expedition leader will command the respect of those in the team, even if they are more experienced. Earning respect is important – it doesn't come with the job title or with any qualification – it is an individual thing. Respect can be earned by treating people fairly and in a friendly way, by being able to make correct decisions, by having the correct knowledge or skills when they are needed, and by being able to take effective control at times when the team are looking for leadership. Above all, respect comes from honesty: bluffing your way through a situation does not work. The foundation stone of good leadership lies in your underlying abilities as a diver and an organiser. The former can be developed with time and experience, the latter is made easier by thorough preparation.

One of the biggest difficulties a dive manager faces, is having too much to do when a situation develops that requires action. This can be prevented by effective delegation. If the workload is spread more evenly, it gives the dive manager time to become aware of developing situations, to plan how they can be addressed and then to act on the plan. By involving the team in managing the diving activities, the team members will be better prepared to assist should they be needed.

As the dive manager on an expedition may change from day to day, the previous dive managers must be prepared to work within the team when someone else is in charge.

In general, during normal diving activities, the dive manager should take the opportunity to delegate tasks and give constructive advice and help when required. When delegating, they should be clear in their instructions. Using a person's name is a good way to ensure that the person knows that they have been selected for the task and there is a need to be clear and specific about the nature of the task. For example, compare 'Can someone tidy up the boat?' with 'John, could you please move those cylinders that are obstructing the ladder and secure them to the bottle rack'. During an emergency situation, the dive manager should take special care to assess who is available, plan how they are going to be used and give clear instructions to each of them specifically.

Success as a leader can be developed using some simple guidelines. The good dive manager and expedition leader share similar characteristics.

- They should be friendly and approachable.
- They should try to treat everyone fairly.
- If someone has a grievance, they should listen to it and try to resolve it.
- Where possible, they should allow their team members the opportunity to become involved in decision making, while avoiding indecisiveness.
- They should give team members credit for their activities and praise when they perform well.

If the team members are having problems, the dive manager should intervene and give help and advice. If an unsafe situation is being promoted by one of the team members, the dive manager needs to intervene to deal with the situation quickly. It is important to stand by any decisions and not succumb to any pressure to allow the unsafe situation to continue. It is essential to explain the reasons for any such decisions clearly to the diver. In a conflict situation, where one of the team members wants to do something differently, the dive manager should listen, evaluate the ideas, consider the advantages and disadvantages and accept the best solution. A good dive manager will give a team member credit for putting forward their idea and will not be afraid to back down over their own ideas if the new suggestion is better. Most of all, it is important that the dive manager does not shout or get angry with the team members.

Not everyone has the personality to be an instant leader, but by employing some simple principles, such as those above, leadership can be just another skill, like mask clearing, that can be learned.

Dive manager's checklist

Tasks

Cox: ....

Assisted by: ....

Cox to ensure that boat is fully prepared and ready for sea.
Confirm to me when this is done

- ☐ Tubes
- ☐ Anchor
- ☐ A-Flag
- ☐ Boat boxes
- ☐ VHF/DSC
- ☐ Electronics working

Fuel estimate amount and duration: ....

Confirm to me this is sufficient for this plan Y/N

Estimated amount/distance/duration/reserve

O_2 administrator: ....

Deputy O_2 administrator: ....

Check O_2 is ready with full cylinder. **Confirm to me that this is done**

First aider: ....

Deputy first aider: ....

First aid: check kit **Confirm to me that this has been done**

Navigation

Point out route on chart, bearing and distance and other navigation information to Cox'n or task Cox'n (navigator) to sort out route, return and safe havens. Communicate to other navigators/Cox'ns.

Confirm this is done

Shot

Prepare to specifications **Confirm to me that this has been done**

The dive plan

Current tissue codes: Has anyone dived in last 16 hrs? **Y/N**

Expected max depth:

Check again: Is this within qualification level of every diver? **Y/N**

Check no-stop time from tables

Divers

Pair	Dive leader	(grade)	Buddy	(grade)
1	....	....	....	....
2	....	....	....	....
3	....	....	....	....
4	....	....	....	....

Depth limits for each dive

- ❑ Ocean: 20m Sports: 20m–35m DL: 35m–50m PO_2 <1.4 bar He to 80m

Are there any problems with the pairings?

The dive leaders' tasks

- ❑ Plan the dive, decompression, gas requirements, max operating depths, gases you will be using, tasks and brief your buddy
- ❑ Conduct a SEEDS brief and buddy check before diving
- ❑ Tell me about any part of the plan that I need to be aware of or if it is outside of usual procedures or safe diving practices

The diving tasks

	Names	Tasks
Pair 1	....	....
Pair 2	....	....
Pair 3	....	....
Pair 4	....	....

At the end of the dive **regain shot/surface on DSMB**

Signals

During the dive: Use usual BSAC signals. Agree any plan-specific signals

such as use of SMB

- ❑ Single orange = OK follow me
- ❑ Yellow or yellow/orange = Problem, help!
- ❑ Yellow plus orange (2 buoys) = Gas required at stop

Personal diving equipment/preparations

- ❑ Buddy lines/delayed SMBs/torches/distance line tokens

Entry and exit

- ❑ I must know you are about to enter the water: On my signal
  Which side?

Checklist

Safety

- ❑ VHF: Channels port control ....
- ❑ Coastguard working channel ....
- ❑ Our call sign ....

- ❑ Ensure word left ashore or coastguard contacted
- ❑ Achieve clearance to dive in restricted areas
- ❑ At end of day, confirm safe return and all well

Confirm to me that each of the above has been done

Summary of the above Main points and tasks are…

Personal dive planning checks

Dive leaders SEEDS briefing has been done

Dive leaders confirm to me/deputy DM before entering water:

- ❑ plan for the dive and separation plan
- ❑ gas requirements

Buddy check done

Pair	Dive leader	Buddy	Plan depth	Plan time	All points covered
1					
2					
3					
4					

Emergencies

Diver recall ❑ Pulls on SMB ❑ Explosive recall

If recalled, signal using buoy that you are ascending. Carry out stops

Coastguard: Channel 16 ....

Chamber telephone

Hospital: ....

Nearest landing: ....

Estimated times

Confirm completed tasks to me by: ....

Estimated time of departure: ....

ETA site: .... ETA back: ....

Chapter 6

Dive site location

Locating a known dive site is, in theory, a straightforward task. You take the boat to the position you intend to dive, check you are in the correct location on arrival and put your divers into the water. However, those who have had the experience and responsibility of finding a site will tell you that it is not necessarily that easy.

Position information needs to be accurate and it must be brought aboard or correctly entered into the boat's navigation system. On site, the sea conditions may make holding your position difficult while you mark the position with a shot line. Also, there is usually a limited amount of time available to locate the site.

Trying to find a site for the first time is an even bigger challenge.

Many divers simply do not do their homework before setting off to find a dive site, which means they cannot find it, or when they do, they discover they have spent too long looking and have missed slack water.

LOWRANCE
RIB LOGAN
235030171
MKGT6

Before setting off, you will need the best information available for the site you intend to dive. Traditional site location techniques through to more advanced electronics all have their place, so the information that you have about a site may include diagrams of visual transits, GPS positions and much more.The more accurate your information is, the more likely you are to find your site.

When you have collected together the information about the chosen site, don't forget to take it with you. You can copy it onto a suitable waterproof slate or into a waterproof notebook.

Grid references

A grid reference, which pinpoints a position on the Earth's surface, is usually expressed as a latitude and then longitude (for more detail, see *Seamanship: a guide for divers*). Note that it is necessary to know whether the latitude is north or south, and the longitude is east or west. It is also necessary to know what system was used to derive the grid reference.

All positioning systems reference a datum point that is the centre of the Earth. However, as the Earth is not a perfect sphere, there is some disagreement between the systems about where the centre is and this has an impact on the co-ordinates derived from each system. A standard datum used on nautical charts in the UK is the World Geodetic System 84 (WGS84).

However, older charts may use a different datum and positions derived using other datums are still published in the diving literature.

Positions are commonly given as degrees (°) and minutes ('), with the minutes expressed using three figures after the decimal point. These are referred to as decimal minutes. For example, WGS84 position 58° 53.841' N 003° 08.545' W is the grid reference for the wreck of the SMS Koln in Scapa Flow, Orkney.

Alternatively, positions can be given as degrees, minutes and seconds. A degree is made up of 60 minutes ('). A minute is made up of 60 seconds ("). Using this notation the position for the SMS Koln would be 58° 53' 51" 003° 08' 33".

It is essential to know which notation is being used when you are given a GPS position for a site.

Other sites, particularly shore dives, may be more conveniently noted using the British National Grid, the UK datum used on land maps. This would be expressed as an Ordnance Survey of Great Britain (OSGB) position read from an Ordnance Survey map. For example, the position OSGB (1936) SY 683733 is a good place to begin a shore dive at Chesil Cove, Portland. (The Ordnance Survey publish good instructions on how to use the national grid on their website.)

Errors

So, depending on the charts, maps or electronic aids that you are using to navigate to the site, you may need to convert position information from one system to another. Care is needed to make sure no significant errors occur in converting the numbers. A formula to convert from one GPS datum to another may be given on the chart. Many of the free programmes available to do these conversions on the internet are not accurate. Most electronic navigation systems can be set up to use a variety of common datums.

If you are reading a dive site position from the chart, remember that errors can be introduced here too, particularly if you are using a small-scale chart. It is best to take GPS position from the largest scale chart available.

Let us consider the size of such errors. A nautical mile is represented by one minute on the vertical scale of a chart, at a particular latitude. One nautical mile is a distance of 1852 metres. The final figure of any GPS latitude position expressed in decimal minutes is one thousandth of a minute (0.001), or one thousandth of a nautical mile – 1.852m. If the latitude of a position is 55° 49.540' N but you actually record 55° 49.550' N (that is an error of 0.01), your position is already 18m out before you start.

When inputting dive site position data into your navigation system further errors can occur. As mentioned above, you need to know which datum was used to derive a position. For example, older nautical charts in the UK were referenced to OSGB36 and if a position is taken directly from that chart and used in a GPS unit referenced to WGS84 there can be a significant error, sometimes up to 100m or more. Correction factors between different datums may be given on the chart.

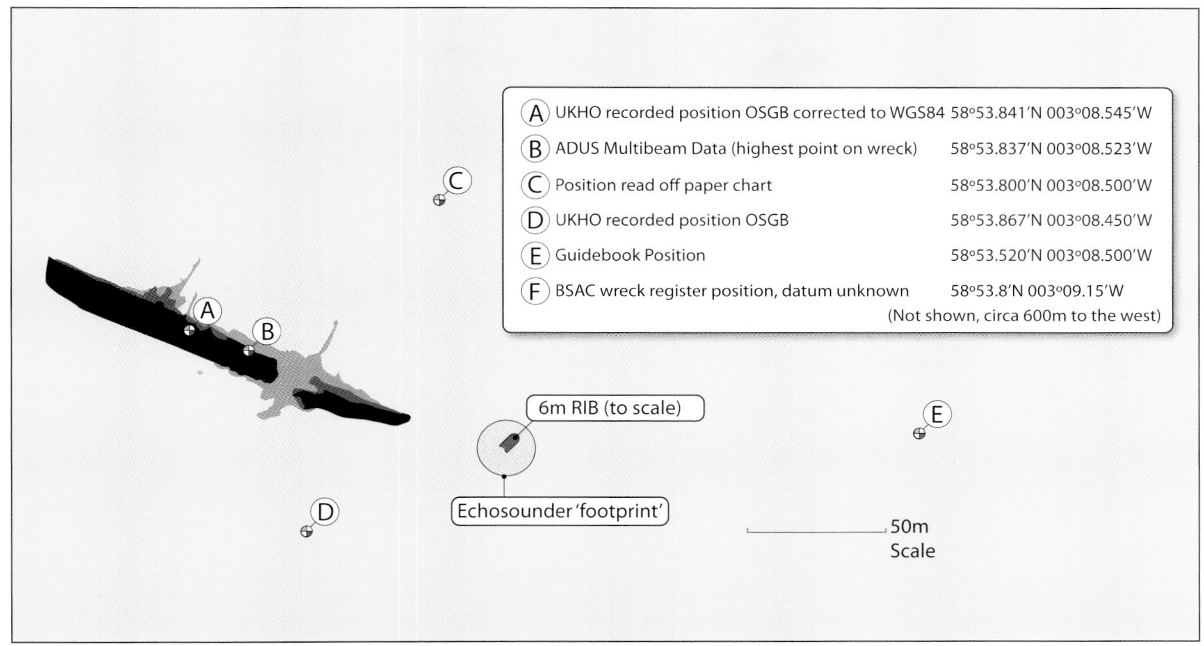

Information from different sources about the position of the SMS Koln does not agree

Accurate data

To get a really accurate position for a wreck may mean going to the source information used to create the chart. The UK Hydrographic Office, for example, sells this information at a reasonable price. However, be cautious when using this source information as it may come from surveys carried out many years ago. Positions acquired using commercial survey equipment today are very accurate and seabed features can be positioned within a few metres. At some point in the future we can expect that most of the seabed will have been surveyed using this equipment, but until then we are reliant on the survey methods used in the past.

To check the quality of this information, ask what the source is. Information about the survey that a chart is based on is always given on Admiralty charts. The more recent the survey, the more accurate it is likely to be.

Depth

Knowing the site depth can add a third dimension to your position fixing.

For example, if you know a wreck is in 30m and you arrive at the estimated position and discover the depth is 50m, you might well be looking in the wrong place.

Remember to take account of the height of tide as this can vary the depth significantly. A site in 30m at low water could be in 35m at high water, for example.

The depth of the site can also have an effect on the type of search pattern you choose to locate the target, given the characteristics of the sonar device you are using. Generally, the shallower the depth the closer together your search grid will need to be.

Wreck information

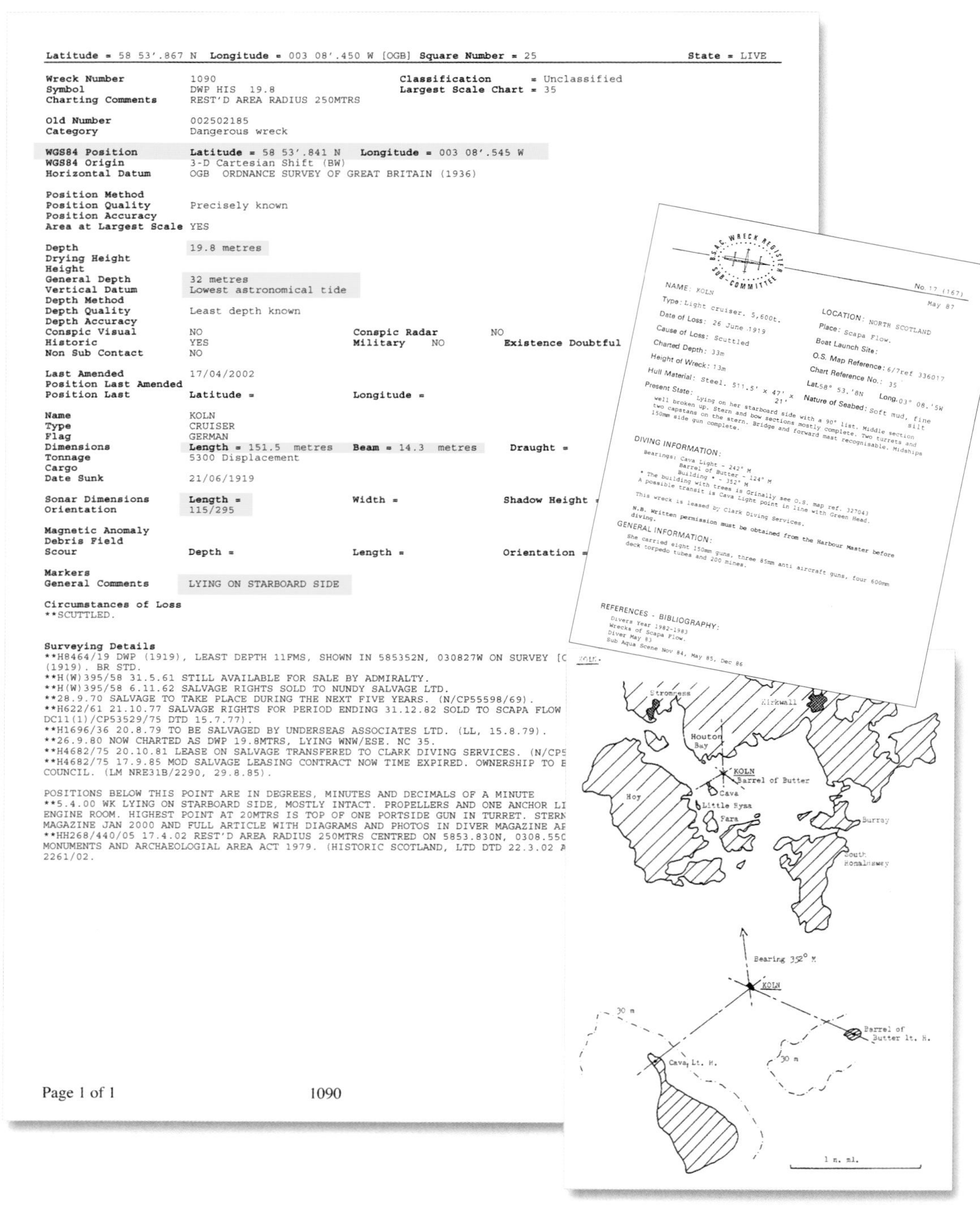

Latitude = 58 53'.867 N **Longitude** = 003 08'.450 W [OGB] **Square Number** = 25 **State** = LIVE

Wreck Number 1090
Symbol DWP HIS 19.8
Charting Comments REST'D AREA RADIUS 250MTRS
Classification = Unclassified
Largest Scale Chart = 35

Old Number 002502185
Category Dangerous wreck

WGS84 Position **Latitude** = 58 53'.841 N **Longitude** = 003 08'.545 W
WGS84 Origin 3-D Cartesian Shift (BW)
Horizontal Datum OGB ORDNANCE SURVEY OF GREAT BRITAIN (1936)

Position Method
Position Quality Precisely known
Position Accuracy
Area at Largest Scale YES

Depth 19.8 metres
Drying Height
Height
General Depth 32 metres
Vertical Datum Lowest astronomical tide
Depth Method
Depth Quality Least depth known
Depth Accuracy
Conspic Visual NO **Conspic Radar** NO
Historic YES **Military** NO **Existence Doubtful**
Non Sub Contact NO

Last Amended 17/04/2002
Position Last Amended
Position Last **Latitude** = **Longitude** =

Name KOLN
Type CRUISER
Flag GERMAN
Dimensions **Length** = 151.5 metres **Beam** = 14.3 metres **Draught** =
Tonnage 5300 Displacement
Cargo
Date Sunk 21/06/1919

Sonar Dimensions **Length** = **Width** = **Shadow Height** =
Orientation 115/295

Magnetic Anomaly
Debris Field
Scour **Depth** = **Length** = **Orientation** =

Markers
General Comments LYING ON STARBOARD SIDE

Circumstances of Loss
**SCUTTLED.

Surveying Details
**H8464/19 DWP (1919), LEAST DEPTH 11FMS, SHOWN IN 585352N, 030827W ON SURVEY [C
(1919). BR STD.
**H(W)395/58 31.5.61 STILL AVAILABLE FOR SALE BY ADMIRALTY.
**H(W)395/58 6.11.62 SALVAGE RIGHTS SOLD TO NUNDY SALVAGE LTD.
**28.9.70 SALVAGE TO TAKE PLACE DURING THE NEXT FIVE YEARS. (N/CP55598/69).
**H622/61 21.10.77 SALVAGE RIGHTS FOR PERIOD ENDING 31.12.82 SOLD TO SCAPA FLOW
DC11(1)/CP53529/75 DTD 15.7.77).
**H1696/36 20.8.79 TO BE SALVAGED BY UNDERSEAS ASSOCIATES LTD. (LL, 15.8.79).
**26.9.80 NOW CHARTED AS DWP 19.8MTRS, LYING WNW/ESE. NC 35.
**H4682/75 20.10.81 LEASE ON SALVAGE TRANSFERED TO CLARK DIVING SERVICES. (N/CP5
**H4682/75 17.9.85 MOD SALVAGE LEASING CONTRACT NOW TIME EXPIRED. OWNERSHIP TO E
COUNCIL. (LM NRE31B/2290, 29.8.85).

POSITIONS BELOW THIS POINT ARE IN DEGREES, MINUTES AND DECIMALS OF A MINUTE
**5.4.00 WK LYING ON STARBOARD SIDE, MOSTLY INTACT. PROPELLERS AND ONE ANCHOR LI
ENGINE ROOM. HIGHEST POINT AT 20MTRS IS TOP OF ONE PORTSIDE GUN IN TURRET. STERN
MAGAZINE JAN 2000 AND FULL ARTICLE WITH DIAGRAMS AND PHOTOS IN DIVER MAGAZINE AF
**HH268/440/05 17.4.02 REST'D AREA RADIUS 250MTRS CENTRED ON 5853.830N, 0308.55C
MONUMENTS AND ARCHAEOLOGIAL AREA ACT 1979. (HISTORIC SCOTLAND, LTD DTD 22.3.02 A
2261/02.

Page 1 of 1 1090

B.S.A.C. WRECK REGISTER SUB-COMMITTEE

NAME: KOLN
No. 17 (167)
May 87

Type: Light cruiser. 5,600t.
Date of Loss: 26 June 1919
Cause of Loss: Scuttled
Charted Depth: 33m
Height of Wreck: 13m
Hull Material: Steel. 511.5' x 47' x 21'
Present State: Lying on her starboard side with a 90° list. Middle section well broken up. Stern and bow sections mostly complete. Two turrets and two capstans on the stern. Bridge and forward mast recognisable. Midships 150mm side gun complete.

LOCATION: NORTH SCOTLAND
Place: Scapa Flow.
Boat Launch Site:
O.S. Map Reference: 6/7ref 336017
Chart Reference No.: 35
Lat. 58° 53.'8N Long. 03° 08.'5W
Nature of Seabed: Soft mud, fine silt

DIVING INFORMATION:
Bearings: Cava Light - 242° M
Barrel of Butter - 124° M
Building * - 352° M
* The building with trees is Grinally see O.S. map ref. 327043
A possible transit is Cava Light point in line with Green Head.
This wreck is leased by Clark Diving Services.
N.B. Written permission must be obtained from the Harbour Master before diving.

GENERAL INFORMATION:
She carried eight 150mm guns, three 85mm anti aircraft guns, four 600mm deck torpedo tubes and 200 mines.

REFERENCES - BIBLIOGRAPHY:
Divers Year 1982-1983
Wrecks of Scapa Flow.
Diver May 83
Sub Aqua Scene Nov 84, May 85, Dec 86

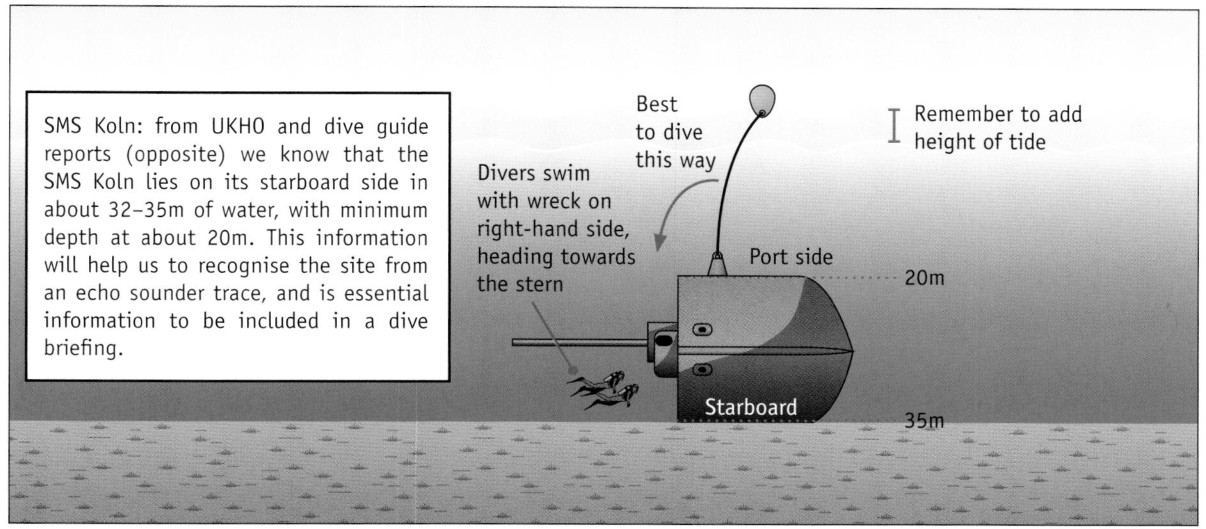

Pulling together detailed information from different sources tells us much about the wreck of the Koln

Site details

Accurately knowing the dive site location is clearly a big part of finding the site. However, knowing what you are looking for once you get there is also important. Generally you will want to put your divers into the water as close as possible to their area of interest. On a large wreck this may be the bridge area of the ship, rather than an empty cargo hold. On a scenic pinnacle you will want to find the top so there is less water to look at on the way down.

Knowing the size and orientation of the feature you are looking for also helps your search. If a dive site such as a wreck or a reef lies east-west, it is usually best to search using north-south passes, hoping to pass over its shorter dimension which will give a distinct, up and then down echo sounder trace. If you know that the best part of a site is 5m off the seabed, you will know that something 2m off the seabed is not the spot although it might be close.

The position of a wreck is not the only relevant information available from the UKHO records. We can find out more about the wreck from the same source. For example the records about the SMS Koln give its orientation as 115°/295° (see report, opposite) and its measurements as 151.5m long by 14.3 wide.

A photograph or sketch of the site is also useful - to help divers orientate themselves. Also further information about the position of the wreck on the seabed and its structural state will help the divers to plan their dive.

A photo of the SMS Koln is more use than words

It is important to know the nature of the seabed around the site. This is of use in planning an underwater search, but can also affect the surface searching techniques that you use.

Knowing if there are gullies in the area about the same size as the wreck you are looking for, or that the seabed consists of shifting sand dunes likely to bury or unbury the site, or whether the wreck sits on hard rock or soft mud will help you to interpret your sonar equipment output.

Compass bearings

Transits and compass bearings

Compass bearings have been used for centuries to navigate on the water, and sets of transits were the method of choice to find dive sites until relatively recently. However, as the accuracy of electronic navigation aids has increased, the use of these more traditional means has diminished. But they should not be forgotten. Expedition leaders re-visiting old dive sites may only have bearings and transits for position references of the dive site, and these are accurate ways of finding any site.

Two objects are said to be in transit when they are in line with one another, and this places the observer on a position line. If you have two sets of transits for the same site, the two resulting position lines cross each other and this gives a position fix.

Some transits are better than others. Ideally the transits should be 'fast', the two position lines defined by the transits should be perpendicular to each other, and the objects used should be easily recognisable and well aligned.

A fast transit is one where the distance from the observer to the object in the foreground is relatively small compared to the distance between the objects. For a small movement of the boat the objects move in and out of alignment quickly. This sensitivity can make a fast transit more accurate (see fast and slow transits, opposite below).

In good surface conditions a set of well thought out transits, used properly, can be an extremely accurate way of locating a dive site, although clearly you need to have found it some other way the first time. There is something particularly satisfying about being able to locate a dive site without having to use modern electronic aids.

Bearings and distance from an object may also be used to fix your position at sea, but are not usually practical in a small, moving boat. However, bearings can be very useful alongside transits, to put the boat roughly in the right location as the dive site is approached.

Using transits can have problems. They are no use when diving out of site of land. They may not be visible due to poor surface conditions such as rain, haze or fog. Transits taken years ago may simply not be there.

It is not always easy to use someone else's transits. Writing down your transits needs care and attention. A clear sketch of each transit is best, alongside the bearings on which they lie.

Looking 180° (south): line up the right-hand edge of the bungalow with corner of the shed

Looking 270° (east): line up radio mast with the boulder on shore

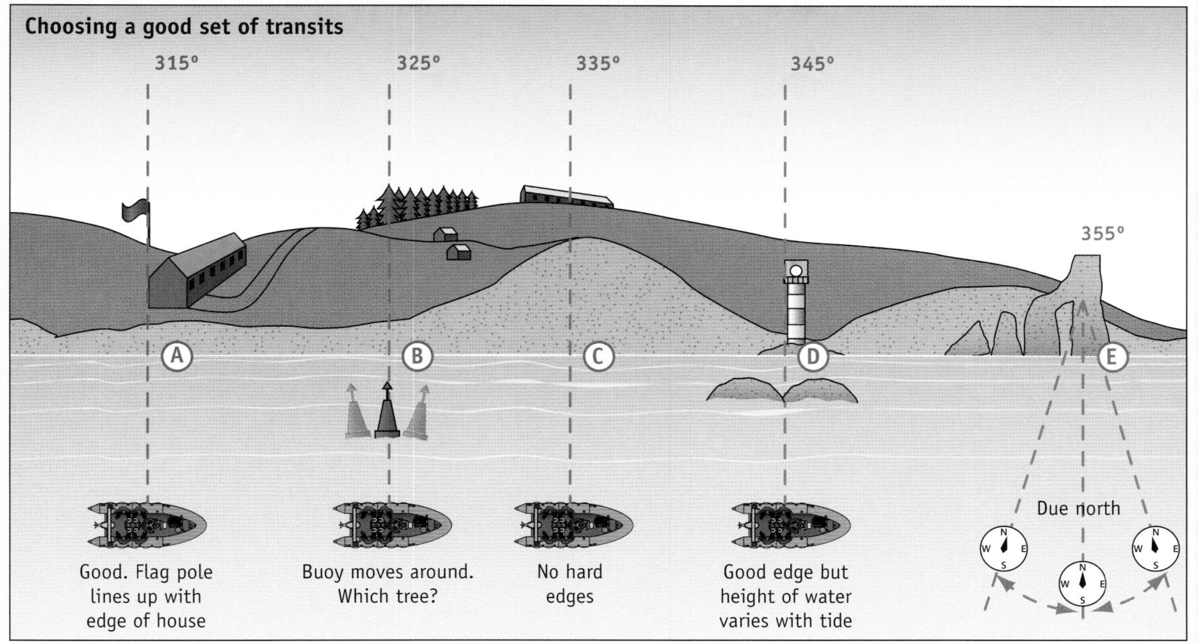

Transit A: good because the thin flag pole can be clearly aligned with the edge of the house.
Transit B: lining up a buoy with the edge of some trees, is less desirable as the buoy will move around in the tide.
Transit C: the middle of the cliff lines up with the middle of the row of houses, but without hard edges this could be difficult to judge.
Transit D: the lighthouse is aligned with the edge of a rock/water interface, but this may only be useful at certain states of the tide as the height of the tide changes the position of that rock/water interface.
Transit E: taking an accurate bearing on an object can be difficult from a small boat. The movement of the boat on the sea means that you are unlikely to be more accurate than +/- 5 degrees. Magnetic variation and deviation also need to be considered.

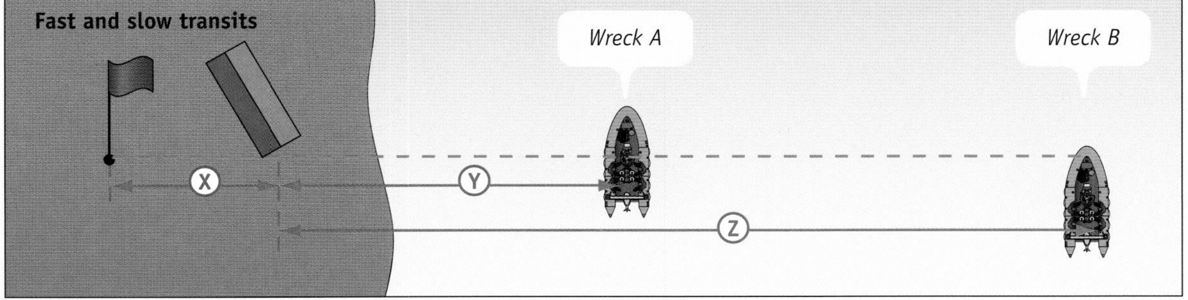

When using this transit, the house appears to move quickly past the flagpole when you are approaching wreck A, and more slowly when you approach wreck B. For wreck A this is a 'fast' transit, the boat has to travel a shorter distance for the objects to come into and out of alignment, so it is more accurate. For wreck B this is a 'slow' transit, and is less accurate. The faster the transit, the smaller will be the ratio of the distance between the wreck and the nearer object (y or z) and the distance between the two objects (x). In this example y/x is smaller than z/x.

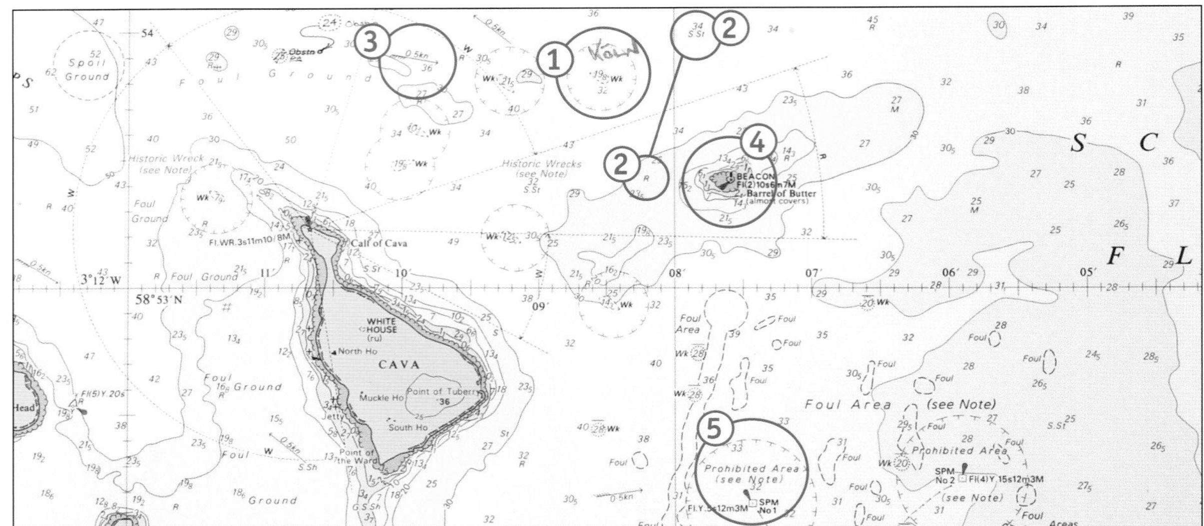

The chart gives you information on what to expect on site, both above and below the water

Other information

When out looking for dive sites, other information may be required for a safe and effective search. It is important to identify hazards in the area.

- Is the site in a shipping lane where other vessels may limit your search area or interrupt your search?
- Is it near to shallow reefs that can damage your boat?
- Do you need to search in the direction of the tide to make your grid searches easier?
- Is the site a protected site or other restricted area?
- Do you need to seek permission or inform authorities of your intentions before carrying out the search?

From the chart (above) we can get some information about the wreck, the surrounding seabed and the local hazards:

(1) The SMS Koln is a protected wreck site.

(2) It lies on a rock or sand/stone seabed, depth 34m.

(3) Tides are weak (as indicated by the 0.5 knot tidal arrow).

(4) Nearest land is about 0.5 miles to the south-east.

(5) The location of the Flotta oil terminal suggests large boat traffic to the south-west of the site.

Surface search techniques

Once you have gathered enough basic information and have used it to arrive at an unknown site, you will need to carry out some sort of search to accurately place your shot line.

Two basic search techniques that are simple to set up are a grid search and a circular search. The start of the search, which will normally be the position you have for the site, should be marked with a datum. This can be a shot line or an electronic marker on the screen of the navigation system.

As the search progresses and evidence of the site is detected with the echo sounder, more datum points should be marked. Gradually the extent of the site will become apparent.

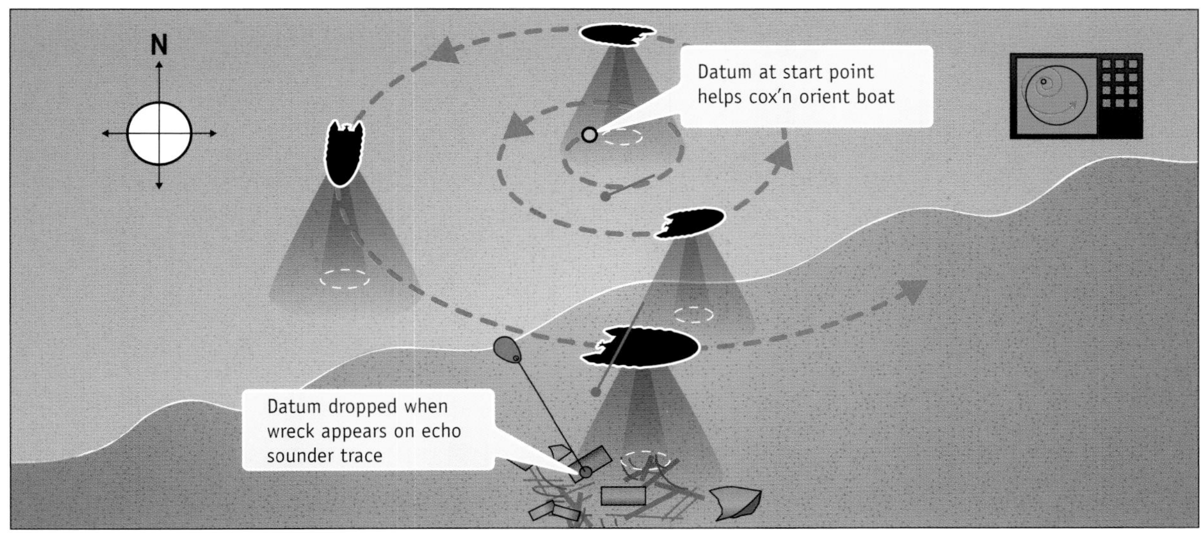

Using GPS tracks called snail's trails to monitor the boat's present and historical position simplifies a circular search

Essential equipment

The bare minimum of equipment required for most site location is a navigation system (usually GPS), a suitable echo sounder and a waterproof copy of your site finding information.

Waterproof slate

One thing about human beings is that they are prone to forgetfulness and making mistakes. Even for locating a well known site, it is not unknown for someone to input the wrong position into the GPS, and/or forget the orientation of the site or layout. So, the main details of the site should be taken with you on a waterproof slate so that you have the position, depth, site details, transits and bearings and any other information.

GPS

The Global Positioning System provides a continuous, accurate worldwide, three-dimensional (latitude, longitude and altitude) positioning system for use in all weather conditions. The system uses satellites managed by the US Department of Defense.

Initially the system was only accurate to 100m, because of a deliberate error introduced into the signal through selective availability. This could be overcome using a differential GPS where separate (relatively expensive) receiver would receive a land-based correction signal to achieve accuracy to with three to five metres.

Selective availability was turned off in 2000, giving an accuracy of 15m for most civilian GPS units. However, growing civilian use, particularly for aerospace, has led to the introduction of WAAS (Wide Area Augmentation System) and EGNOS (European Geostationary Navigation Overlay Service), which can increase accuracy to within 3m with suitable receivers.

It is important to bear these changes in accuracy in mind when using older GPS position fixes for dive sites. For most sites, getting within 15m is more than acceptable.

Many GPS receivers are able to track their position on the screen. Known as a snail's trace, this is useful for monitoring where you have searched. The principles of the search are the same, either circular or grid-based, but you can track your progress more easily and 'drop' electronic markers when passing over something of interest. It can take considerable boat handling experience to counteract the effect of tides and waves to navigate the perfect search pattern.

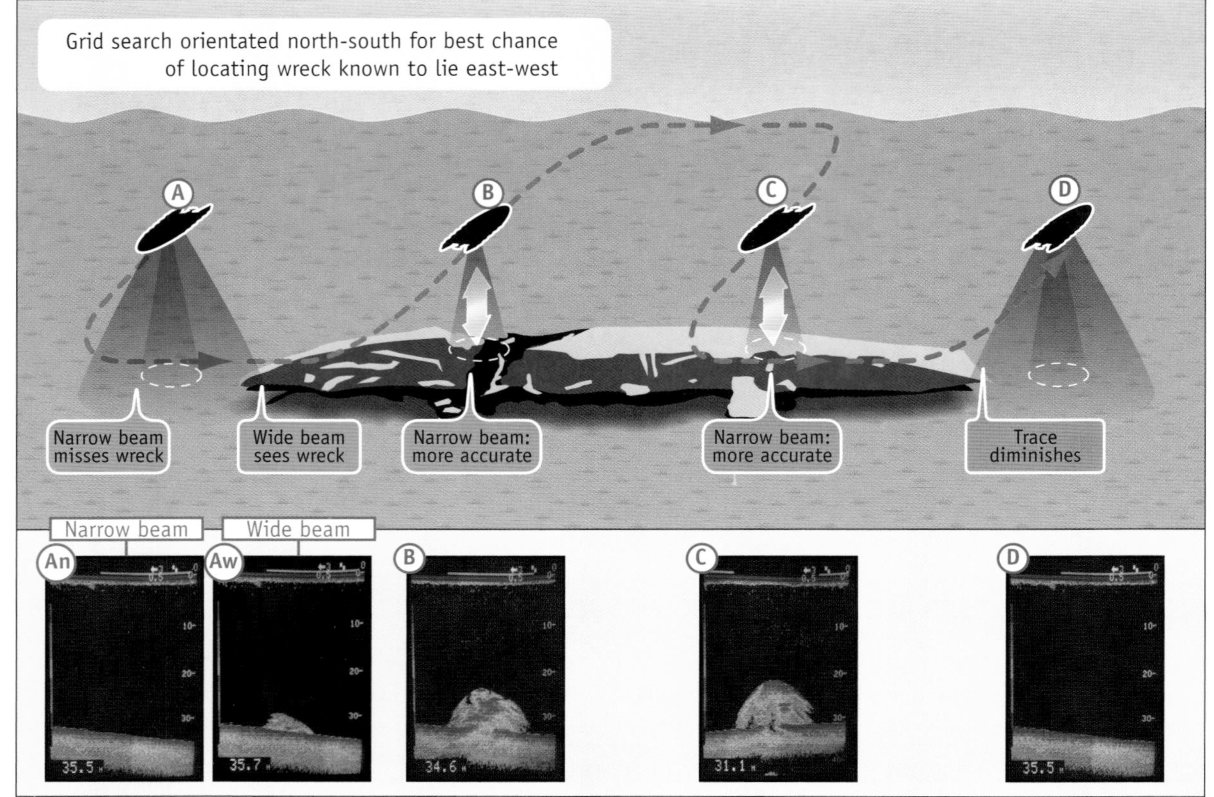

A rectangular search pattern generates information from an echo sounder that helps to locate a large wreck

Echo sounder

When you have arrived at a fixed position using a GPS mark or transits, an echo sounder (also known as a sonar or depth finder) can be used to confirm the depth and underwater profile of the site. It consists of a transducer, typically fitted into the boat's hull on larger boats or mounted on the transom on smaller boats, and a display unit.

The acoustic pulses are sent out from the transducer, reflected from the seabed and detected by the transducer before being interpreted and displayed on a screen.

When using echo sounders as part of a site location, the boat's speed should be kept low in order to obtain a clear depth trace of the seabed features on the echo sounder screen. Also, you should make appropriate use of a dual beam transducer if you have one. For example, using a wide beam angle such as 60° will scan a wide area of the seabed – in 20m of water the width is 22m increasing likelihood of detection. If greater accuracy is required a narrower beam can be selected. A narrow beam angle such as 20° will scan a smaller area of the seabed, helping identify specific areas of an object such as a wreck. A 20° beam would have a scan width of 7m at a depth of 20m and 17m in 50m.

A narrower beam concentrates the power of the beam giving better results in deeper water, although some echo sounders also offer a choice of high or low frequency.

In some ways, errors in the surface positioning of the boat can be made up for by the choice of beam and therefore the area scanned by the sounder.

Enlarged image of scan B

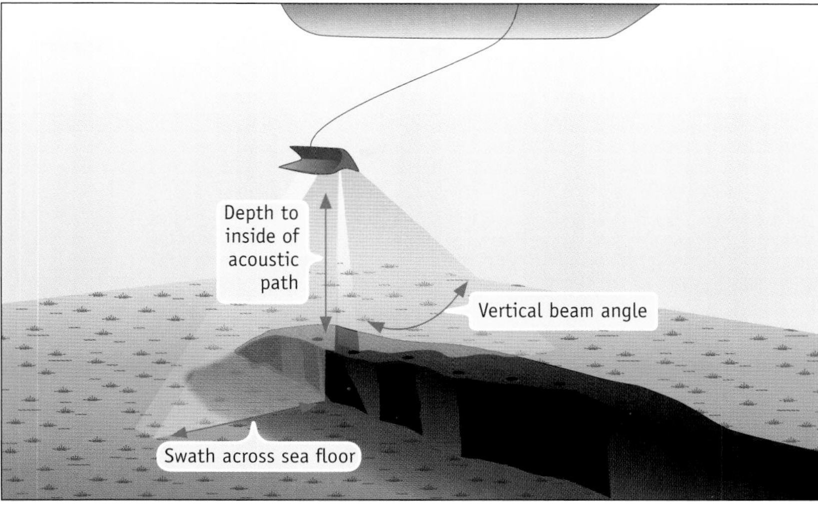

Side-scan sonar shows the shape of a strip of the seabed

Using an echo sounder to help locate a wreck

- When initially looking for a wreck, the wide beam is selected to maximise chance of locating the edge of the wreckage. If narrow beam were selected you could drive very close to the wreck and not realise it (as shown by both An, Aw and D, opposite).
- If you drive over edges, you may see multiple traces as the echosounder receives multiple signals back of wreck and seabed (see enlarged version of B, above).
- Switching to a narrower beam permits more accurate location of specific parts of the wreck as the beam is covering a smaller area. This allows more accurate location of the shot line for divers.
- As the grid search continues the height of the trace increases, identifying the highest (and usually most interesting) parts of the wreck (see C, opposite). A strong solid trace is seen over the centre part of the wreck where there is a strong reflection from the metal.
- As the boat moves towards the stern the height of the trace diminishes (D, opposite).

Using the zoom facility on an echo sounder allows the operator to view the lower part of the water column in detail on the display, rather than the whole water column. This is particularly useful for deeper wrecks; for example, a 3m high wreck in 20m will show up well on the echo sounder trace but a 3m high wreck in 60m may be harder to see on the trace without the zoom facility.

An echo sounder can be used to gain information about both man-made and natural underwater features. Sonar waves will reflect more strongly from acoustically hard materials such as metal and rock, but will also reflect from sand and shells.

The gradient of any underwater slope can also be assessed using the echo sounder, but remember that the trace is moving at a fixed speed regardless of the boat speed. Even a shallow slope will look steep when you are travelling at speed.

The echo sounder is a versatile tool, but it is limited in the area of the seabed that it scans. It is generally the appropriate tool to locate something in a small search area rather than a large one, although echo sounders are becoming more advanced with some units generating three-dimensional traces or looking forward as well as underneath.

Advanced equipment

Side-scan sonar

Side-scan sonar was developed the early 1960s but it is only recently that this technology has become available to the average diver.

A side-scan sonar unit produces a narrow fan-shaped acoustic pulse perpendicular to the direction of travel. A typical beam might be 2° wide but fan out over 100° on

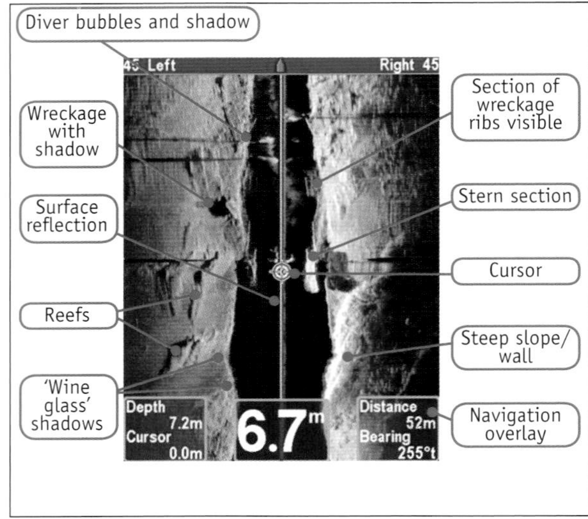

Interpretation of side-scan images needs practise

This side-scan sonar image of the wreck of the SMS Koln shows its stern structure, wreckage sections (ribs), and divers' bubbles (and shadows). The cursor can be moved to find the position of an object

either side of the transducer so it can 'see' almost a full 180°. However, the beam strength is usually concentrated in the middle.

The transducer can be mounted in a towfish, towed along behind the vessel. This isolates it to some degree from the vessel motion and also permits the transducer height above the seabed to be adjusted by increasing or decreasing the length of tow. Hull-mounted transducers are more susceptible to boat motion.

As with an echo sounder, acoustic pulses are reflected from objects on the seabed and detected by the transducer before being interpreted and displayed on a screen. Each pulse is represented by a single line across the screen and by stitching these together an image of the seabed is created.

How much sound is reflected back depends upon the composition, shape, slope and features on the seabed. The information on the screen is usually displayed in black and white. Areas of high reflectivity, such as metal, rock and vertical edges, are one colour (white in our example) and areas of low reflectivity in another colour (usually blue or black). With experience, a side-scan sonar operator can gain a great deal of information from the image.

The dark central gap in the centre indicates the height of the transducer above the seabed (although some transducers also have a depth sensor built into them). A smaller gap means it is closer to the seabed. No gap means you have probably crashed the tow fish into the seabed.

Seabed features can cast acoustic shadows. These can not only help the operator to identify features of interest but also to estimate the height of them with some basic mathematics, although some systems have sophisticated software to allow measurements on screen.

If the side-scan system is interfaced to a GPS system it can be possible to obtain the actual position of an object on the seabed. However, remember that you may need to correct this position if the towfish is being towed 100m behind the boat.

For a clear side-scan sonar image a number of conditions must usually be met:

- The boat must proceed slowly, between one to six knots depending on the range of the side scan unit. The larger the range the slower the speed needed.
- If the transducer is too close to the seabed the shadows will be large and distorted and might hide features behind them.
- If the transducer is too high above the seabed the shadows might be too small to help locate features on the seabed.
- Calm conditions are needed to keep the transducer

A computer-generated multi-beam sonar image of the SMS Koln gives enough detail to assess its current state

steady in the water and also help reduce the risk of sea-sickness among operators looking at the screen.

- A grid search is the best pattern to adopt as turning the transducer in the water creates a distorted image that is harder to interpret.

Side-scan sonar is undoubtedly a powerful tool to help locate underwater features. However, to learn to use it effectively does take time.

Multi-beam sonar

Multi-beam sonar has some similarities with side-scan sonar. It sends out a fan-shaped beam perpendicular to the direction of travel, processes the reflected signals and then displays the image on the screen.

However, it is far more sophisticated than side-scan sonar. The transducers are usually mounted on the boat itself, which means the coverage area is dependent on the depth (usually two to four times the depth). As the name suggests it sends out multiple beams extending not only to the side but also underneath. Thus using multi-beam sonar is more akin to mowing the lawn.

Unlike side-scan sonar, where the strength of the return signal is interpreted, the multi-beam system measures the time taken for signals to travel from the transducer to the seabed and then back again.

The multi-beam system not only records the sonar information, but also the motion of the boat on which it is mounted. A computer on board the ship then uses this data to calculate the depths of the seabed along each scan line and then generates a two- or three-dimensional map to show the shape of the seabed and features on it.

The complexity and computing power required by the current systems limits its use to larger boats with room to install the equipment and the capability to provide the electric power required.

Multi-beam sonar systems, at the time of writing, are very expensive to buy and maintain and are used predominantly by commercial survey companies, particularly those involved in providing data to produce more accurate nautical charts.

However, the technology has been adapted to record shipwrecks. A project was completed to map the wrecks of Scapa Flow using this technology (see picture, above). The results highlighted how well the technology could be applied to build up images of wrecks and monitor how they degrade with time.

In time the cost and size of the technology will probably fall. However, at present only well-funded expeditions will be able to utilise this equipment, maybe by hiring a unit and an experienced operator.

Magnetometers

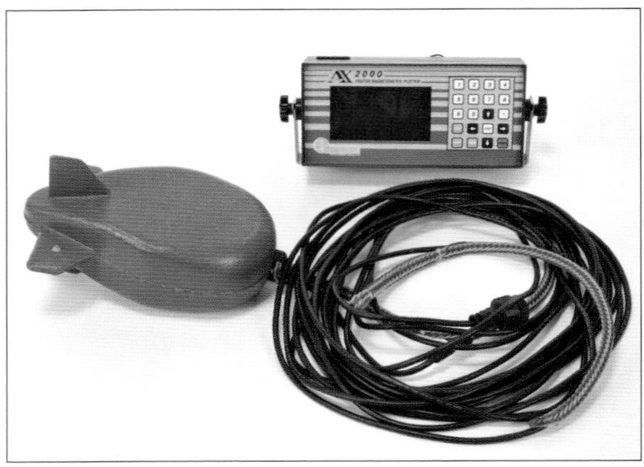

A proton magnetometer measures magnetic anomalies caused by local geological features or ferrous metals

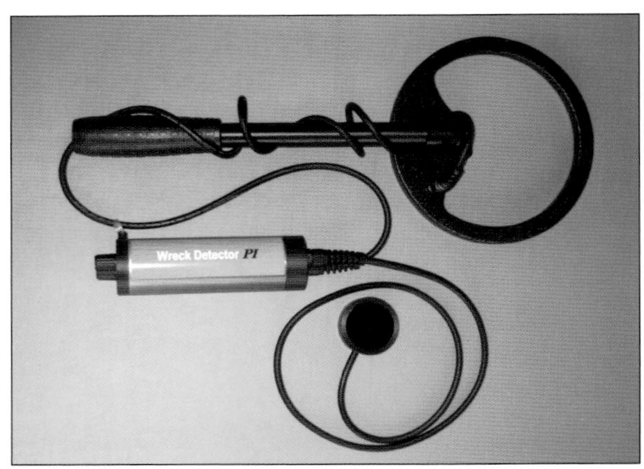

A hand-held metal detector can be used to find a variety of metals

Magnetometer

A magnetometer measures magnetic field strength. This is generated by both natural and man-made objects, such as ferrous metals, and detecting a distortion in local field strength, known as an anomaly, can help to locate a wreck when only an approximate position is known. A modern ship's hull is a huge ferrous target, but on older wrecks the only metal may be the anchor or cannon, although even the magnetic properties of ballast stones that are not native to the wreck's location can be detected with care.

The rule of thumb with magnetometers is that any field variation, or anomaly, varies inversely with the cube of the distance. In practice, if you halve (1/2) the distance between the detector and an anomaly you will detect a signal that is eight times stronger (2x2x2, two cubed). So the magnetometer should be operated as close to the target as possible - the smaller the object the deeper the tow will need to be.

The size of the distortion determines the distance at which it can be detected and, therefore, also the size of the search grid spacing required to find the wreck. For larger wrecks, you may use a search grid spacing of hundreds of metres. Large areas can, therefore, be searched relatively quickly.

The common types of magnetometers used by divers are proton precession and fluxgate magnetometers. Both have advantages and disadvantages - including their sensitivity to interference, whether they suffer from heading errors, and their cost. The equipment consists of a towfish housing the transducer, which is towed behind the boat, and a display unit. The proton magnetometer must be set up before use and tuned to the local strength of the Earth's magnetic field, ideally away from any magnetic distortion - this can be tricky. There will be interference from metal aboard the dive boat, so the towfish will need to be at least 20 to 30m from the boat. Once calibrated, the display will normally show a flat trace, or on older units the needle will be stationary on the dial. Every couple of seconds the magnetometer pulses to energise the transducer in the towfish.

The search strategy used with a proton magnetometer is a modification on those discussed so far. Searching east to west on a grid is the best (this is essential for some cheaper sensors), deciding on how far apart to space the grids by knowing the target weight of metal that you are searching for, and the depth, and with reference to the magnetometer user guide.

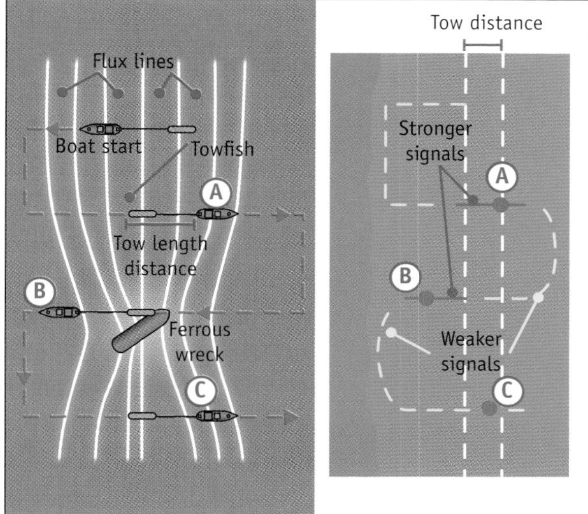

The strength of the magnetometer readout indicates how close to the anomaly the towfish is

As you move backwards and forwards past a magnetic anomaly, you will see a kick in the trace or the needle will move from one side of its rest position to the other as the field groups and then decays. Mark the position of the kick on your GPS or chart. As you move to and fro on different east-west gridlines, you should build up a staggered line of positions. The kicks will be stronger the nearer you are to the anomaly, so you should be able to narrow down the search area sufficiently to start using your echo sounder.

Rather than proceed straight into a well-defined search pattern, you can narrow the search area first. For example, start your search a suitable distance south of the approximate position, which could be 250m, 500m, 750m or more depending on how confident you are of the position. Now head north. You should see a small kick next to the anomaly. Record this latitude on the plotter and head east-west along it until you notice a larger kick. You should now have a longitude as well as a latitude for the anomaly.

The GPS and echo sounder are also still required to effectively manage your search pattern and check to see if there is anything on the seabed. Some magnetometer systems can interface to your GPS system and also to a computer, thereby allowing post-processing of your searches to be conducted on shore. Magnetometers are not wreck detectors – they are magnetic anomaly detectors and will detect anomalies due to the rock strata in the Earth just as well. In practice, considerable experience, planning and patience is required to use this equipment effectively and efficiently. It is worth trying the equipment on known dive sites first, to get the feel of the equipment.

Magnetic gradiometers

Unlike magnetometers, which measure the Earth's magnetic field at a given location, gradiometers measure how quickly the field varies from one location to another. They can be thought of as being two magnetometers a fixed distance apart, measuring the rate of change of field between them. The main advantage is that changes in the local magnetic field that affect both sensors equally do not appear as an anomaly, and such changes stem largely from the natural sources of field distortions.

The field gradient falls with distance much faster than the total field. The rule of thumb for gradiometers is that the field gradient varies inversely with the fourth power of the distance, in practice if you halve (1/2) the distance between the detector and an anomaly you will detect a signal that is sixteen times stronger (2x2x2x2, two to the power of four). In practice this means that the gradiometer is less sensitive to distant objects, which may seem to be a disadvantage, but can be an advantage if you need to resolve several smaller anomalies close together. Also, a gradiometer will record a wreck and largely ignore the more distant underlying geology, which could mask the wreck when using a magnetometer.

Metal detectors

Metal detectors can be used to find a variety of metals, unlike magnetometers, which only respond to ferrous metals. Metal detectors use their search coil to transmit a magnetic field and they measure the distortion to it caused by the electrical and magnetic properties of nearby objects. In general, the distance at which objects can be successfully detected is related to the diameter of the search coil. For small items such as coins, the detection distance will be similar to the coil diameter for search coils up to about 200mm. Above 200mm diameter, as the search coil is made larger it becomes better at detecting large items but worse for small objects. For general search purposes, a 200mm

Large areas of seabed can be searched by divers using underwater scooters

A circular search requires minimum equipment and is an effective way to search a small area

coil is a useful size. For large items the detection distance is likely to be about three to five times the diameter of the search coil.

Generally, metal detectors that work well in the sea cannot differentiate between different metals, as land-based metal detectors can.

In use, the metal detector produces a tone that varies in pitch and/or loudness with the strength of the signal being detected. The operator scans the seabed and listens to the tone on a headset or watches an indicator, which moves to a maximum when the object is at the centre of the coil. A type of earphone known as a bonephone can be used. This is a piezoelectric sounder or loudspeaker embedded in a solid block of plastic to protect it from water pressure. Held in place behind the ear by the diver's hood or mask strap or by a suitable head band, vibrations from the bonephone are transmitted to the ear by conduction through the skull, hence the name, allowing the tone to be heard.

Underwater search techniques

Despite all the technology available sometimes there is no substitute for just getting in the water and looking for your dive site. For example, many old wrecks, in clear shallow waters, have been located by simply diving or snorkelling the entire length of the search.

When searching for a site in this way, the principles behind searching must not be lost. You need to know exactly where you have looked, so you do not miss anything. This may be as simple as a pair of divers following the contours of the seabed at suitable depth intervals along a slope from a known start point to a known end point. The distance between the search lines is determined by the underwater visibility.

Covering large areas by swimming or snorkelling can be quite arduous. Underwater scooters increase the distance covered. Care should be taken by divers using scooters not to ascend too quickly or become separated.

There are a number of simple, easy to set up search techniques that can be used to locate an object on the seabed. For example, a circular search using a distance line or compass grid search can easily be carried out by a pair of divers. A circular search moves out from a known point.

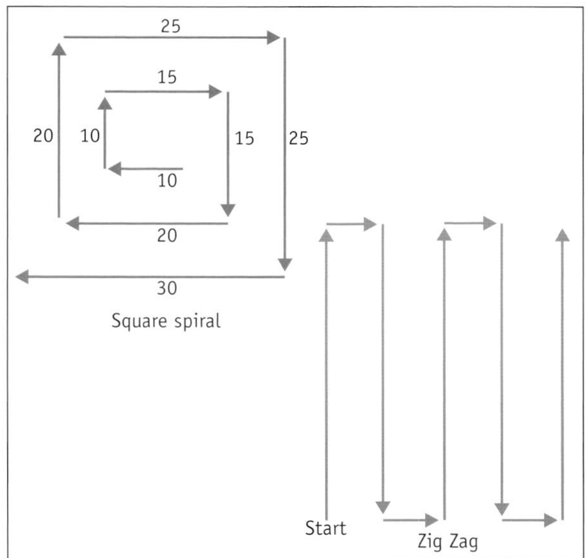

Divers carrying out a compass grid search follow a strict pattern. Each leg of the search is no further away than the limit of the visibility

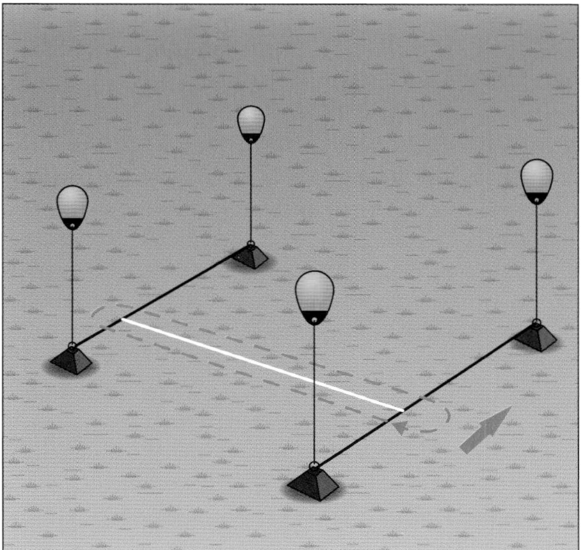

A jackstay search can be used by teams of divers to cover large areas

It is an effective method for searching small areas and total coverage can be ensured if the distance between circles is chosen carefully in conjunction with the underwater visibility. This search technique can also be used to cover only part of a circle, as a pendulum or sweep, depending on the area to be searched

A simple reason for carrying out such a search is that the shot line has not been placed precisely enough and divers have to locate the site of interest.

If there is a need for a very thorough search of the seabed, as may be the case on an archaeological project, a jackstay search may be required.

Two jackstays are deployed in parallel on the seabed as baselines from which a grid can be laid for a larger scale search. The divers swim up one side of a moveable jackstay and down the other. Then the jackstay is moved along the baselines a suitable distance, depending on the underwater visibility, and the process repeated.

More details on search techniques can be found in the BSAC manual *Dive Leading*, the BSAC skill development course Search and Recovery and the Nautical Archaeology Society's suite of courses (see the NAS website).

Recording details of the dive site location

We started this chapter with a list of information that you would ideally like to have when setting out to find a site; position, depth, site details, transits and bearings and any other information.

Having dived a site, it is well worth correcting any errors in your initial information and filling in any gaps so that you can find it quickly next time.

Many expedition leaders also fill in the appropriate wreck forms to inform the UKHO of particular sites, especially where the original data is missing or inaccurate. If the UKHO finds the information useful, the expedition leader may be given some other information in exchange, and the fee waived.

Of course, expedition leaders may wish to tell other divers about the site and information collected on the site can be much more than basic dive details and location. One way to do this is to write an expedition report (see *Collating your information*, page 141).

Chapter 7

Equipment and dive support

For many years most divers had breathing apparatus consisting of a single tank, a buoyancy compensator device of some kind and a regulator. From an expedition leader's point of view this kept the logistics of expeditions simple.

While single-cylinder diving remains popular, divers can now choose from a range of different equipment configurations from open-circuit equipment, through semi-closed-circuit to closed-circuit equipment. The benefits for expedition leaders, and divers, are that new equipment has opened up possibilities for expeditions to carry out diving to greater depths and for longer times.

There are challenges though for the expedition leader, who needs to ask; what equipment does a diver need to carry out the diving, and if a range of different equipment can be used, how can I manage the divers using it.

Here we look at the basic ways equipment can be configured, their relative merits and uses, and some of the dive management issues that these set ups raise. We also examine some dive support systems and safety equipment that should be considered for expedition diving.

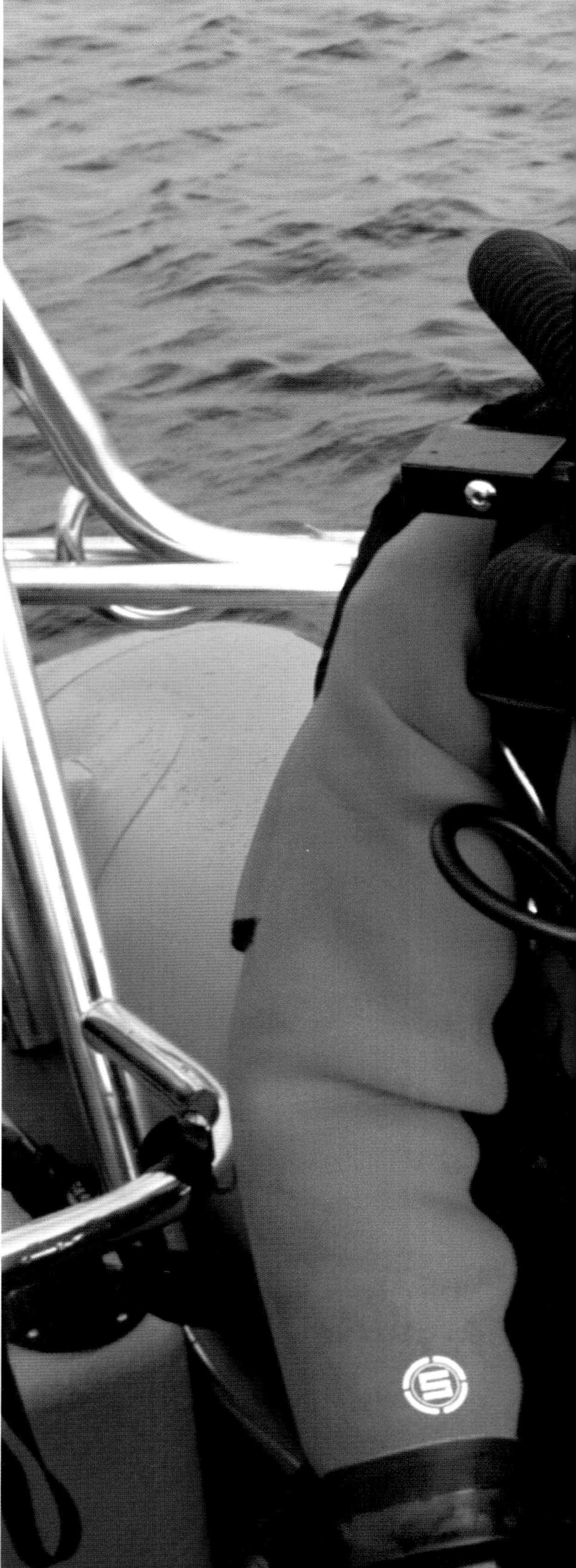

OUTEREDGE
UTEREDGE

Equipment

Equipment configuration

Having the latest diving technology seems to be the goal of many divers today. This can have a negative effect on expeditions and those who partake in them, as more effort is focused on the equipment than on the purpose of the expedition itself.

If you want to run an expedition to produce a detailed survey of an ancient shipwreck in a depth of 6m, for example, do you really need an expensive rebreather or will a conventional tank filled with rich mix of nitrox be sufficient and less hassle overall? On the other hand, if the aim is to photograph fish normally scared by exhaust bubbles in the same depth then a rebreather might be the perfect tool. If your dive team only own rebreathers then this argument is a little academic.

Comparison of typical equipment configurations

Configuration	Uses
Single cylinder	Universal diving equipment, anywhere the world Good for the majority of no-stop dives
Single cylinder with Y-valve	Not a common configuration in the U
Single cylinder with pony cylinder	Gives added safety, particularly in conditions where regulator free flows buddy separation more likely
Twin set	For deeper and longer dives
Inverted twin set	Usually more common in military and commercial diving than sports diving
Twin set with stage cylinder	Standard equipment for extended rang diving and some mixed gas dives
Twin set with twin stage cylinders	Standard configuration for open-circu trimix diving
Semi-closed-circuit rebreather	Suitable for nitrox diving up to 40m
Closed-circuit rebreather	Suitable for all types of diving but particularly useful for deep trimix

ntages	Disadvantages
le, easy to assemble and use pact, easy to use in a RIB tweight der can be readily hired in most locations simplifying travel ngements	Limited gas supply, limits dive time and depth Reliant on buddy for emergency gas supply
for cold-water diving, two separate regulators off the same der reduces gas expansion cooling effects through each pact, easy to use in a RIB tweight	Limited gas supply, limits dive time and depth Reliant on buddy for emergency gas supply
ted bailout in case of regulator failure gets you to your buddy pact, easy to use in a RIB tweight	Limited gas supply, limits dive time and depth Reliant on buddy for emergency gas supply if a deep dive or a dive with extended stops Extra clutter if the extra pony regulator not stowed correctly. Pony cylinders not easy to hire abroad
gas available be manifolded to provide a single large tank with isolation s to manage regulator failure ces the amount of weight that needs to be carried by the diver	Heavy Reduced mobility in the water because of the added inertia and drag Half empty cylinders cost more to fill at commercial air stations, which usually charge per bottle
gas available. be manifolded to provide a single large tank with isolation s to manage regulator failure ces the amount of weight that needs to be carried by the diver s are easy to access for gas shutdown in the event of a ator failure	Heavy Reduced mobility in the water because of the added inertia and drag Half empty cylinders cost more to fill at commercial air stations, which usually charge per bottle Longer hoses required Can affect in-water trim as centre of gravity of cylinders is lower
gas available be manifolded to provide a single large tank with isolation s to manage regulator failure. ces the amount of weight that needs to be carried by the diver ys use of a richer nitrox mix in the stage cylinder to accelerate decompression phase of a dive	Heavy and cumbersome Reduced mobility in the water because of the added inertia and drag Half empty cylinders cost more to fill at commercial air stations, which usually charge per bottle
gas available be manifolded to provide a single large tank with isolation s to manage regulator failure. ces the amount of weight that needs to be carried by the diver ys use of two richer nitrox mixes in the stage cylinders to erate the decompression phase of a dive delivery not reliant on electronics routine maintenance than a rebreather	Heavy and cumbersome Reduced mobility in the water because of the added inertia and drag Half empty cylinders cost more to fill at commercial air stations, which usually charge per bottle Expensive trimix gases used Needs much storage space
tly extended times underwater for the given gas supply tively simple to set up and use tively compact thing air moist and warm exhalation bubbles	Greater level of training and dive discipline required than for open-circuit Separate bailout stage cylinder may be required Harder to stow away on a small boat Requires disciplined and regular user maintenance Access to nitrox required Duration limited by the chemical scrubber life
low gas consumption compared with open-circuit mum oxygen mix at all stages of the dive efore, greatly extended times underwater for a given gas ly thing air is moist and warm exhalation bubbles ble of using mixed gases	Greater level of training and dive discipline required than for open-circuit Separate bailout stage cylinder may be required Not as robust as open-circuit equipment Requires disciplined and regular user maintenance Access to nitrox required Duration limited by the chemical scrubber life Electronically controlled Expensive

Rebreather divers need time to carry out extensive pre-dive checks

Working with different equipment configurations

Expedition leaders and dive managers need to consider the various requirements that divers using different equipment configurations will have during an expedition.

From a logistics point of view, everyone using the same equipment has some advantages. It helps divers plan similar dive profiles, particularly for technical dives, and minimises the number of spares that need to be carried on the expedition.

However, on many expeditions the type of breathing apparatus used will not be as critical and there will be a mixture of open, semi-closed and closed-circuit equipment. The equipment being used by divers will influence the time they can spend underwater and may dictate their decompression requirements.

Special considerations for rebreather divers

Both semi-closed-circuit and closed-circuit rebreather divers need more time to prepare their equipment before a dive than those using open-circuit equipment. Routine maintenance, including correct packing of the rebreather scrubber material and a set of pre-dive checks, is best done on land the day before the dive. This should give adequate time for fault finding and solving.

On the day of diving, the dive manager should ensure adequate time is allowed for rebreather divers to kit up, which usually means they start getting ready a few minutes earlier than others.

The correct pre-dive checks are more extensive than for open-circuit divers and the equipment should be breathed on the surface for a few minutes to confirm it is operating correctly. Fatalities have occurred where rebreather divers have rushed or omitted their equipment checks, for example, by forgetting to turn on their gas bottles or the electronics.

Buddy pairing of rebreather divers can also be an issue. The dive manager should make sure that the buddy chosen is capable of rescuing the rebreather diver and that both divers have sufficient emergency gas between them to deal with an out of gas situation. or equipment failure of either diver

The current BSAC guidelines for selecting a buddy for a rebreather diver are set out in the *Safe Diving* guidelines (see BSAC website).

Should a rebreather diver need to bail out onto another system this can considerably increase the amount of decompression they need to do.

CASE STUDY 7.1

Mixed up

A group of divers with a mixture of different equipment configurations have come together for a dive. Their chosen site involves a dive to 40m for 20 minutes bottom time.

The problem

- Diver A is using a closed-circuit rebreather with air as the diluent gas plus a bailout.
- Diver B is using a semi-closed rebreather with the rebreather set to 27% nitrox plus a bailout.
- Divers C, D, E are using twin sets (2 x 15 litres) with air as a breathing gas.
- Diver F, G are using twin sets (2 x 12l) with air and a stage cylinder of nitrox 60%.
- Diver H is using a twin set (2 x 15l) with a nitrox mix of 27%.

Using a proprietary decompression software package the following dive profiles were calculated for 40m maximum depth and 20 minutes bottom time.

Equipment	Diver	Total time (mins)	Deco time (mins)
Open-circuit air	C, D, E	58	33
Open-circuit nitrox 27%	H	43	19
Semi-closed-circuit 27%	B	43	19
Open-circuit air, with nitrox 60% deco gas	F, G	38	14
Closed-circuit pO_2 1.2 bar	A	32	9

The solution

The advantages of various equipment configurations in terms of decompression requirements can be seen but this can make buddy pairing a problem.

One approach is to match total times and profiles.

This gives the buddy pairs A and F, B and G, C and D, which looks reasonable as their total timings are close. Consideration should be given to making sure that the divers do not become separated from each other as they complete their respective decompression stops.

Unfortunately E and H will not be closely matched, with diver E needing to spend 14 minutes more in the water decompressing. Diver H will simply have to wait a bit longer for his buddy.

If a closed-circuit rebreather diver has to bail out onto another system at the furthest point into the dive (worst case), there will be a significant increase in dive time.

Each diver will also need to consider his or her breathing gas requirements. The final dive plans may be limited by the divers' gas consumption.

Equipment	Total time (mins)	Deco time (mins)
Closed-circuit pO_2 1.20 bar A – bailout to air after 20 minutes	42	18

How they did it

The open-circuit air divers only just have enough air if you assume a surface breathing rate of 20l/min and 1/3 air in reserve.

- Note that for this dive a single cylinder would be completely inadequate.
- The different dive times can be used to the dive manager's advantage.
- If diving from RIBs, for example, some of the divers might be required to drive the boats (assuming they are appropriately qualified). In this case divers A and F could enter the water first and be out early to take over and allow those divers remaining in the boat to have a dive.

Stowing kit

Stowing equipment

Expedition leaders and dive managers need to consider how to properly stow equipment aboard the boat. Incorrect stowage can lead to damage of equipment and injury to the dive team at worst, and inefficient and frustrating kitting up of divers at best.

Correct stowage of equipment is particularly important when conducting dives that are kit intensive such as extended range or trimix dives, but the principles apply equally well to other types of dive.

Guidelines for stowing equipment

Stowing equipment sounds obvious and simple, but it is amazing how such a simple thing can descend into chaos.

You need a way of stowing the equipment so that those getting kitted up first have their equipment to hand first and buddy pairs are next to or opposite each other to facilitate a buddy check.

- Stow equipment securely and safety as even gentle boat rocking motion can send equipment flying.
- Ensure regulators and other delicate equipment are not lying on the deck or floor waiting to be trodden on.
- Rebreathers are generally not as robust as open-circuit equipment and should be treated accordingly.
- If the boat is about to enter rough water, double check that everything is secure and not likely to come loose or be lost overboard.
- Liaise with the boat skipper who may have his or her own way of stowing equipment for their boat.
- Organise the dive team to load the boat in an orderly way, giving clear directions as to how the boat needs to be loaded.
- Setting up a human chain can load or unload a boat in minutes.

Records

The correct completion of dive records, which usually means the dive slate, is not the sole purpose of dive management. However, dive records are important.

For the dive manager the information on the dive slate has various levels of importance. Of prime importance is the information about who is in the water and when they are due to surface – name, time in and time out.

The dive slate is usually used to collect more information than that, but with the many equipment variations encountered a slate can become complicated.

Opposite is an example of a partially completed log sheet for the groups diving in case study 7.1 (see page 99). It is designed to cater for a range of equipment types.

We see here how details of all the cylinder gases carried and scrubber durations are recorded. For expedition leaders, the dive records can be a useful and important document after the diving is complete, often used as supporting evidence for grant claims or for the benefit of the expedition team to complete their own dive logs.

Basic diver safety equipment

The expedition leader needs to make sure that their divers have appropriate basic safety equipment for the diving that is planned. In particular, it is necessary to ensure divers can be located on their return to the surface. Even in the most perfect surface conditions, divers can be difficult to spot. All that is often visible of the diver above the water is the diver's head, which is roughly the size of a football.

There is a range of basic equipment that a diver can carry to help others locate them on the surface.

Brightly coloured hood

Black is the favourite choice of colour for wetsuits, drysuits and in particular hoods. Unfortunately, it is not the easiest colour to spot against the sea. Brightly coloured hoods are more easily seen.

DATE	14 Jul 09	SITE	Unknown wreck	Dive Manager	Diver C	Tide times	Time (BST)	Height (m)	Time (BST)	Height (m)	BSAC Diving for divers
Weather Forecast/Actual F 2-3 WESTERLEY, VIZ GOOD				Assistant DM	Diver A	LW	4.15	2.0	5.05	1.7	
				Skipper/ Cox'n	BOB	HW	10.33	4.4	11.16	4.1	DIVE MANAGEMENT SLATE

Name	Qual	OC SCR CCR	Gas 1 Mix	Gas 1 in Bar/ Size	Gas 2 mix	Gas 2 Bar/ Size	Gas 3 Mix	Gas 3 Bar/ Size	Gas 4 Mix	Gas 4 Bar/ Size	Scrubber Time (mins)	Plan Depth (m)	Plan Total Time (mins)	Time Down	Time Up	Max Depth (m)	Total Time (mins)	Total Deco (mins)
DIVER A	AD	CCR	230	AIR / 3	200	O2 / 3	200	40% / 10	-	- / -	180	40	38	11.00	11.38	39.5	38	9
DIVER F	FC	OC	230	AIR / 12	230	AIR / 12	230	60% / 7	-	- / -	N/A	40	38	11.00	11.38	39.5	38	14
DIVER B	AD	SCR	230	40 / 10	-	- / -	-	- / -	-	- / -	100	40	48					
DIVER G	DL	OC	230		230		-		-		N/A	40	48					

The dive log forms the dive manager's record of the state of the diving at any time

A brightly coloured hood is easily seen on the surface

Delayed surface marker buoy

This is such a valuable piece of equipment that it is hard to understand why any diver dives without one. Its obvious use is to mark the location of the divers underwater to enable surface boat traffic to avoid them.

If each DSMB is marked with its owner's name, it will help the dive manager or boat skipper track each diver. It is important on some dives that every diver launches their DSMB even if their buddy has already launched theirs, in order that the boat can effectively track every diver.

There has been much debate about what colour is best for locating divers. Recently, a convention has started whereby red or orange DSMBs are used for marking divers, and yellow in conjunction with the red for a diver in distress. It is also a generally recognised convention that two DSMBs, regardless of colour, deployed together forming a V on the surface is an indication of distress underwater.

Slates can be attached to the top of some makes of DSMB so signals can be sent to the surface. This might be a useful technique in some diving projects, as well as in an emergency. All signals to be used on any dive should be agreed beforehand and mentioned in the briefing.

Flag

Collapsible flags can be strapped to diving cylinders and deployed on the surface if required. If diving on open sites or when there is a swell, the extra height of the flag allows the boat cover to see the divers' position on the surface more clearly. There is again some debate as to whether a darker or brighter colour is preferable. A brighter colour is more visible against the dark sea, but a darker colour or indeed a thicker material may make a better silhouette against the sky.

Tracking systems

Mirror or other reflector

Small, reflecting (non-breakable) mirrors can be used to attract the attention of the boat by reflecting sunlight. Old CDs or DVDs can be used for this purpose.

Whistle or air horn

Many BCs are sold with a simple whistle to attract attention. Also available are gas-operated whistle units that can be connected to a BCD inflator hose.

Personal flares

These are smaller version of the emergency flares carried by all dive boats. Housed in a waterproof container, they can be taken on dives and used at the surface in case of distress. However, the integrity of the waterproof housing needs to be checked regularly and also the life of the flares themselves. Being rarely used, they are often forgotten until they are needed, when it is too late for any maintenance.

Strobe

These are small, flashing waterproof lights. They can be switched on both underwater and at the surface, but a flashing light on the surface signals distress, so they should only be used on the surface in an emergency.

EPIRBs

Emergency position-indicating radio beacons, when activated by a diver, will relay a signal to satellites linked to the Global Maritime Distress and Safety System (GMDSS). There are small versions of EPIRBs used by boats in life-threatening situations. For obvious reasons they should only be used if divers are separated from their boat and lost on the surface. Two frequencies are generally available 121.5MHz and 406Mhz. The former has now been phased out and is not monitored by satellites but can be detected by most search and rescue aircraft when in the vicinity.

Underwater tracking systems

For expeditions diving in remote areas or in demanding conditions, where the risk of the boat losing contact with divers is higher, the expedition leader may consider using an electronic tracking system in addition to the more basic equipment to help locate divers underwater or on the surface. Some of these systems can track more than one diver at a time.

Underwater tracking systems have been developed using technology used widely to track the location of remotely operated underwater vehicles (ROVs). Using acoustic signals, the relative position of a diver from the boat can be calculated, and using a basic search pattern the diver can be quickly located and their depth determined.

Some systems can be linked to a GPS system to provide and absolute position of the diver. Some systems include a distress signal – the diver activates an emergency signal by pulling a cord.

The underwater systems work using line of sight so they may not detect the diver if they are behind or inside a large object.

Surface tracking systems

Surface tracking units are also becoming available based on EPIRB technology. In this case a surface unit looks for radio signals from the unit carried by the diver.This radio signal carries the GPS position of the diver embedded within it enabling their position to be displayed on the surface unit. Such devices could be used in non-emergency situations as well as emergencies.

Dive support systems

A 'dive support system' is a wide-ranging concept more commonly encountered in commercial and military diving environments. It covers all dive equipment including personal equipment, saturation systems and large purpose-built dive support vessels, along with the procedures to operate them and carry out tasks safely.

With the advent of technical diving, the term has started to become more widely used by divers on deeper diving expeditions to refer to the system of equipment and procedures they use to carry out their diving in as safe as way as possible.

Although these systems have grown up in support of deeper diving, many of the equipment and procedures can be applied to shallower diving expeditions.

The buddy system

The incident statistics and their analysis support the buddy system of diving as the safer way to dive. The buddy system means you dive with someone else, closely together and in support of each other. If one diver has a problem the other can help. The most obvious instance of assistance is an out-of-gas situation, particularly where the pair are diving on single cylinders. However, the presence of a buddy can very often avert a major incident in the first place. This might be through such simple a thing as an occasional gas check, or sorting out a very simple problem underwater before it becomes a major incident.

Over reliance on a buddy, however, can be a problem, particularly if the divers become separated. For example, both divers should carry surface location aids rather than sharing them. This is not an argument in support of solo diving, which for most diving cannot be justified. Rather, divers in the buddy pair should be capable of diving independently (and so able to deal with becoming separated confidently) but should dive in support of each other as a team.

Team diving

Most dives require a dive team to make them happen. Divers underwater usually need someone on the surface to monitor and track them. Team diving is a term that usually refers more to the way in which the actual dive is executed.

Certain dives, particularly the more technical ones and dives in demanding conditions, require something in addition to the buddy system. Support divers may be used, for example, to monitor divers during the decompression phase, taking excess equipment, such as cameras, to the surface and bringing extra gas from the surface.

Stand-by divers usually wait on the surface and enter the water only if there is an emergency, for example, if a signal is received reporting a diver out of gas. Additional surface support may be required to handle extra equipment on the dive support boat or assist the divers in and out of the water.

Dive plans may also need to be unified. It is a good idea for a group of bottom divers to agree a certain depth and time and stick to the plan. This has a number of benefits.

DSMBs are an essential piece of safety kit

First, as the group ascend, divers can not only monitor their buddy but also keep an eye open for other buddy pairs in the group. Second, support divers if used will also know what time they need to enter the water. Third, a set time for divers ascending may also help surface cover to locate and follow them. This is particularly important if diving near shipping lanes, where the dive support boat needs to protect the divers and warn other vessels of their location.

For team diving to work, the expedition leader needs to balance the needs of the individual with the overall team objectives and team members need to accept that they may have to take on the role of support diver, stand-by diver or surface support.

If there is a mixed ability team where a couple of divers may want a deep dive but others don't, then the roles of bottom divers and support divers/stand-by divers can be easily defined. If all divers are capable of the dive, then they may simply need to take it in turns, returning to the same site later with the roles reversed.

Some dive systems also require divers to carry the same gas and or use the same equipment. It can be argued that this has some advantage as the divers will be more familiar with their buddies' equipment and so better able to assist. It probably has more advantages for the expedition as a whole, as it simplifies the spares that are needed and what gas mixtures need to be prepared.

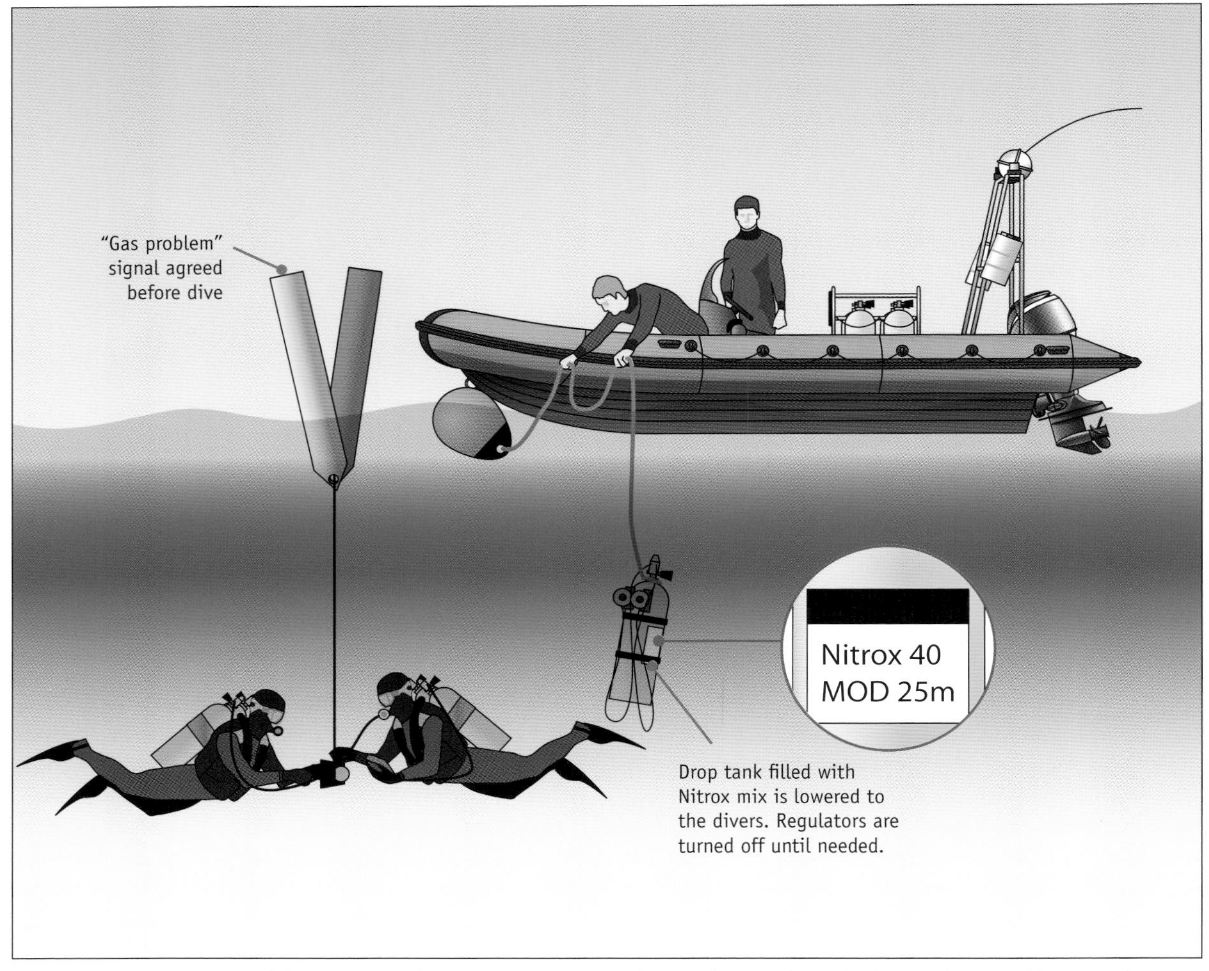

If divers signal that there is a gas problem, a drop tank can be lowered to provide extra deco gas

Drop tanks

Drop tanks are used to provide divers who are running low of gas during the decompression phase of the dive with extra gas. Pre-prepared tanks of gas (usually air or an appropriate mix of nitrox) are fitted with regulators and attached to a buoyed rope, ready to drop to any divers signalling the need for more gas. The buoy clearly needs to be sufficiently large to support the weight of the cylinder, and the rope long enough to reach the divers at their deco stop. Drop tanks may be deployed on a shot line in anticipation of the divers returning up the line.

However, if the divers are not returning up a shot line, then the drop tanks could be deployed upon a pre-arranged signal. It is important that any emergency signals are agreed before the dive. It could be a colour-coded delayed surface marker buoy (yellow is usually taken to mean emergency, nature unknown), or two DSMB's deployed together, or a DSMB with a message written on a slate. Surface support will respond accordingly.

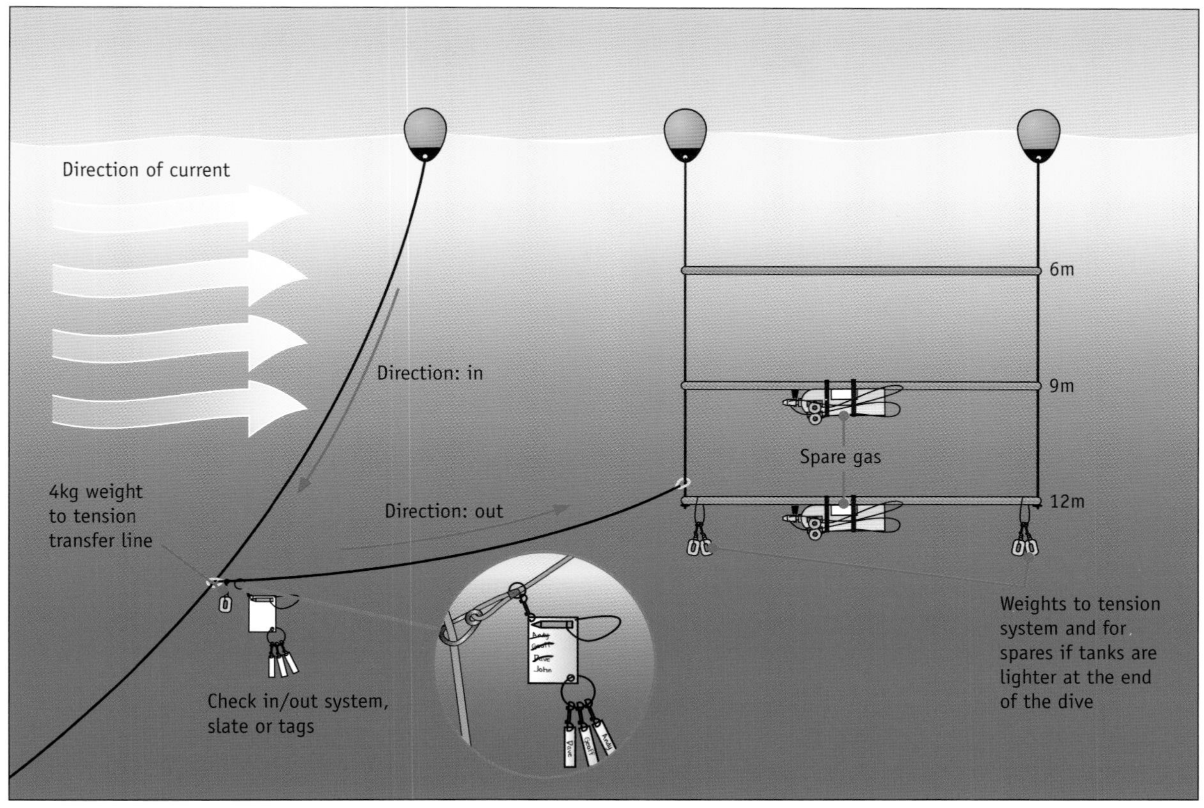

Using a detatchable trapeze decompression station such as this increases the comfort for decompressing divers

Decompression stations

Decompression stations keep divers together during prolonged deco stops. Spare gas and weights are often deployed on the decompression station for decompressing divers to use if required.

A trapeze is the most common design, consisting of a series of horizontal aluminium or plastic bars supported under two buoys on ropes at decompression stop depths of, for example, 12m, 9m and 6m. Weights on the ends on the ropes maintain tension and, providing the buoys are not too buoyant, help reduce the amount of wave motion transmitted to the horizontal bars.

The decompression station is connected to the shot line with a transfer line and a quick-release clip. Once all divers have returned to the station, it can be released from the main shot line and allowed to drift with the current.

A checking in and out system is useful to verify that all divers have returned to the decompression station. A popular checking in and out system consists of a name tag, which each diver clips to a ring on the transfer line on descent. As divers ascend they remove their own tags. Once all the tags have been recovered, all divers will be on the decompression station, which means it can be released from the shot line.

If any divers fail to return to the decompression station, the usual procedure is for the decompression station to remain attached to the shot line for a pre-arranged time before releasing. A system needs to be agreed beforehand to handle divers who do not return to the shot line on time. It is usual for them to deploy a DSMB and carry out their decompression below that.

Portable compressors have slow charging rates but offer the chance of getting air in remote locations

Compressors

The proliferation of dive centres in most popular diving locations around the world means that to fill cylinders may simply be a question of where to take the bottles, when to leave and collect them and how much it will cost. There are dive locations, however, where this is not an option and the expedition will have to consider taking a portable compressor.

Compressors are available in all shapes and sizes. A balance has to be struck between the charging rate (usually expressed in litres per minute) and the weight and portability of the device. Typical portable compressors are capable of filling at around 100l/min and weigh about 45 to 50 kilograms.

Filling cylinders from a portable compressor can be a lengthy business. The time taken to fill all of the cylinders must be built into the overall daily timetable. Taking two compressors would halve the time spent filling cylinders each day. Organising a rota for filling cylinders is a good way of sharing the workload and avoiding any one becoming burdened with what quickly becomes a boring job. The second compressor would be a back up in case of problems with the first.

Consumables required such as filters, lubrication oil, and fuel must be brought along. Training to ensure the dive team can operate the compressor will need to be provided. The compressor filters need changing at regular intervals as stated by the manufacturer. Chemicals within the filter will eventually become fully saturated with the contaminants that they are designed to remove and will no longer be effective. Filter life can vary considerably, depending on the operating environment, and is usually quoted as a maximum numbers of hours or maximum volume of gas to be filtered.

All compressors should have written procedures for filter changing. Most compressors use filter cartridges, which can be quickly and simply changed. Although it is possible to refill filters with fresh material, it is usually more convenient and safer to use new filter cartridges. Careful records need to be kept of the hours the compressor has run in order to ensure the compressor filter life is not exceeded.

Most portable compressors have a petrol or diesel engine. It is important to avoid drawing fumes from whatever source into the air intake of the compressor as this will lead to contamination of the cylinder fills. This is accomplished by setting the compressor up so that it is not in a confined area, the exhaust is downwind and the air drawn into the compressor is fresh.

Electrically-driven portable compressors are also available and reduce the risk of contamination with exhaust fumes. Care still needs to be taken to ensure any other fumes are not drawn into the compressor. Also, the power supply that the unit is being connected to must be capable of carrying the electrical load and there must be plenty of ventilation around the compressor to cool it, otherwise it could easily overheat.

Finally, compressors are generally noisy and operators should wear ear defenders for their own protection and think of others when operating the compressor.

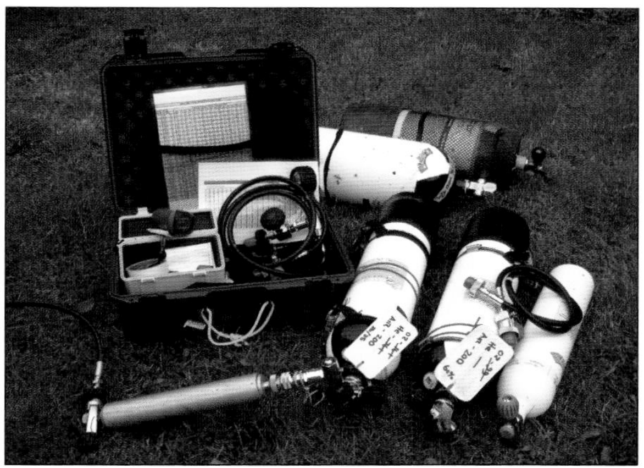

Gas-blending equipment is portable

A booster pump back at base enables efficient use of gas

Portable gas blending equipment

Some expeditions will want to use nitrox or trimix gas mixtures. With suitable equipment there is no reason why these gases cannot be blended in the field.

Again, the expedition leader should allow plenty of time for blending gases and ensure the blending is carried out by properly qualified people to ensure their safety. Records should be kept of the gas mixtures that have been blended, when, by whom and that they have been analysed and checked by the end user.

A typical blending kit comprises an in-line filter (for double filtering compressor air), a hose assembly for decanting gas from storage bottles to diving cylinders fitted with a needle valve to control flow, and an accurate gauge to monitor gas pressure and a gas analyser to measure oxygen and if necessary helium content. These items can usually be fitted inside a protective case along with waterproof marker pens and tape to mark the cylinder with its gas mixture and depth restrictions.

Of course, in addition to the small quantity of blending equipment, the gas also needs to be considered. The amount required will need to be calculated in advance to ensure there is sufficient gas for the mixtures required. Rather than completely draining the diving cylinders, it may well be possible to top up diving cylinders. Calculations, or look up tables, will be required to determine the additional amount of oxygen required and a sufficiently high pressure of oxygen will be required in the storage cylinders in order that oxygen flows to the diving cylinder. A booster pump helps to make the most of the contents of the storage cylinders as the pressure in them drops.

Diving grades of oxygen and helium are available from gas distributors. Typically, the bottles are substantially larger and heavier than scuba cylinders and do not fit into the average car. Where possible it is usually best to contact a local distributor to arrange for delivery of the gas to the place where you will be blending. For more remote locations this will probably mean ordering ahead. If the expedition has to take gas with it, then clearly the suitability of the transport and any local laws restricting the movement of these cylinders will need to be considered.

Booster pumps

Booster pumps are used to take lower pressure gas from a storage cylinder and pump it to a higher pressure in another cylinder. This permits more efficient use of expensive gases such as helium.

However, some booster pumps are driven by compressed air of which a considerable quantity could be required. With a large compressor the time required may not be an issue, but for the adventurous expedition using smaller portable compressors, the increase in compressing time may make the use of a booster pump impractical.

CASE STUDY 7.5

A 'most memorable' expedition

Diving HMS Victoria

In 2008, after a year of planning, an experienced expedition diver led a team of BSAC divers on a mixed gas expedition to dive the wreck of the HMS Victoria, maximum depth 144m, off the coast of Lebanon.

The story

The primary purpose of the expedition was to dive the wreck of the HMS Victoria. Secondary objectives were to:

- accurately check depths and map them onto a ship's plan to see how much of the vessel is buried in the seabed.
- record video and still pictures of the wreck for reporting but also for the Ministry of Defence (Heritage Section) and the Hydrographic Office.
- check for damage caused by explosive fishing methods and deterioration.

The expedition leader faced a number of challenges to achieve his aims:

- getting permission to dive the wreck.
- getting all people to Beirut at the same time with the right gear on the same flights and sorting the accommodation.
- setting up the support equipment and gases for a deep technical dive.

Sixteen divers came together from different clubs, including some commercial diving instructors to form the dive team. All were trimix divers with a minimum certification to 80m, either closed- or open-circuit. The expedition leader was personally aware of the experience and capabilities of each member of the expedition. They typically had at least 30 logged dives to >80m, 10 of them within the last two years. The expedition leader was prepared to take a small number of divers who had qualified to 80m within the last 12 months on the basis of personal recommendation and ability to *'cover with experienced buddy'.*

How they did it

Expedition leader planned the expedition in consultation with whole group via email.

The diving platforms were two day boats from the dive centre, one 10m boat in Beirut and a 13m boat in Tripoli. Both were open speedboat-type vessels with twin 200hp and 225hp outboards respectively. Room was at a premium with 12 technical divers, 24 stages, four drop tanks and four video camera rigs on board. The gear had to be stowed around the boat and kitting up took place sitting on the gunwhale. The boats were less than ideal for this sort of diving and had no diving ladders; re-entry was a climb over the stern after de-kitting. The boats were not suitable for heavy weather but that is usual in an area of generally calm weather. The cheerful willingness of the crew allowed them to overcome these problems.

Gas was supplied by NISD Beirut. The expedition took a helium/O_2 analyser and used laptop-based gas mixing programmes. Standard bailout mixes of 10% oxygen/53% helium (10/53)and 20/30 were used to facilitate common bailout plans. A mix of 6/72 heliair was used as diluent for ease of filling and common decompression schedules devised so that if anyone needed to bail out any diver could help. The centre did not have a booster pump; 80% nitrox was used as the shallow bailout gas and O_2 fills for on-board tanks were never more than 180 bar.

There was a fair amount of heavy kit. A pallet (32 x 20kg tubs) of Sofnolime was transported via ship to Beirut in advance. Rebreathers and general diving kit were taken individually and excess baggage allowance was purchased from the airline. Cylinders were mostly hired from the dive centre although some dedicated 3l and 2l tanks were taken out on the flight. Video and lighting equipment was also taken as excess baggage.

Diving logistics

All divers were to use closed-circuit rebreathers, except for one open-circuit diver. Mixed gas was used on the >60m wrecks. There were 12 APD Inspirations, one MkVI Cis Lunar and one Megalodon.

The team leader planned to alternate the diving so that a team of six or eight divers would dive the wreck with the rest acting as surface support, shallow and deep in-water support. These two teams would alternate so that each team would get three dives on the wreck a week.

Local knowledge was used to find the dive sites. But they did take a hand-held GPS and a GPS position for the HMS Victoria obtained from the UK Hydrographic Office just in case. This position was within 30m of the wreck.

Costs

In order to determine what gas and Sofnolime would be required, the expedition leader needed to accurately consider the expected dive times and kit configurations of the dive team in advance (see Gas planning box overleaf). Cylinder hire was $7 per tank (usually a minimum of four tanks per diver were needed). Nitrox and O_2 cost $12 for any sized fill, helium was $0.10 per litre.

Other costs included:

hotel accommodation at	$37.50/night/person;
road transport (Beirut – Tripoli) at	$175/day ($22/person/day)
taxis at	$2/person/day
boat hire at	$525/day ($66/person/day)
dive centre charge at	$25/person/day
food at approximately	$30/person/day
flights at	£430 per person
	£120 excess baggage charges

The cost per week based on three dives on HMS Victoria was approximately **£1314**

There was no sponsorship, as such, but Custom Divers provided and shipped the Sofnolime at cost.

Problems

- Local politics – when the expedition landed, the Lebanese authorities had placed a ban on diving HMS Victoria. After about 10 days of meetings with the Military Attaché at the British Embassy and high-level negotiations with the Lebanese army plus communications by phone and email with UK Ministry of Defence, the expedition got permission to dive the wreck.
- The team had to modify the diving plans, including rethinking the support equipment and gases for a deep technical dive, to enable all divers to dive at the same time once permission was granted to dive the wreck.
- There were logistical problems getting the Sofnolime to Lebanon.
- As the team didn't get permission to dive the wreck until the Wednesday of the second week, the diving plan had to be modified to enable everyone to dive the wreck at the same time.
- A decompression station with transfer line was attached to the shot line for each dive.
- The first pair took the transfer line and attached it using a prussic loop at 40m.
- The crew fed in the deco station with a bar at 6m and two cylinders of 80% at 9m with regulators, from the boat.
- A further two tanks of 80% were kept in the boat for use as drop tanks.
- The second pair followed down with an 11l 20/30 cylinder and reg and attached it via a prussic loop to the shot line at 60m. Diver ID tokens were placed on this cylinder.
- The last pair up removed their tokens, brought up the tank and disconnected the transfer line. Each diver carried an 11l 10/53 stage and an 11l 20/30 stage, enough to ensure a safe bailout return to the 80% on the deco station for one diver of each pair.
- The wreck is vertical and the visibility was in the order of 20m on the wreck so pairs of divers would be in sight of one another should any problem arise.
- Surface signalling via red and yellow DSMBs would indicate requirement for drop tanks or other assistance.

Gas planning

Gas planning		
Open-circuit divers, mean gas costs:		
Back gas	2 x 12l x 200bar of 10/53	$252.00
Travel gas	1 x 11l x 200bar of 20/30	$73.00
Deco gas	1 x 11l x 200bar of 80%	$12.00
Dive gas		**$337/dive**
+ share of stage/drop tanks		**$3.60/person**
Total gas cost		**$340.60/dive**
Closed-circuit rebreather divers, mean gas costs:		
Diluent	1 x 3l x 200bar of 6/72	$42.60
Diluent serves two dives		$27.00/dive
O_2	1 x 3l x 200bar 02	$12.00
Air fills for suit inflation		free
Total gas cost		**$39.00/dive**
Sofnolime	£108/week/diver	**$36.00/dive**
Total consumables		**$75.00/dive**
Bailout gas	1 x 11l x 200bar of 10/53	$115.50
Bailout gas	1 x 11l x 200bar of 20/30	$73.00
Deco and drop tanks	4 x 11l x 200bar of 80%	$12.00
Deco stage tank	1 x 11l x 200bar x 20/30	$73.00
Bailout gas and deco/stage tanks only used in an emergency so they are a one-off total cost shared between eight CCR divers		
+ share of stage/drop tanks		**$34.00/person**

The dive sites

Typical visibility in open water >30m

Visibility on the wrecks varied, 20m-30m on HMS Victoria, 3-4m on the SS Lesbian

HMS Victoria was sunk 1893 in collision with HMS Camperdown, the lives of 358 men were lost in the tragedy. She lies vertical and unsupported with her bows sunk approximately 30m into the seabed. The deck faces south, the stern is at 77m and the seabed 144m. The wreck is largely intact and the 10″ stern gun, the 6″ guns and 6 pounders are all still in position. The forward turret with the two 16.25″ guns has fallen out and is somewhere off the wreck on the seabed. It is possible to enter the gun deck at 140m and swim up through the guns, which are still on their carriages and through the Admiral's quarters in the stern, exiting via the Admiral's stern door onto his walkway.

When descending onto the wreck the outline of the stern is visible from approximately 53m and the props and rudder are clearly visible from 57m. A little deeper than 60m the brass letters 'Victoria' can clearly be seen on the stern. Penetration through one deck at 110m gives access to the ward room pantry and there is much intact crockery and glassware lying about. Portholes are still in place. The funnel holes are clearly identifiable at 132m, these are memorable since they lie across the ship rather than in line with the keel. Masts, spars and other debris are littered on the seabed standing about 3m high. The ship appears to be buried in the seabed up to just aft of the centre line of the main forward gun turret mount.

A shoal of very large jacks seems to be permanently circling the stern and large scorpion fish lie about the wreck, these are coloured red to blend in with the red sponge that seems to cover the wreck. Two free swimming moray eels were also spotted at about 115m.

The temperature on the wreck is 18°C and the visibility averages at least 20m, increasing to 40m near the surface. There is a thermocline at about 60m and again at about 25m, so the temperature warms progressively to 26-27°C at 6m. Deepest depth recorded on the wreck was 146m in the scour at the side, longest dive was 6 hours 33 minutes with a bottom time on the wreck of 42 minutes and a maximum depth of 144m.

Vichy French submarine Souffleur a Second World War wreck in 38m and in two halves having been torpedoed by a British submarine. Visibility approximately 40m and penetration through the wreck was possible in both halves. This was a memorable dive.

The torpedo boat a Second World War freighter carrying torpedoes as cargo, wrecked off Tripoli, in 60m. A superb dive in 40m vis. The wreck was pristine, upright and complete with ship's wheel, steam whistle, portholes, engine room telegraph and gauges all still in place. Add to that two eagle rays circling the wreck made this a memorable dive.

The **wall off Beirut** was not particularly interesting. It served as a depth build-up dive before diving HMS Victoria. The maximum depth on the wall was more than 300m, most dives were between 90 and 110m, but one pair went to 152m.

SS Lesbian a Second World War wreck off Beirut. Silty, but compared favourably with UK channel sites. If you did a similar wreck in UK at 65m you would consider it a good dive.

MV Alice B is upright and intact in 38m. She is a single hold, rear bridge motor vessel that was sabotaged during the civil war of 1996. Visibility was about 20m but the wreck was a little silty. Penetration in and through the engine room was possible with care. This would be considered a good dive in the UK and the warm water and good visibility enhances it.

Russian freighter in 38m is on its starboard side and very silty. Visibility is in excess of 20m until the silt is disturbed. All portholes were still on the wreck but nothing much else of interest. Penetration was possible but distance lines advisable.

Team verdict

The three best dives of the trip were: HMS Victoria, absolutely awesome – to quote the expedition leader *'In 32 years of diving this is without doubt the most memorable wreck I have dived'*; the submarine Souffleur; and the torpedo boat.

Diving achieved

4 days' diving on **HMS Victoria**	31 person dives
3 days' diving on **SS Lesbian**	27 person dives
1 day on the **torpedo boat**	11 person dives
3 days' diving on the submarine **Souffleur**	20 person dives
1 day on the **Alice B**	12 person dives
1 day on the **Beirut wall**	12 person dives
1 day on the **Russian freighter**	12 person dives
Total person dives	**125**
Total days diving	**14**

Chapter 8

Dealing with diving emergencies

Diving expeditions are often adventurous and challenging for those taking part. Statistics demonstrate that even on the most conservative of diving expeditions, incidents happen. In this chapter, we set out to highlight the issues that expedition leaders must take into account so that if an incident occurs the expedition team is capable of taking appropriate action.

Incidents happen for a reason and when you understand the reasons you can help to prevent them. It is also important to be able to recognise an incident, respond to it appropriately and resolve it. Coordination of activities is an essential part of dealing with an emergency; this is best achieved by nominating a rescue manager.

The expedition leader needs to carry out some planning and preparation for dealing with emergencies as part of the general expedition planning. Rescue philosophies will vary when emergency services are likely to be on scene quickly to assist and when they are not.

This chapter builds on detail found in other BSAC publications, such as *Seamanship: a guide for divers* and *Safety and Rescue for Divers*, putting everything in the context of an expedition.

135D

Incident pit

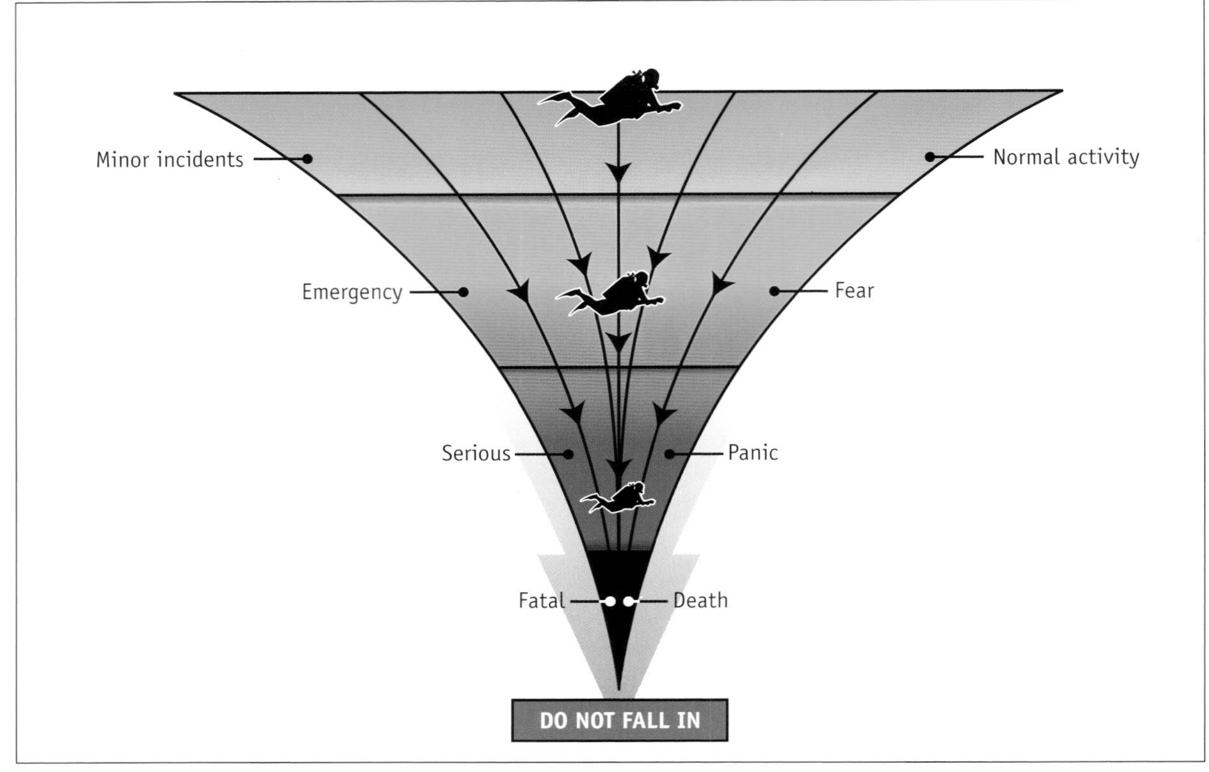

Prompt resolution of minor problems prevents the slide down the steep sides of the incident pit

The incident pit

The incident pit is often used to describe how a number of minor things can combine to generate a much more serious incident. It is far easier to resolve each of the minor problems in isolation, than to allow them to escalate. This concept is normally associated with an individual diver but can be equally applied to an expedition.

Resolving problems, particularly early on if underwater, does prevent more serious consequences that could occur. Incidents rarely happen as the result of one factor but, more commonly, are the result of a combination of factors. Each factor in isolation may be quite innocuous but, as the combination builds, the stress on the diver increases until it is beyond their capabilities.

The effect has been likened to a pit whose sides become steeper and steeper the further one descends. While the slope is gentle it is easy to retain your footing and to climb back out - minor incidents can be resolved.

As you descend further in, your footing becomes less sure and it becomes more and more difficult to climb out. Minor incidents escalate into emergencies, which become more difficult to resolve.

Ultimately, all grip is lost and the resulting slide into oblivion at the bottom of the pit is irreversible - as the severity of the emergency exceeds the ability for resolution, the incident becomes increasingly serious and ultimately may be fatal.

The moral: resolving an underwater problem promptly prevents more serious consequences.

CASE STUDY 8.1

The slippery slope

A diver is still using a drysuit even though the suit inflator has occasionally been sticking.

The story

On a dive the inflator sticks open again causing the diver to disconnect the drysuit feed. But dumping too much air from the suit causes the diver to sink. Finning upwards to stay level is an effort. Water now starts to leak into the suit and the diver begins to get cold. Stress levels rise, resulting in panic. To compensate for a lack of buoyancy, the diver inflates his BCD, but putting too much air in results in a fast ascent.

The solution

By addressing each minor aspect as it arises, the potential for the development of the serious incident is reduced. Climbing out of the pit while the slope is gentle is the easiest option.

Some maintenance on the drysuit feed would have avoided a cold diver and a fast ascent.

Anyone who has read the annual diving incidents report produced by the BSAC, or articles in the diving press, will find many examples of other divers falling into the incident pit to varying degrees.

Avoiding incidents

Incident avoidance starts well before the actual diving begins, at the planning stage of the expedition. Prevention is definitely better than cure. We have already seen, in earlier chapters, how potential hazards can be identified through a process of risk assessment and how we can then find ways to avoid harm.

If the actions to avoid the incidents or help cope with them if they happen, are not put into practice, the risk assessment process has failed.

If a diver needs to rely on their buddy for surface detection aids (i.e. DSMB) and then they become separated, they are climbing into the incident pit before they have even entered the water.

Anticipation of incidents, however, should not be limited to a planning exercise on paper. It should continue throughout the expedition. Everyone on the team, especially the expedition leader and dive managers, should constantly be aware of all that is going on around them. This can provide vital information about members of the team that can help in the recognition of a potential problem before it happens and hence reduce the chances of an incident happening. If a problem is identified, it should always be rectified.

Before a dive, observe the actions and attitudes of the members of the expedition. Check for signs of nervousness and reluctance, such as making excuses, appearing stressed, repeated questions, slow kitting up or constant fiddling with equipment.

During the dive, continually monitor depth, time, air supply and your buddy. Be aware of other divers around you who might be in need of assistance. Be alert to changing conditions, resolve small problems before they have a chance to grow and don't hesitate to terminate the dive early if necessary.

While on the surface, monitor changes in sea and surface conditions. Do not be afraid to change plans and move location or abort the dive if necessary. It may be necessary to recall divers, although this can be difficult to achieve in practice.

Remember that the safety of the dive boat is also critical to the safety of the divers. If conditions are too rough, not only may it be difficult to recover divers but the boat and crew may be in danger.

CASE STUDY 8.2

Lost on the surface

A group of divers is conducting some adventurous diving from a hard boat in an area known for its strong tides.

The story

After completing a boat briefing and radio checks with the coastguard the boat heads to the first site for shake-down dives.

Weather conditions are good and the boat moors up in the shelter of an island out of the tide, the tender is prepared and the first wave enjoy their dive.

The second wave enter the water having left dive times with the dive manager and each taking a DSMB with them just in case they get caught in a current.

What actually happened

- t=0: divers fail to surface at the agreed time.
- t+5mins: tender sets off from hard boat to search.
- t+15mins: attempts are made to contact coastguard, but although the radio was checked before departure there is no reply.
- t+40mins: contact with coastguard made. Helicopters scrambled, lifeboats launched and all available shipping in the area diverted in a coordinated effort to look for the divers.
- t+50mins: first missing diver is located and recovered safety. This diver became caught in a current and deployed a DSMB immediately, but became separated from his buddies. Surfacing on time, he was south-west of the boat, which was about 750m away.
- t+9hrs: strobe light and torch of remaining two divers spotted by helicopter north of the main search location. Divers airlifted to hospital suffering from exhaustion and hypothermia. They surfaced on time but some distance to the south-east of the boat. Despite inflating a large lifting bag to supplement the DSMBs and blowing whistles they were not seen. They watched the entire rescue operation looking for them in the wrong location. The divers had been caught in a different tidal stream, which ultimately took them back in a northerly direction. As night fell they turned on their strobes and torches and were found soon afterwards

Lessons learned

A risk assessment had been completed, conditions were good, the team was experienced and had anticipated some of the problems. However, with the benefit of hindsight, they would have done some things differently.

- Remain vigilant during the dive and continually try to track your divers.
- Notify the coastguard as soon as you suspect something is amiss.
- Carry out a radio check if you have doubts about reception.
- Use a DSC radio, rather than conventional VHF, which can transmit a digital emergency signal further than the analogue voice transmission.
- Search in the direction of the wind and tide, but take into account the local topography.
- Divers to carry location aids appropriate to the risk. In this case an EPIRB would have been most effective (see *EPIRBs* page 102).

This summary is based on a real incident.

The basic rescue plan

Risk assessment can be a useful tool for thinking through potential incidents and how to resolve them. Wise expedition leaders will plan for the worst case: this usually means dealing with an incident in which one or more of the team's lives are in danger.

If the worst happens there are three basic tasks to consider: the rescue, the first aid to be administered and the evacuation of any casualties.

These three phases comprise the rescue plan

Rescue

Divers can get into difficulty underwater or on the surface. Underwater, the rescuer is likely to be the diver's buddy. For deeper or more technical dives, stand-by divers may be the best rescuer, as they are monitoring divers during the decompression phase. Once on the surface, additional help may be required, for example, from snorkel divers to tow casualties back to the dive boat or to help recover the divers from the water.

Of course, the incident may not happen on the water, it could be on land.

During a rescue it is important that dangers are properly assessed so that rescuers do not become casualties themselves.

First aid

The principles of first aid are to preserve life, prevent worsening of an injury and promote recovery. While an incident on a diving trip is likely to be the result of a diving-related injury, this is not always the case.

The first priority of the first-aider is to establish whether a casualty is still in danger, and if so to remove them from danger. As soon as that has been done, the casualty's airway and breathing should be checked to see whether basic life support is needed.

Following this, stem any severe bleeding. Then consider diagnosis and treatment of any of the diving-related conditions such as decompression illness, cerebral arterial gas embolism and poisoning. Finally look for other problems, such as broken bones.

Shock will inevitably accompany, to a greater or lesser extent, any of the above. The casualty should be monitored for signs and symptoms of shock and appropriate action taken as soon as possible, compatible with the above priorities. To treat shock, remove the primary cause, reassure the casualty, lay them down and administer 100-per-cent oxygen. The rescuers' attitude towards the casualty often has a significant effect on the casualty's response and well-being. At all times the casualty should be reassured, and given tender loving care. This is true even for apparently unconscious casualties, many of whom may still be aware of what their rescuers are saying about them. People suffering from shock should always be evacuated to medical care.

Evacuation

On any expedition, there needs to be a plan in place to get casualties to proper medical attention if it is required. Also, there should be a plan ready to evacuate the entire team to safety. The proximity and ease of communication with the emergency services will clearly determine the amount of detail, planning, equipment and training required to effectively carry out each of these tasks. For a typical UK-based expedition the coastguard is contacted to arrange for evacuation whether by air, sea or land.

Rescue management

We do all that we can to prevent accidents, but it is inevitable that some incidents still occur - that is their very nature. When they do, there are a number of activities to be carried out. Without proper management any rescue will at best be inefficient, possibly making it harder than it need be, and at worst diverting resources away from the rescue.

The natural reaction when someone is seen to be in danger is to want to help. The urgency of the situation can make people take risks that they would otherwise not take, some of which may put them in danger. A rescue manager needs to look out for such reactions. If a rescue is to succeed, the most important people involved are the rescuers, not the casualty. Their safety is paramount. A rescuer who takes unnecessary risks, in the heat of the moment, may end up becoming a second casualty. Not only is this of no help to the original casualty, but it places additional demands upon the remaining rescuers.

From an expedition leader's point of view, remember that a casualty could mean divers in the water, on the surface or even in the boat. Regardless of the nature of the casualty, the rescue follows the same pattern.

Stop

When an incident happens, normal diving activities cease so that the team can concentrate on the rescue. Someone needs to take charge and that person is the rescue manager. They need not be the expedition leader or the dive manager. In practice it often falls to the most senior diver on the scene to manage the rescue, but could be anyone with rescue management skills.

The rescue manager is there to do exactly that - manage, not to carry out all the rescue activities.

Assess and plan

In an emergency, a few seconds spent considering the overall situation may well result in more effective help being provided to the casualty more quickly - less haste can often mean more speed.

Ideally, the rescue manager should be able to stand back from the rescue activities to assess the overall situation, identify all the activities that are needed and formulate a plan based on the resources available. Tasks can then be delegated to suitably qualified personnel. As the rescue progresses, the rescue manager should retain strategic control of all activities, monitoring progress and making any adjustments to the plan as circumstances evolve.

With a large team, many tasks can be delegated. For example, divers can be directed to the removal of the casualty from the water, if appropriate, others can prepare resources to administer first aid, such as the oxygen equipment and first-aid kit, and someone can be made responsible for contacting the emergency services and putting the evacuation plan into action.

It may be possible to give everyone a duty to perform, even if it is something small, so that they feel that they are contributing to the rescue, which helps to keep everyone's emotions under control.

Many of these tasks need to be carried out in parallel. It should not be forgotten that other divers may still be diving, and unaware of what is happening. They still need to be monitored and, if required, recalled.

Incidents attract attention from the public who can often be a distraction to the rescuers or even, by ill-advised though well-intentioned efforts, actually impede the rescue. Where an incident occurs in a public location, there may be a need to dedicate resources to keeping people who are not involved, clear of the rescue activities. This will need very firm, but tactful, handling.

In reality the rescue manager might not be able to delegate all the tasks and will have to be directly involved in some capacity, in which case they will need to remember to prioritise their actions: rescue, first aid, evacuation.

Act

The next step for the rescue manager is to put the plan into action. Remember that the plan is likely to evolve as the situation develops, and the situation may need to be re-assessed and plans modified.

CASE STUDY 8.3

Suspected decompression illness

A mixed group of technical divers are diving a wreck in 60m of water, seven miles offshore. A trapeze system is in use for decompression stops and there is a tag system. The boat skipper has crew to monitor and help recover divers.

The story

One of the divers loses control of his buoyancy during decompression and misses some 20 minutes of stops. Seen by the other divers below, the diver is recovered into the boat by the crew. He breathes 70-per-cent nitrox from his rebreather for a while. He convinces the crew he is fine and his buddy is OK on the trapeze. There is no need to contact the emergency services, he says, as he feels fine. Thirty minutes later, the other divers surface and find the diver very quiet and concerned in the corner.

What actually happened

- t=0: incident occurs underwater.
- t=+20mins: other divers surface.
- t=+30mins: STOP a senior diver takes control and makes the decision to make sure the casualty gets medical attention. The senior diver has just become the rescue manager.
- t=+31min: ASSESS the rescue manager quickly gathers the facts from the casualty and skipper, to find out what happened.
- t=+32min: PLAN the casualty is advised to breathe oxygen as a precaution and told that the team will contact the coastguard and get a doctor's opinion.
- t=+33min: ACT diver 1 is asked to prepare the oxygen kit. Diver 2 monitors the casualty. The remaining divers are asked to pack away diving kit and start clearing the deck. The boat crew are tasked with contacting the coastguard, to advise them of the situation and get medical advice. Diver 1 administers the oxygen and Diver 2 is tasked with getting the casualty's details.
- t=+34min: the coastguard requests more details about the casualty and requests confirmation that there are no other casualties. The rescue manager advises them to stand by for more detailed information which is being gathered by Diver 2.
- t=+36min: further details are relayed to coastguard.
- t=+39min: medical guidance is received which confirms the need to evacuate the casualty by helicopter. The skipper is instructed to start proceeding back to port.
- t=+40min: divers not directly caring for casualty are instructed to prepare for helicopter evacuation.
- t=+58min: helicopter arrives on scene and requests smoke to identify the dive boat among other vessels.
- t=+60min: boat crew set off flare.
- t=+65min: winchman on board and casualty evacuated.
- t=+95min: vessel reaches port.

Lessons learned

- This is a situation where the diver is not complaining of any symptoms, but is clearly concerned.
- There is often a reluctance to contact the emergency services in case it turns out to be a false alarm. If in doubt, make the shout!
- Although the whole incident takes about 65 minutes from the diver losing buoyancy control to being evacuated, the initial rescue actions take very little time once someone has taken charge of the situation.
- Within a couple of minutes first aid is being administered in a tactful way while the big decision to evacuate is being taken by doctors.
- Effective use of crew and dive team means that other tasks can be done efficiently.

This summary is based on a real incident.

Emergency services

Contacting the emergency services

The expedition leader should make sure the expedition team members are clear about how the emergency services can be contacted. This is especially important when diving abroad where contacting emergency services and the way they operate is likely to be different to home. A waterproof slate containing the relevant contact numbers and procedures should be kept to hand.

The bare minimum of information you usually need to give to the emergency services is:

- **The nature of the problem, for example, a diver suffering DCI.**
- **Your location, as a GPS position, grid reference, or address.**
- **The size of the problem – how many casualties there are.**

The acronym MIPDANIO highlights all the information that you need to include in your mayday message (see What to say in a mayday call, page 121). Not only should everyone in the team know whom to call, but they should know how to call them as well. Make sure the expedition team have the knowledge and confidence to operate the communications equipment you have, regardless of whether it is a radio or a satellite phone. A good way to build confidence in using equipment is to get your team to make any appropriate routine calls.

Emergency services on land

In the UK, for incidents occurring at inland sites (such as lost divers or near drowning) the police and ambulance services will be required. All are contacted by the normal 999 or 112 emergency telephone call.

For assistance with decompression illness, advice in the UK can be obtained from the appropriate National Decompression Illness Helpline.

Use the following 24-hour telephone numbers:

- In England, Northern Ireland or Wales call 07831 151523 to be connected to the BHA/RN Diver Helpline.
- In Scotland call 0845 408 6008 to be connected with the Aberdeen Royal Infirmary.
-

When diving outside of the UK, ensure that you know the local emergency contact procedures. Specialist international rescue agencies or diving insurance companies usually have an emergency contact number. These can be useful if you are abroad particularly if you are not fluent enough in the local language.

Emergency services at sea

For incidents occurring at sea in the UK all contact, including that with the BHA/RN Diver Helpline, will be via the coastguard using VHF radio channel 16. The coastguard will coordinate the other emergency services.

A Mayday call is used where life is in imminent danger, for example, suspected decompression illness or the boat sinking, and a Pan Pan call is used for other urgent calls. Don't worry too much about the exact proword, the coastguard will make an evaluation of the situation.

Radios with Digital Selective Calling (DSC) send an emergency alert on Channel 70 if you press the red button labelled 'distress alert' or 'SOS'. If the set is connected to a GPS, your position will be sent automatically as well. The distress alert should be followed up by a voice call on channel 16 to give details of the emergency.

Further details on VHF procedure can be found in the BSAC manual *Seamanship: a guide for divers*.

Mobile phones

Close to land, mobile phones may well work but VHF radios have some important advantages. Everyone nearby listening on the emergency frequency can hear your call and can respond appropriately by relaying your call or offering assistance. Also, the position of the vessel can be approximately determined by radio direction-finding equipment on shore and aboard lifeboats.

What to say in a mayday call

	Mayday procedure	Example
M	Mayday proword	MAYDAY MAYDAY MAYDAY
I	Identity of boat, followed by Mayday proword and repeat the boat's name	This is Diveboat 1, Diveboat 1, Diveboat 1, MAYDAY, Diveboat 1
P	Position [give from known object, distance in nautical miles, bearing away in degrees]	My position from St Mary's Light, 1 nautical mile, bearing 045 degrees
D	Nature of Distress	I have a diving emergency
A	Assistance required	Request urgent medical assistance
N	Number of casualties and people onboard	One diver suffering from suspected decompression illness. Thirteen people onboard
I	Information (anything else useful)	All divers out of the water
O	Over, end transmission	Over

CASE STUDY 8.4

Without power

When something goes wrong it can often happen at the most inconvenient moment. Having the correct safety equipment onboard helps to deal with the situation.

The story

A group of divers are diving in 40m of water, near shipping lanes a mile offshore from a harbour entrance. Divers are in the water when the boat engine fails and cannot be restarted. The boat starts to drift into the shipping lanes. The VHF radio remains operational. The sea is relatively flat although there is a long lazy swell and a slight surface breeze.

What actually happened

- t=0: engine cuts out and fails to restart. Divers are in the water and not due to surface for 30 minutes.
- t=+1min: cox'n starts to carry out checks for any obvious causes of the problem. The kill cord is in place and has not been accidentally pulled out. The fuel supply is connected, there is plenty of fuel and the tank bleed valves are open. There are no engine alarms for overheating or low oil. The electrical supply to the engine appears to be OK but the engine is not making its normal turning-over noise.
- t=+2min: The boat is starting to drift into the shipping lanes and an anchor is deployed but the seabed is not good holding ground for the type of anchor they have and the boat continues to drift.
- t=+3min: the cox'n surveys the surroundings to check for shipping traffic. There is no shipping traffic in sight.
- t=+4min: radio operator makes a VHF call to Humber Coastguard with urgent safety traffic
- t=+5min: the coastguard respond and channel 67 is given as the working frequency.

The dive boat relays the following information:

'We have broken down ½ mile due east of Tynemouth Pier
Two persons on board. Four divers in the water.
We have anchor deployed but are drifting into shipping lanes.
We are attempting engine repairs.
Request assistance.'

- t=+5min: the coastguard acknowledge the message, confirms details and tells the cox'n to stand by.
- t=+6min: the coastguard advises that the lifeboat is being launched.
- t=+6 to 10min: The boat crew double checks the engine but still cannot restart it, even manually with a starter cord.

- t=+11min: the coastguard updates the crew on progress of the lifeboat. Crew maintain lookout for divers and surface traffic. White anti-collision warning flares are taken out of the flare box just in case.
- t=+30min: divers surface some 500m away from boat and deploy flags to mark their position.
- t=+32min: divers are picked up by lifeboat.
- t=+35min: dive boat taken in tow.
- t=+55min: dive boat arrives back at port.

Lessons learned

Engine failure is potentially quite serious; without power, the boat and its crew are liable to drift into danger and are also unable to cover their divers in the water. Regardless of how reliable your boat normally is, there is always a potential for a breakdown for which you need to be prepared. It should be noted that in this case having experienced diver cox'ns on the boat helped ensure a swift and satisfactory outcome to the incident.

- In this case we see some calm, quick and positive actions from the boat crew.
- Engine checks are conducted quickly, their rate of drift slowed by deploying an anchor.
- They then assess the situation, formulate a plan and carry it out.
- Given their position on the edge of the shipping lane and the depth of water, at this stage there is no imminent danger to the boat and diver. However, large vessels can travel surprising quickly and from the perspective of the RIB the horizon is actually not that far away so in 20 minutes or less a large vessel could be upon them.
- The crew did not make a Pan Pan call, although had there been more shipping traffic in the area it might have been justified. But they did want to communicate the problem quickly to the coastguard, who decided to request a lifeboat to be sent to their assistance.
- While waiting for the lifeboat they remain vigilant, maintaining a lookout for their divers, large ships and the lifeboat.
- The fault was later traced to a faulty starter motor.

Routine calls to the coastguard

Of course, you do not just have to contact the coastguard in emergencies. In the UK, the coastguard actively encourages divers planning a sea dive to advise of their intentions. After the initial call to make contact with the coastguard, the radio operator should indicate that there is routine safety traffic to convey and give the following details:

- Departure point.
- Destination.
- Number of divers/crew aboard.
- Expected time/duration of diving operations.
- Expected time of return to point of departure.

The coastguard is now aware of your plans for the day. The information will be useful if there is an emergency. You should inform the coastguard of your safe return to port at the end of the day.

Rehearsing rescues

Incidents are few and far between but when they happen you need your rescue and rescue management skills to be automatic. Expedition leaders should make sure their team are prepared and this can be achieved in a number of ways.

Skill development courses

Skill development courses are very useful ways to learn particular rescue skills such as oxygen administration, lifesaving and advanced lifesaving, practical rescue management, first aid for divers, or use of an automated external defibrillator (AED). Indeed, an expedition leader may need to use these as a way to get more people qualified ready for the expedition.

Other courses may also be of benefit when considering the wider rescue situation such as VHF operation and boat-handling skills.

Practise

Skills deteriorate over time if not used. Divers who have sound knowledge and whose skills are regularly practised, are less likely to get into trouble in the first place and if they do get into trouble, are more likely to be able to cope.

Exercises

Individual skills can be learned on courses and then practised. However, as we have seen rescues require teamwork to be really effective. Exercises are a good way to check how the expedition team cope with mock incidents.

For example, why not conduct an exercise to locate a missing diver, try rescuing an injured diver into a RIB or arrange an exercise with the emergency services.

Mock incidents can identify any major shortcomings in the expedition team's response, individually or collectively.

Care needs to be taken to ensure that no one gets too carried away and causes the mock incident to turn into a real one or be identified as one. For example, a football might be used for the search instead of a real diver. Also if a real incident does arise during the course of the exercise it must be able to be identified as such and dealt with appropriately. For example, find alternative signals in your exercise to signify help required, so that 'Help!' really does mean 'Help!'

Rescue exercises keep your skills up to date

Expedition first aid

The general principle of rescue management and dive planning is that prevention is better than cure. Risk assessment, both formal and informal, is a tool that is used by expedition leaders to achieve this – and it can be used to assess the first-aid provision on an expedition.

There are many medical conditions, in addition to specific diving conditions, that need to be considered. Where these are pre-existing they will need management. Other conditions might emerge during the course of the expedition. These are usually covered in first-aid training, for example, heart attack, fits, faints, fractures/sprains, and burns.

The location of the expedition will determine the likelihood of endemic illnesses, typical gastrointestinal upsets, hazardous organisms and marine life, risks of illness due to climate such as hypo/hyperthermia. Travel health risks and vaccination requirements should also be studied.

Should an incident occur, standard diving training provides rescue and first-aid skills to be applied until professional rescue services arrive and evacuate the casualty to medical attention.

Ready access to emergency services does not mean that the expedition leader relies on the emergency services to meet every need that may arise. For some expeditions, the evacuation distances involved and times to access to emergency services will be significant. This is not necessarily restricted to overseas expeditions, but could also encompass more adventurous diving within UK waters. In such instances, serious thought must be given to the evacuation plan to ensure that any casualties can be given first aid over the longer periods involved and still be evacuated safely.

The expedition medic

The qualifications required of an expedition medic will clearly depend on the medical conditions expected. For many expeditions, divers who hold diving oxygen administration, first-aid courses, lifesaver and practical rescue management courses will be the 'expedition medics'.

However, for some expeditions, such as those in very remote locations or those catering for people with certain special medical needs, the expedition medic would almost certainly need to be a suitably qualified doctor or paramedic. For such expeditions, they would be expected to have a major role to play in planning the expedition first aid and medical requirements from diver medicals, equipment and supplies needed and training.

The expedition leader will also need to consider what to do if the expedition medic becomes ill themselves. Will remaining members of the team be able to treat them or are 'spare' medics required.

Specialist expedition medical training, not only for doctors and paramedics but other members of the team as well, may be required.

Medicals

With typical diver medicals or self-declaration forms, you may not recognise conditions that could be potentially life threatening in an expedition situation but do not interfere with fitness to dive, such as allergic asthma and food allergies.

Also, a significant aim of the expedition might be to accommodate people with special needs or minors, in which case extra information may be required specific to their needs.

A more thorough pre-expedition screening questionnaire may be required that considers things such as regular medications, allergies, pre-existing conditions.

Care needs to be taken to ensure any medical records are treated confidentially and sensitively. For example, the expedition leader, having accessed the team's medical information for planning purposes, could keep everyone's medical details in sealed envelopes only to be opened in an emergency.

Confidentiality is particularly important if the official medical records of an expedition team member need to be examined. A confidentiality waiver may be required. Where access to medical records is required, it is likely that the expedition medic would be a qualified doctor.

In some instances, however, the entire expedition team may need to be briefed on a particular medical condition of one of the team members so that the expedition team are aware and prepared to deal with it if required. For example, a diabetic may wish to brief the team on what to look out for should they become ill and how to treat an episode.

First-aid kits

First-aid kits need to be designed for the conditions under which they are to be used, taking into account the size of group and the diving location. Suitable lists can be found in *Seamanship: a guide for divers, Safety and Rescue for Divers* and other relevant diving manuals and first-aid manuals. The first-aid kit should be placed in a water-resistant container, with its contents sealed and easily identifiable. Ready-made kits from high street stores or chandlers may need augmenting with diver-specific items such as fresh water, high-energy chocolate bars and vinegar and alcohol to treat jellyfish stings.

Waterproof diving first-aid booklets are available that detail essential instructions on diving first aid and procedures and are a valuable addition to the first-aid kit.

Advanced first-aid kit

A first-aid kit suitable for more remote locations will require considerable thought. For example, a basic first-aid kit may need augmenting with more dressing so not only the initial trauma can be treated, but also that there is sufficient stock to allow the wound to be dressed daily if required.

Expedition members who use medication regularly should be prompted to bring along a spare supply. There will be legal requirements for possession/export/import of any drugs, which will need to be adhered to.

Intravenous cannulae and needles may be required where sterility of local ones is questionable, even if professionals use the expedition supplies.

Oxygen first-aid equipment is readily portable

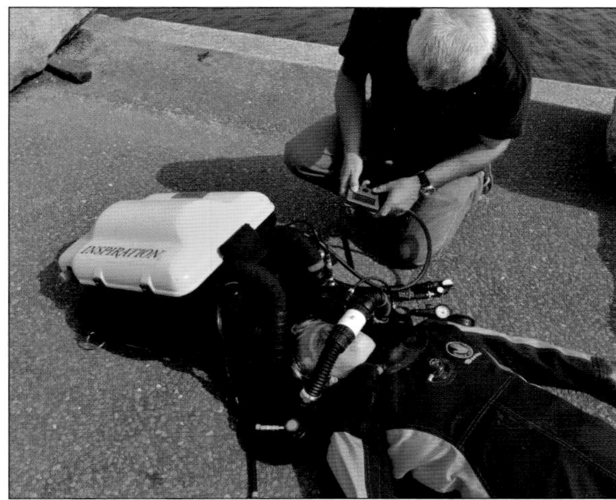

A rebreather can be used to give oxygen-rich first aid

An expedition medic who is a doctor or paramedic is likely to be the only person with the appropriate qualification to define what is required for an advanced first-aid kit. Not only that, but they might be the only ones qualified to use the contents, not only because of their skills but also in the eyes of the law.

Oxygen equipment

An oxygen kit is an essential piece of diving first-aid equipment.

The British Sub Aqua Club specification for an oxygen kit is a follows:

- Standard medical oxygen cylinder, size D or E.
- Oxygen regulator incorporating a cylinder contents gauge and providing an outlet for at least one demand unit, and an outlet capable of delivering oxygen at a constant flow of 10-litres/min
- Demand unit, hose and oro-nasal mask
- Pocket mask incorporating an oxygen connection elbow, and a suitable hose for the delivery of oxygen at a constant flow of at least 10-litres/min
- In demand mode, the unit should be able to deliver a maximum demanded flow rate in excess of 100-litres/min.

The equipment should be stored in a robust, waterproof container to protect it from the diving environment. Ideally it should be possible to leave the oxygen kit equipment assembled ready for use within the container. An overpressure valve is required on the container to prevent inadvertent build of pressure from a gas leak.

The expedition leader needs to give some thought to how long the oxygen will last. A D-size cylinder with hold between 370 and 540 litres of oxygen, lasting 37 to 54 minutes on constant flow or slightly longer on demand. Furthermore, a stressed diver may use more oxygen thus reducing the time further. Looking at our earlier case studies where there was a rapid response from the emergency service, this amount of oxygen will probably be sufficient for one casualty. However, if the buddy needed treatment as well, extra oxygen would be required. For this reason either a larger E-size cylinder or extra D-size cylinders are usually carried.

If you have nitrox or rebreather divers in the expedition team, there is automatically a back-up plan in the case of multiple casualties or running out of oxygen. Breathing as rich an oxygen mix as possible is better than air for treating a conscious casualty.

Adaptors can be purchased to allow the connection of oxygen equipment to nitrox bottles. Care, however, is required if adopting this approach to make sure the adaptors, and the nitrox bottles, are in oxygen service to minimise the risk of oxygen fires.

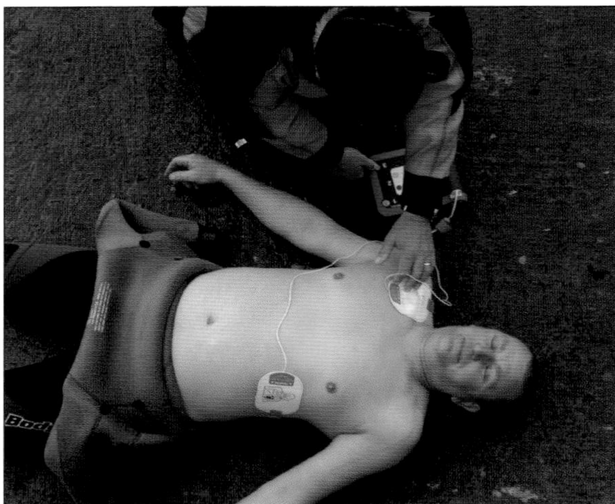

An AED is an invaluable addition to an expedition first-aid kit, especially in remote locations

Automated external defibrillators

Defibrillation is the only treatment proven to restore a normal heart rhythm in an abnormally beating heart. When used on someone who has suffered a cardiac arrest, an automated external defribrillator will administer a potentially life-saving electric shock that, if delivered quickly enough, can restore the heart's rhythm to normal and enable it to contract and pump blood again.

AEDs are designed to allow properly trained non-medical personnel such as divers to save lives. Although many of us may have seen them strategically placed in airports and public buildings, only recently have units and skills courses started to make an appearance in sport diving market.

The best place to learn about using an AED is on a course. However, it is worth mentioning some of the safety considerations here for rescue managers to consider:

The AED and the rescuer should be the maximum distance from casualty - as far as the leads attached to the pads attached to the chest will allow.

No one should touch the patient when the shock is delivered, otherwise they too may receive a shock. This is important at all times, but especially so in the damp environment of a dive boat or water's edge.

There is a risk that the electric shock may result in a spark and this has a risk of enhanced combustion of clothing, hair etc. Diving casualties may be being given oxygen, in which case it should be turned off while shocking.

Boat radios may interfere with the AED while it is analysing the heart rhythm and so should be turned off at this stage.

Portable recompression chambers

For diving in extremely remote locations, it may be necessary to consider taking a recompression chamber with you. Some larger dive vessels may have small recompression chambers on board and hyperbaric stretchers are available.

These are beyond the affordability of most expeditions and, even if they are available, there must be properly trained personnel to operate them available too. Clearly this needs to be someone who knows how to operate the controls but also how to care for the casualty.

It should be also remembered that decompression illness is, after all, a medical emergency and therefore deserves to be treated as such.

Incident record sheet

Incident history, signs and symptoms, and subsequent first-aid actions taken are important. A casualty's condition is dynamic in nature, perhaps improving or worsening or staying the same.

A written record of such symptoms, with approximate timings, can assist in the subsequent treatment of the condition by qualified medical staff. Where practical, written records should be kept. This is available on the BSAC website.

Waterproof copies of this incident sheet are a useful addition to the first aid equipment.

Incident follow-up procedure

After an incident, members of the dive team may have to deal with friends and relatives of the casualty, the media, and the authorities.

Personnel issues

Relatives and friends of the casualty and even the rescuers themselves will suffer some degree of shock either at the time of or after an incident. In more serious incidents, particularly where fatalities are concerned, relatives may require significant comfort and support.

These emotions need very sympathetic and tactful handling. Ensure that relatives know that the offer of help is there if they need it, but do not force it on them. Similarly, if they want someone to talk to, be prepared to listen but do not encourage them to talk if they do not want to. Also be aware that support is best given by listening; do not get involved in debating the incident or giving your own opinions as these may only aggravate the situation. As soon as possible after the incident, all concerned should ensure that their own relatives are informed that they are safe. If news of the incident is broadcast on radio or television, relatives of the rescuers could be worried needlessly.

Media

The media have their job to do but the nature of that job can be unhelpful where incidents are concerned. While any rescue activities are under way, the media should be kept away from any personnel involved in those activities, so that they are not distracted from what they need to do. Even after the event, if you are approached by the media do not offer any comment. Editing constraints may mean that comments are taken out of context, and consequently may appear to mean something quite different to what was intended. Comments can also be sensationalised to provide attention-grabbing headlines. It is also possible that they can be portrayed as criticism or blame, which causes distress to the people concerned and/or their families.

Above all give out no personal details of any individuals, especially any casualties. Doing so could result in the relatives of any casualties hearing of the incident through the media before they have been personally informed.

Incident reporting

After an incident there will usually some sort of paperwork to complete and this should be filled in while all the details are fresh in participants' minds. Depending on the nature of the incident, there could be a considerable amount of paperwork, for example, police statements and insurance claim forms.

Whatever the incident, it is important to learn from it to help avoid the incident occurring again. In the UK, the BSAC has a confidential reporting system, which enables the club to maintain a comprehensive database of incidents. Incident reports are analysed to determine trends or common causes, to monitor the effectiveness of diver training or to indicate where revisions or additions to training procedures are required.

There is a tendency to consider incidents to be incidents only when the outcome is adverse. Reports for successfully resolved incidents are just as important as much can be learned from them. The feedback from incidents is an important part of maintaining and improving the safety record of sport diving.

Fatalities

The safety record of the sport means that fatalities are fortunately rare events. Whenever a sudden death occurs from any cause there is a legal process to be followed. In the UK, the Coroner (or the Procurator Fiscal in Scotland) will request the police force where the death occurred to investigate the incident and present their findings. This investigation will be carried out by experienced officers who may be from the underwater search unit. The police will look at four main areas:

- The medical and past history of the deceased - did the person have a current medical and was there a past history of medical problems?
- The dive profile and past history of dives - what was the profile of the last dive? Was this the type of dive usually done by this person or were they diving beyond their capabilities?
- The diving conditions -were they safe conditions to be diving in?
- The casualty's diving equipment - this will be examined by police technicians and checked for faults, lack of maintenance or misuse. Specialist equipment such as rebreathers may be examined by outside experts, perhaps by people from the BSAC.

This process highlights the importance of following safe diving practices and planning and executing any dive meticulously.

For expedition leaders planning expeditions abroad, it is wise to consider and plan for the worst. Local laws and police may well operate differently than in the UK when dealing with fatalities. It is advisable to seek legal advice and insurance to ensure an appropriate plan is in place.

Chapter 9

Diving with a purpose

Sport diving always has a purpose: it is a recreational activity and the purpose is to enjoy the time spent underwater. However, expeditions often have a task-oriented purpose, which gives the trip a theme. This purpose can be anything from a simple task, such as diving to find out whether an anomaly on an echo-sounder trace is a wreck or a rock, to a complex project such as raising a wreck or conducting a detailed survey of a large area of seabed.

In general, we need to match the scale of resources and expertise needed with the nature of the task. In some cases, the purpose may be easily achievable within branch diving, in others it needs the back-up support of specialist expertise and significant amounts of specialist equipment.

THREE
GEMINUS
10
20
30
40
50

Diving projects

Diver capturing video footage

Commercial divers must comply with diving-at-work laws

Projects may involve the use of extra equipment

Photography can be a means or an end in project diving

Types of diving projects

There are many different types of diving with a purpose, for example:

- marine life identification and surveys
- measurement of visibility or water quality
- recording the effects on the marine environment of fishing, fish farming, diving or other human activity
- recording seabed quality or type
- recording underwater geology
- making physical or oceanographic measurements (waves, tides and so on)
- underwater searches
- wreck discovery
- identification, surveying and measurement
- salvage or lifting
- mapping of dive sites
- producing a dive guide
- drawing and recording dive sites
- setting out underwater dive routes
- underwater photography and video
- evaluating diving equipment
- experimenting with new diving techniques
- building underwater structures (such as artificial reefs).

Expeditions and the law

Before considering dives with a purpose, we need to make the distinction between commercial diving and amateur divers undertaking a project. This distinction is not artificial; it is defined in the law.

As a guiding principle, if there is any remuneration, either in monetary terms or in kind, then a dive is classified as a commercial dive and will be subject to the law. This legislation will, of course, vary from country to country but, in the UK, it is governed by the Health and Safety Executive.

We will only be considering diving in an amateur context. However, care is required to ensure that an expedition is organised in accordance with applicable law. This is certainly based on the location where the diving is taking place, but also possibly the country in which it is organised and those which are travelled through en-route to the final destination.

There may be restrictions on diving specific sites; permits may be required to dive others. There may be different requirements for diving medicals; self declaration is acceptable in the UK, for example, but not in other countries. There may be different laws on transportation and identification of diving equipment.

It is the responsibility of the expedition leader to plan for, and prepare to meet, the requirements of the law. In the UK, there is a clear distinction between commercial diving and recreational diving for sport. The UK's HSE is concerned with all matters relating to health and safety at work, and their diving division is a specific department that oversees all diving matters that are considered commercial. The 'at work' situation covers any diver receiving payment for the provision of an 'undertaking' or 'contract'. This provision is often known as a 'project'. For example, a scenario where an expedition will come under the HSE jurisdiction is where the trip photographer is taking photos to illustrate a magazine article or for the publication of a book/dive guide

Diving at work regulations (1997)

Diving at work was first defined under the Health and Safety at Work Act (1974) in which commercial diving was defined as 'working under a contract of employment, or otherwise working for gain or reward'.

Any diving that comes under this definition is now subject to the more recent Diving at Work Regulations (1997). Compliance with these regulations can be expensive and requires particular risk management procedures (for example, appropriate commercial diving qualifications and timely access to a recompression chamber on stand by). These obligations are well beyond the scope of the amateur diver.

It is therefore important to establish, before carrying out any activity, whether the purpose of the dive involves any 'gain or reward' and therefore comes under the diving at work regulations. It should be noted that 'gain or reward' can also include benefits in kind.

Any dive with a purpose should document all legitimate expenses, so that if any monies change hands these can be clearly reconciled with legitimate expenses. For example, a dive boat required for a dive is booked and paid for by the expedition leader. The dive team then individually reimburse the expedition leader (who pays a share also). The expedition leader is receiving legitimate expenses as long as the amount of money paid to them does not exceed that paid for the boat hire. If the expedition leader gets a 'free trip' that could be construed in a court of law as receiving 'gain or reward'.

To assist in the understanding of, and compliance with, the regulations, the HSE has produced a set of guidelines. These are the Approved Codes of Practice, known as ACoPs. The Diving at Work Regulations 1997 has a series of ACoPs depending on the type of commercial diving operation that is being undertaken – scientific, recreational, media, and so on. The Recreational Diving Project ACoP is one of this series and provides guidance for those operators and team members involved in providing recreational diver training or guided dives on a commercial basis to their clients.

The HSE and recreational diving

The HSE is only interested in a recreational diving project if it is commercial. The HSE's interest is in commercial diving centres, or instructors, who provide diver training services, at all levels of training, in return for a payment from their client. The HSE sees that there is an 'undertaking' by the centre to provide a defined course of training to those paying clients. All diver training schools are commercial centres, since they are offering recreational diver training to clients for a payment. Those commercial centres operating in the UK therefore need to comply with the Diving at Work Regulations 1997 as do their instructors, even if they are not being paid.

Diving centres overseas do not need to comply with UK regulations but may have similar local legislation that they must comply with.

All diving agencies in the UK support a network of branches and clubs that are primarily involved with the provision of diver training. The HSE regard diving clubs as amateur and not commercial.

Provided the branch or club is not involved in a commercial operation, then the Diving at Work Regulations 1997 and the Recreational Diving Project ACoP guidelines do not apply. However, the HSE would expect diving associations to put in place suitable training and safety measures and for the members in their branches to follow these guidelines. In the case of BSAC, these recommendations are contained in the publication *Safe Diving* (see the BSAC website).

As a group, amateur divers have the potential to contribute greatly to underwater projects. It is sometimes possible for the two worlds of recreational and professional diving to meet. The Mary Rose project, which successfully raised the remains of a Tudor warship that sank in the Solent, is an example of an expedition that started out as a recreational diving project but later moved to a professional basis, although it was still able to use volunteer divers.

Another example is the raising of the Victorian steamship Gitana from Loch Rannoch in Scotland in the 1980s. She was raised in two stages from 30m to 20m, then to the surface. Many volunteer amateur divers from BSAC, Scottish Sub Aqua Club and Sub Aqua Association joined the professionals to help with this project. Painstaking work ranged from front-line tasks such as fixing strops and lifting bags, to important support work, filling cylinders and running compressors. Unfortunately, in this case, the work was to no avail as insufficient backing and protection was provided to ensure the survival of the raised wreck and it was not long before she was left breaking up on the shores of the loch. This example illustrates the need for care, professional consideration and long term planning before such a project should be undertaken.

Organisations such as the Nautical Archaeological Society are instrumental in working with volunteers to ensure a clear understanding of approaches to marine archaeology and a clear understanding of the role of amateurs.

The Seasearch project, which started over 20 years ago, is another example of volunteer diver involvement, and perhaps one of the most extensive ones. Begun by Bob Earll (Marine Conservation Society) and Roger Mitchell (Nature Conservancy Council) in the mid 1980s, this project is attracting more and more volunteer divers to contribute to building up a picture of the marine environment. Seasearch was formalised in 1999 by a steering group covering all of the major marine conservation groups, diving organisations, independent groups and relevant government organisations. It offers amateur volunteer divers the chance to make a very real contribution to our underwater heritage.

Protecting our underwater heritage

Divers have a responsibility to protect the maritime heritage in the waters in which they dive. Respect our Wrecks is an initiative in the UK designed to do this (see the BSAC website). The BSAC, the Professional Association of Diving Instructors (PADI) and the Sub Aqua Association (SAA) endorse the principles of this initiative.

Almost all wrecks have an owner – this may be the insurer at the time of sinking, the Ministry of Defence or other individuals. The law protects the owner against unlawful salvage. Some wrecks are designated war graves and wrecks of historical interest. These may be protected by law and you should seek advice before considering diving them. Other wrecks may have sunk with loss of life but are not necessarily protected – these should also be treated with respect. If you discover a wreck site which you suspect may be of archaeological interest, then you should report it and avoid any disturbance on the site. If in doubt, organisations such as BSAC and the Nautical Archaeology Society can provide advice.

The current law affecting wreck diving in the UK can be summarised as follows.

Merchant Shipping Act 1995 S236

The Merchant Shipping Act establishes the role of the Receiver of Wreck and requires individuals to report all items of wreck to the receiver. Wreck means any items of flotsam (floating material), jetsam (material thrown overboard on purpose), lagan (material lying on the seabed) – in fact, any material of or from wrecks. The Receiver of Wreck will then try to find the rightful owners. A salvage award may be payable when this happens, although this then turns the dive into a commercial dive. If the owner cannot be found or doesn't want to keep the items, then the salvor can keep them in place of a salvage award. This is what happens in 90 per cent of current cases. If the wreck is of archaeological or historical importance, the finder may receive the monetary value from a museum.

Section S230 of the Act allows salvage of British warships in UK waters, but you need to consider your moral duty to the survivors and next of kin (see also 2006 amendment to the Protection of Military Remains Act).

Protection of Wrecks Act 1973

The Protection of Wrecks Act exists to protect historically important wreck sites, such as the Mary Rose in the Solent, and sites which have been deemed dangerous to dive, such as the Richard Montgomery in the Thames estuary. Once a site is designated under the act it can only be dived under licence. Decisions about protection are taken by the Advisory Committee on the Historic Wreck Sites. The licensing system is administered by English Heritage. Four types of license can be granted: visitor, survey, surface recovery and excavation. In 2008, there were 60 sites in the UK designated under this act.

Ancient Monuments and Archaeological Areas Act 1979

This act covers both land-based sites and underwater sites of historic interest that are not shipwrecks anywhere up to the 12-mile limit of UK territorial waters. This act gives rise to scheduled site status. Public access to sites is allowed. The only underwater site currently protected by AMMA is Scapa Flow. The whole of Scapa Flow seabed is protected and divers are not allowed to bring any material up at all.

Protection of Military Remains Act 1986

The Protection of Military Remains Act is designed to minimise the interference with wrecks that are the last resting places of military personnel from military conflicts, including the two World Wars. The designation of these wrecks does not prevent access to the majority of them but recognises and encourages responsible behaviour by visiting divers. These designations effectively identify last resting places but do not, in most cases, prevent visiting divers from paying their respects. The vessels involved are not just those with an HMS prefix, but any ship requisitioned by the Crown, or under contract to deliver materials or otherwise on official business.

There are two classifications:

- Protected Place: access to these wrecks is allowed on the understanding that divers look and do not touch or disturb the site.
- Controlled Site: these wrecks may not be dived without a license from the Ministry of Defence. At present there is no clear process for obtaining a licence. An example of a Controlled site is the wreck of HMS Royal Oak in Scapa Flow, which sank with the loss of more than 800 crew.

This Act prevents any salvage of warships without the consent of the relevant government. For example, this means that it is not possible to salvage U-boats in UK waters without specific permission from the German government. Also, no salvage of Crown vessels in international waters is permitted without the specific consent of the Ministry of Defence.

Project principles

There is always the possibility that further legislation on wrecks and on marine life will affect recreational diving in the future and the BSAC website is a source of up-to-date information.

There are other aspects of the law that may affect recreational divers.

The Theft Act

A clubhouse full of undeclared wreck may lead to the charge of stealing by finding.

The Firearms Act

This act may be contravened by the possession of live munitions

Health and safety legislation

Health and safety legislation comes into effect when diving for profit or reward (see *Diving at work*, page 131).

In addition to the laws described above, there may be local arrangements for permission to dive or gain access to a site. For example, diving in lakes within National Parks or launching across privately owned land may require specific permits. Before undertaking your project you should seek out such information. The websites or headquarters of the various diving organisations may be a good starting point.

General consideration for other water and land users is important also. Not just from a point of view of courtesy, but also safety. For example, if your diving objectives have resulted in you leaving survey lines on a dive site, you have a duty of care to makes sure that they are left in a safe manner and that you inform other divers using the site of the possible hazards.

Principles of diving projects

So, if you are planning a diving project with a purpose, whether it is a small, localised, one-dive project or a larger scale project, you will need to think about the impact the project will have on the marine environment, the divers themselves and other users. A project should follow some key principles.

Clear aims and objectives

The diving team needs to be fully aware of what is expected of them, what they need to achieve and what outcomes should arise from the objectives.

Consideration of safety for the divers

Divers who have a task to accomplish underwater face additional risks compared with those carrying out a recreational dive. These extra risks must be planned for. They may be due to the use of new equipment or they may be psychologically induced risks associated with the desire to achieve. A simple example of the latter is forgetting to monitor breathing gas levels due to concentrating on a task.

Consideration of our underwater heritage

Most diving activity creates underwater disturbance and attempts should be made to minimise this. Respect for the marine life and underwater archaeology (old and recent) should be an overriding principle. Objects of historic interest are often better left where they are found, having been properly recorded. If they are removed from the water they will deteriorate rapidly without proper conservation. This can be time-consuming and costly.

Diving within the law

Salvage and other such activities are covered by the law – if these are a necessary part of a project they should be conducted within the law. Permits may be required for some activities.

Consideration for others

A diving project may have effects on other water users, and your land-based activities will certainly affect others on land. You must give due consideration to others. This may range from simple respect to seeking permission from authorities and other user groups.

Choice of appropriate diving techniques and equipment

There are various ways of discovering information about a site. Some are more invasive than others. For example, an annotated photograph of an object is a better record than a measurement alone, which is better than removal for measurement. The most appropriate techniques should be used.

Careful planning is essential

This may involve surface-based dry runs, team co-ordination and careful preparation. If it doesn't work on the surface, it won't work underwater!

Preparation of tools before the dive

A pre-prepared slate that prompts the user to record the desired information is much more effective to use than a blank one. Lines and measuring tapes can be difficult to manage underwater. You could consider using pre-measured lines. Equipment can be delivered to the site contained in a bag for easy handling.

A clear outcome

Finally, the outcome of any project should be recorded in some way. This could be a written report, or a slide show or other visual presentation. This can be kept and shown in the future. It may become the starting point for another project.

Defining your aims and objectives

The success of a dive or expedition with a purpose is to clearly define what it is you want to achieve. Try to simplify the objectives to reduce the complexity of the task. This often works best if you can do most of the legwork before the dive or expedition.

For example, an unidentified wreck may be one of two known wrecks. You could dive the site and make notes on and measurements of the features you see during your dive and then try to identify the wreck later. A better way to distinguish between the two would be to look up some specific key features in advance that differ between the two wrecks, such as the length of the wreck, distance from bow to anchor winches and so on.

Then your dive objectives are simplified. You will need to find the features you are looking for - objective 1 - and take the relevant measurements - objective 2.

Turning objectives into underwater tasks

To accomplish a more complex project, even specific objectives can be broken down further and carried out by several pairs of divers if neccessary.

For example, if your objectives are to measure the distance between the anchor winches and the bow, and the length of a wreck, you will need to place a shot, lay distance lines to the points of interest, mark or measure them, and recover the equipment. These tasks can be divided up between diver pairs.

- Dive pair 1 ensures that the shot is on the wreck and secure.
- Pair 2 lays a distance line to one end of the ship (bow), measures it and marks it with a weighted DSMB.
- Pair 3 lays a distance line to one end of the ship (stern), measures it and marks it with a weighted DSMB.
- Pair 4 measures the distance from bow to anchor winch, and recovers bow line.
- Pair 5 recovers the stern line and prepares the shot for lifting.
- On the surface the lengths of bow and stern distance lines can be measured to the marked points thus enabling the length of the wreck to be determined.

Safety procedure

Diving with a purpose introduces new safety aspects to a dive. These can broadly be grouped into two types: psychological aspects of safety and use of new equipment or techniques.

Diving with a purpose can introduce a new state of mind to the diver - being task fixated. This is where a diver will tend to focus on achievement of the objectives of the task sometimes at the expense of other important aspects of the dive, such as monitoring gas consumption and buoyancy control.

It is common to see task fixation in divers under training - for example, the first time that a diver uses an underwater compass they are likely to swim off at a fast rate, intent on following the compass and ignoring their buddy and others around them.

Task fixation can potentially be very dangerous and it is important to understand the effect it can have on divers, especially if they are inexperienced at working underwater. The effect is compounded if the dive is being carried out at depth where the effects of nitrogen narcosis can further limit the divers appreciation of their surroundings.

Typical problems that can arise from task fixation are:

- Failure to monitor breathing gas.
- Failure to monitor dive times and depths.
- Loss of buoyancy control.
- Poor/lack of communication with buddy.

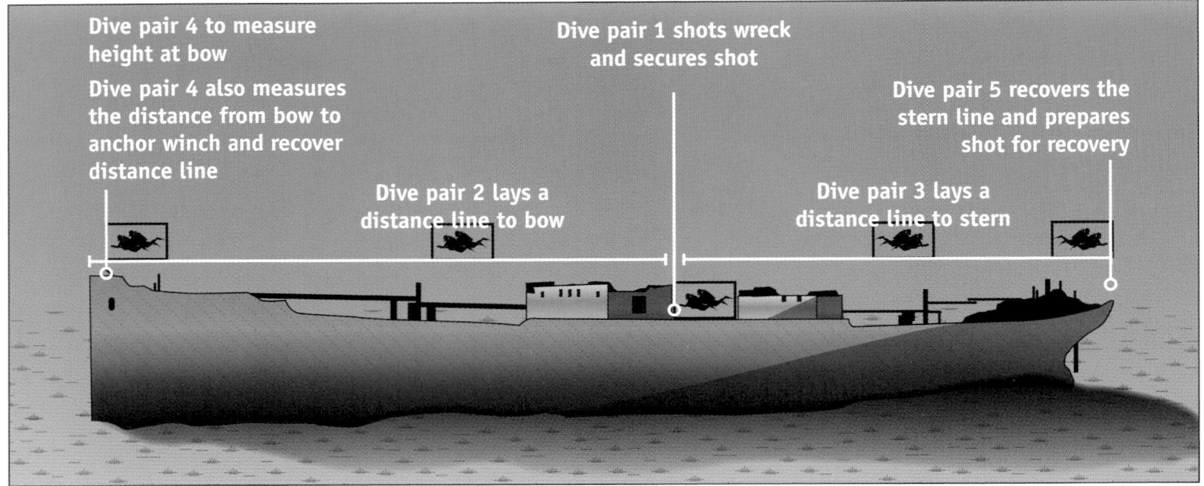

A complex operation to measure a large wreck is achieved by breaking it down into manageable tasks

- Separation.
- Disorientation, inability to relocate shotlines/exit points.
- Lack of awareness of developing situations (such as entanglement in ropes or lines).
- Unaware of own developing stress (such as tiredness or breathlessness from overwork).
- Unaware of developing stress in the buddy (or other members of the dive team).
- Poor decision making.

There are a number of ways of overcoming these problems, but it all comes down to good planning and preparation. It is always good to prepare a task plan – a run time of what is expected during the dive.This can be built up in stages.

First develop a run-time plan covering the overall running of the dive – this will include the times and depths of the dive, and any key points.

- ascent time.
- descent time.
- decompression stops.
- breathing gas check points.
- gas/cylinder exchanges (in the case of mixed gas dives).
- rebreather checkpoints.
- diver to diver communication checkpoints (to monitor stress levels, tiredness and general diver wellbeing).

Second, consider what background steps need to be in place to support the dive. For example, if the divers can get quickly to their point of work and, importantly return to the shot line this removes the need for underwater navigation and reduces the risk of disorientation. Setting up shot line and distance lines prior to the dive can be useful if appropriate.

Third, plan the key stages in the run time of the underwater task. The purpose of this is to superimpose the working activities onto the dive plan, to plan how the underwater work fits into the key stages in the dive plan. In this plan, any decision points can be built in – for example, if a plan needs to be modified based on what is found on the dive, key decision points can be identified and planned for.

The fourth stage is to identify the role of each diver. In general it is safest if one of the divers in a buddy pair conducts the task while the other monitors the activities and the checkpoints on the plan. Of course, a planned swap-over of these roles would ensure both divers get to contribute to the objectives.

When working in a dive team, such as in a large survey or swimline search, it is still advisable to work as pairs but an additional level of awareness and communication is required to ensure co-ordination between dive pairs. This is the job of the swimline controller in a swim line search. This communication is best achieved if the diver monitoring the buddy pair's activity is also responsible for monitoring how the pair is working in relation to neighbouring pairs.

The fifth stage in the plan is to review the plan and decide on escape points – points in the plan where the dive pair can safely leave the task should any issues arise or should the task take longer than anticipated.

Finally, the overall plan should be transferred to slates/notebooks so that both divers can refer to them if necessary during the underwater activity.

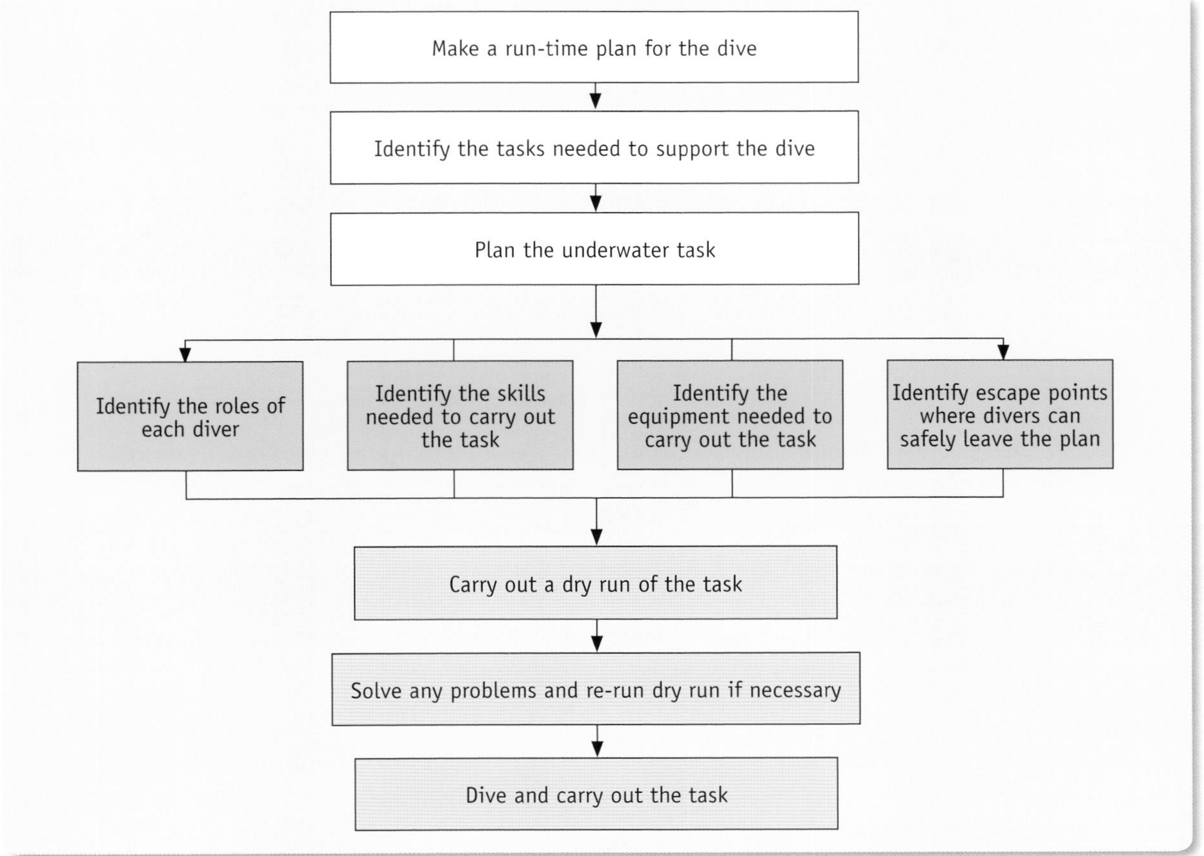

Managing equipment

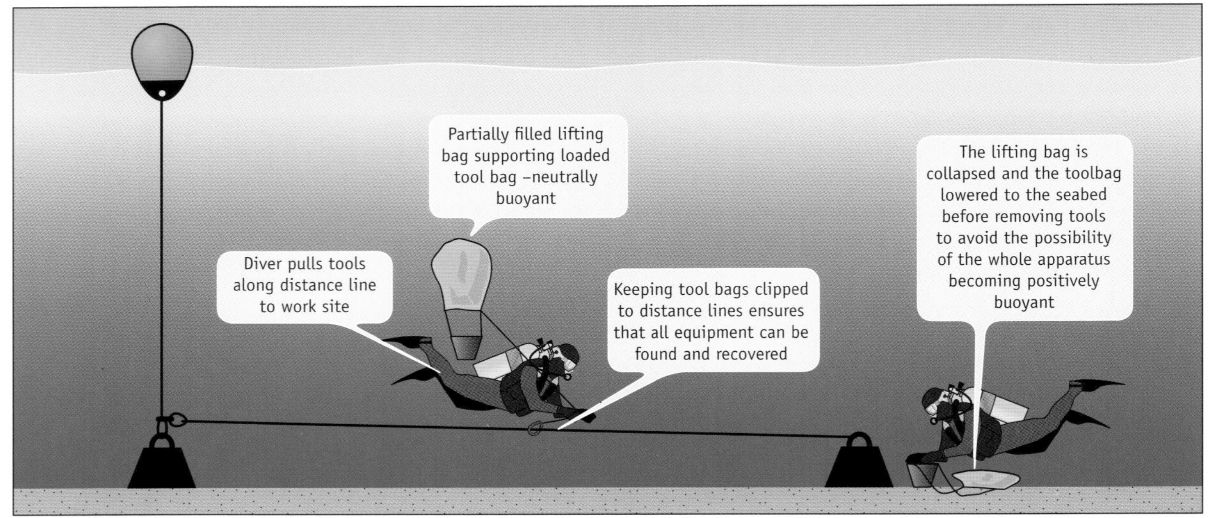

Moving tools around underwater is made easier using lifting bags, but safety must be considered

Using equipment underwater

Using new equipment or unfamiliar diving techniques can also compromise safety. In a lot of cases diving with a purpose requires the use of equipment underwater. This can range from simple equipment such as a slate for recording details, through ropes, tools, cameras and tape measures to underwater vehicles. It perhaps seems obvious to stress the importance of practising with new equipment in safe water before using it in earnest. There are two aspects of using equipment – transporting it to the site and using it.

Heavy equipment can be difficult to move around underwater, especially if it is clipped onto, and dangling from, the diver. Heavy equipment can cause buoyancy changes as it is unclipped for use – possibly leading to problems. In general, it is most useful to package tools and equipment into a bag or sack, and where possible to lower it down a shot line directly to the site of use. If it is necessary to move it onsite, then partly-filled lifting bags can be used to support the weight of the equipment. With more planning, lifting bags can even be used to support the equipment a short distance, for example 1m, above the seabed, perhaps by clipping it onto a distance line when it is being moved – this has the advantage of reducing any damage to the seabed and reducing any effect on the local visibility. Using this system, all the tools can be found and recovered at the end of the task. The lifting bag is collapsed and the toolbag lowered to the seabed before removing tools to avoid the possibility of the whole apparatus becoming positively buoyant.

The main problems associated with using equipment underwater result from entanglement in ropes, lines and measures or buoyancy problems caused by picking up and putting down heavy tools. Both of these types of risks can be reduced by practising using dry runs, or in safe water, by thinking ahead and being aware underwater.

Choice of diving techniques and equipment

It is not the scope of this book to describe detailed methods of underwater work techniques – these are covered elsewhere in manuals and courses run by BSAC and specialist organisations such as the Nautical Archaeology Society and the Marine Conservation Society. However, there are some general principles that will improve the success of your underwater work and mimimise risks.

Planning and preparation

Try to prioritise your approach and complete as much of the task before diving as you can. Underwater time is short so try to maximise what you can do on the surface.

An example of a task plan

Time (mins)	Dive plan	Underwater task	Diver role	Escape plan
0	Descend		Diver 1 leads	
2	Reach max depth (24m) Gas check	Locate distance line to bow	Diver 1 leads	
5	Buddy check	Arrive at bow	Diver 1 leads	Surface if problem no stops required
6		Lay tape measure from bow to anchor winch, measure and record	Diver 2 lays tape Diver 1 monitors	
10		Photograph anchor winch	Diver 1 photographs Diver 2 monitors	
13		Recover tape and return to bow	Diver 2 recovers tape Diver 1 monitors	
15	Gas check and buddy check			If problem, return to shot or deploy DSMB and surface no stops required
16		Lower weighted tape over bow to measure height above seabed	Diver 1 measures Diver 2 monitors	
20		Photograph bow and determine if anchors have been released	Diver 1 photographs Diver 2 monitors	
24		Return to bow		
25	Gas check and buddy check			If problem, return to shot or deploy DSMB and surface
26		Release a DSMB to mark the bow at the surface. Secure the SMB to wreck with weights.	Diver 1 deploys Diver 2 monitors	If problem, surface using DSMB no stops required
30		Return to shot, recover distance line	Diver 2 recovers line Diver 1 monitors	
35		Arrive at shot		
36	Gas check and buddy check			If problem, surface using shot – deco stop of 1min @ 6m
37		Unsecure shot and prepare lifting bag on shot for shot recovery	Diver 1 deals with shot Diver 2 monitors	
39	Leave max depth ascend to stop		Diver 1 leads	
41	Start 6m deco stop (1min)	Check decompression	Diver 1 leads	Add decompression stops if necessary
43	Surface		Diver 1 leads	

Where possible try to work off the bottom. This has the advantage of reducing silt disturbance, reduces damage to the seabed, wreckage or marine life and can reduce the risk of entanglement. This may require you to set up distance or guidelines at a distance above the seabed and, of course, requires good buoyancy control.

Plan your work in relation to tidal streams. Clearly strong tidal streams can make life hard work and are to be avoided. However, gentle streams can be useful. For example, working into a gentle tide can serve to wash away any silt that may be disturbed. Swimming with a gentle tide can assist if your work involves movement, for example, if you are taking video clips of seabed sites.

Site location

If you are working on a particular part of a site, try to use your electronic navigation, sounders, skipper and local knowledge, and other resources to get your shot line as close to the work site as possible. Careful sounding can help you to obtain detailed information about your site such as depth, wreck orientation and extent of wreckage. This can help you to map out your dive site before you start. Transits are a very precise way of locating a dive site. They can be used to pinpoint one part of the site, as can GPS positions.

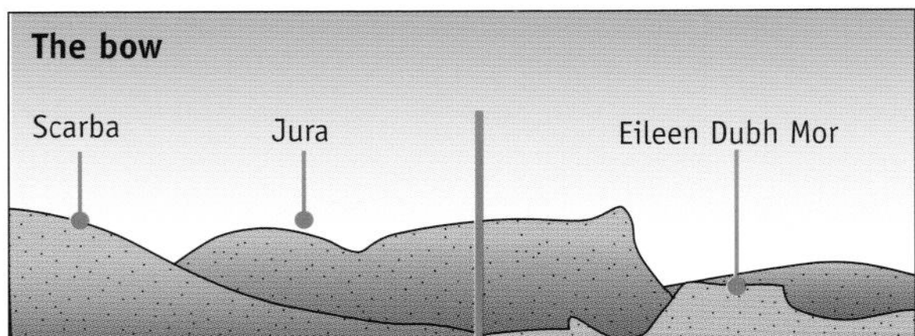

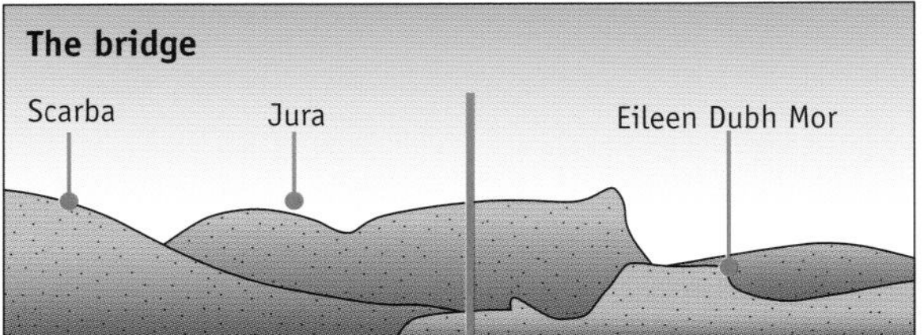

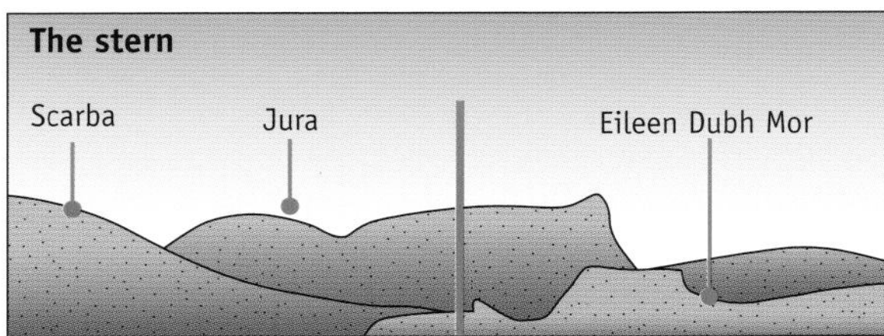

Precise transits for the wreck of the SS Helena Faulbaums, near Oban, can be used to find parts of the wreck

Shot lines

A carefully constructed and placed shot line can ensure an efficient vertical descent. Noting the exact position of a vertical shot line using GPS or transits will help you relocate the site, and with GPS may allow you to accurately plot your work site onto a chart.

A traditional shot line (A) works in a current, but will be distorted in tides or if used to send down heavy toolbags (shown on the line, above), leading to long swims down the line.

A shot line tensioned with a non-collapsible buoy just below the surface (B) allows the surface buoy to rise and fall in the tide and maintain a vertical line. A top-tensioned, self-adjusting shot line is fed through a loop below the surface buoy and a counter weight of a few kilogrammes added to the hanging end to maintain the tension. With this type of shot, in a current the two lines can hang apart from each other and there is a risk of following the wrong one down and ending up at the self-tensioning weight.

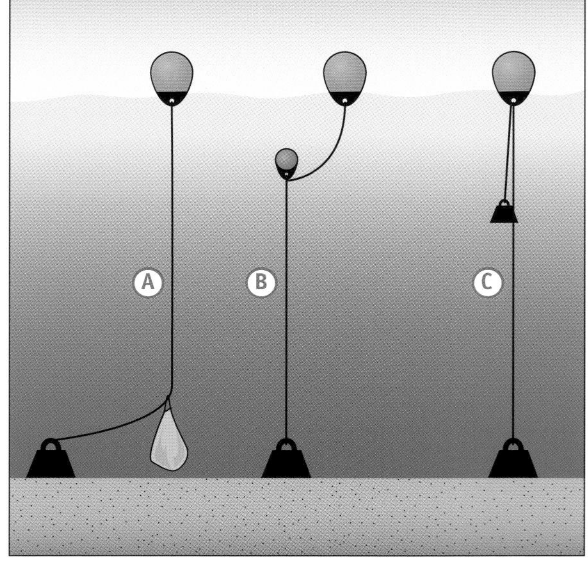

Traditional (A) and top-tensioned (B,C) shot lines have different uses

Equipment

Prepare your tools before going down. For example, predetermined lengths on reels can be measured, slates can be preprepared with diagrams, questions to be answered, keys to marine life, data tables to be filled in, depending on the nature of the work.

When using tape measures and ropes underwater, try to set up as much as you can before you dive. Clearly set out a slate with prompts as to which measurements are to be taken, what lines are to be laid and any other information to be collected.

Practise your task on the surface first.This is especially important if you are working as a dive team – an understanding by everyone of their roles is very important. A good dry run can very quickly identify any problems and allow you chance to sort them out. It also allows you the chance to develop special communication signals, to sort out positioning of divers and to prepare ropes and equipment. If it doesn't work on the surface, it will not work underwater.

Think carefully about the way you will be conducting your work. Underwater activities such as measuring, laying ropes, carrying out detailed surveys, and recording information can often be difficult to achieve.Try to think of ways that will minimise the work. For example, availablility of digital underwater cameras and video cameras means that it is possible to record information photographically rather than manually on a slate or in a notebook. It is then possible to analyse the data after the dive on the a boat or at home.

For example, a detailed plan of a broken up wreck can be achieved by laying a marked grid and photographing from different angles. Similarly, a marine survey could be conducted by photographing quadrats or taking video footage samples of areas of seabed. Clearly these approaches require good visibility.

Collating your information

Having successfully completed your task, it is important to record your study.This can be done either as a written or verbal report.

For a written report, it is helpful to structure it as follows

- Title
- Introduction
- Methods
- Results
- Conclusions (sometimes called the discussion).

The title should clearly describe your project and should name the authors of the report and the participants of the study.

The introduction should include the aims and objectives of the project, what you set out to do and why you did it. It may also contain background information relevant to the study (for example, the history of a wreck).

The methods section should explain how you did the work and, if possible, should be in sufficient detail to allow someone else to repeat your work.

The results should contain the data you have collected, any tables of results, figures containing diagrams (of sites, wrecks, marine organisms and so on) and relevant photographs. It should also describe the key results in the text.

Finally the conclusion, or discussion section, should draw out the key findings of your study. It may 'discuss' any limitations or difficulties you encountered with your project and how they might be overcome in the future. It may comment on how certain you are that the conclusions you have drawn are accurate. For example, you may have surveyed an historic wreck and your conclusions state that 10 cannons were found. However, in your comment you might point out that you encountered a large mass of concreted material and you cannot discount the possibility that further cannons might be obscured within that matter. In the discussion you might compare your findings with those of others who have done something similar. Finally, you might propose 'future work' – what still needs to be done.

Your report may also contain a set of references if you have used other people's work or used diagrams or information from other sources. Sometimes it is also helpful to have a summary at the beginning which provides a description of what you have done in a single succinct paragraph.

A good report is very useful for future reference and could even be published if of sufficient general interest.

Expedition awards

Most expedition leaders are quite modest and take their reward from the satisfaction of having completed the aims of their expedition safely, successfully and, perhaps more importantly, knowing that those participating in the expedition enjoyed the experience.

However, BSAC consider that exceptional expeditions should be more formally recognised; hence the BSAC Expeditions Trophy, which is awarded to an expedition that promotes the true spirit of adventurous diving and discovery of new and interesting diving locations.

In order for an expedition to be judged for the award, a report is submitted to the BSAC Expeditions Officer (see BSAC website). Participants in expeditions with particularly modest expedition leaders may apply on behalf of their expedition leader, but must follow the same submission process and should seek approval from the expedition leader.

The Peter Small Jubilee Trust Award is an award for the most worthwhile and ambitious BSAC project conducted in British waters. The recipient will receive a prestigious medal and a cash prize.

Peter Small was a well known science journalist and co-founder of BSAC. He promoted and was involved in 'inner space' research; a passion that would sadly ultimately claim his life. In December 1962 Peter tragically died aged only 35, during a pioneering deep diving experiment to 1020ft in the Pacific Ocean.

Eligible diving projects should promote the advancement of underwater exploration and the education of the public by encouraging safe diving, while conducting underwater study, research and exploration.

This award is only be made if the project is considered by the British Sub-Aqua Jubilee Trust to be of a satisfactory standard.

The Duke of Edinburgh's Prize by BSAC is an annual prize for the best underwater scientific project carried out by members. When he was President of the Club the Duke offered this prize to BSAC. By agreement with the Club, the Jubilee Trust administers the Prize. Applications are sent to the Trust and the trustees, who represent a wide range of scientific expertise, select a short-list and submit these to the Duke for his final selection.

HRH the Duke of Edinburgh awards the annual Duke of Edinburgh's Prize to the Jurassic Shark team in 2007 for the best scientific project carried out by BSAC members that year

CASE STUDY 9.1

National heritage

One of the finest examples in the world of a wreck survey is that of the Tudor warship the Mary Rose in the Solent on the south coast of England. This was a project that had humble beginnings but became of national importance.

The story

The Mary Rose, one of King Henry VIII's warships, was built in 1510 (although there has been some debate as to the exact dates). She sank on 19 July 1545 during a battle with the French fleet in the Solent. Nearly 500 sailors were lost in the sinking.

Some 400 years later, the discovery of the wreck is a result of the hard work of Alexander McKee. In 1965 he initiated a project with Southsea Branch of BSAC to explore the wrecks of the Solent – with a particular interest in finding the Mary Rose.

The usual diving survey and search techniques available at the time proved unsuccessful and McKee, in collaboration with others, utilised recently developed side-scan sonar techniques. In 1967, they discovered an unusually shaped structure beneath the silt of the Solent that was possibly consistent with the wreck of the Mary Rose.

A committee was set up to manage the project, the Mary Rose (1967) Committee, which included McKee and Margaret Rule, an archaeologist whose name would become forever linked with the Mary Rose.

Between 1968 and 1971 a team of volunteer divers worked exhaustively to establish that the wreck was indeed the Mary Rose. In the winter of 1968, the presence of something under the silt was finally confirmed. The excavation continued with a dredger to remove the top silt layer and divers using water jets and air lifts began to reveal the structure under the silt.

Early on, the discovery of an iron gun and pieces of timber provided stronger evidence that this was the Mary Rose. The discovery in May 1971 of timber frames and decking confirmed her identity.

The project began on a shoe-string budget but by 1979 it had grown and moved onto a professional footing, culminating in 1979 with the formation of the Mary Rose Trust. HRH Prince Charles was the president and Margaret Rule was the Trust's Archaeological Director. By this time, the importance of the discovery had been fully appreciated and it was necessary to professionalise the excavation.

Between 1979 and 1982, Margaret Rule managed volunteer divers from across the world to help with the excavation. Reportedly some 27,800 dives were carried out during this period (a significant proportion of which were amateur volunteers) with some 20,000 artefacts and 3,000 timbers removed for conservation. Both Alexander McKee and Margaret Rule have written books about the project.

One of the original objectives of the Mary Rose Trust was to, if possible, raise the Mary Rose and conserve her for future generations to see. After major engineering achievements by archaeologists, salvage divers and engineers, the Mary Rose was brought to the surface witnessed by 60 million people worldwide, live on television. She was finally towed into Portsmouth Harbour on 11 October 1982. This fantastic achievement was due, at least in part, to the contribution of volunteer divers.

The preserved remnants and artefacts of the Mary Rose are now a major tourist attraction in Portsmouth.

How they did it

- You can see that the expedition had a clear purpose driven by an expedition leader with a determined dive team.
- Some expeditions like the Project Solent Ships do have the potential to become major projects in their own right.
- Such projects usually require substantial and proper funding, and a core of paid full-time staff, although they are often supported by volunteers who realise the project.

Chapter 10

Overseas expeditions

Overseas expeditions can lead to spectacular and stunning diving. They vary from package diving holidays, through self-designed packages to independently organised expeditions.

A package expedition is relatively easily achievable for most divers, as most elements are provided by the travel company. The self-designed package can vary from sourcing your own flights, accommodation and dive package, to a more individual approach involving different dive packages and bespoke diving. The independently organised expedition requires much more organisation and planning, but can result in diving in exotic locations inaccessible to the package diver.

The logistics of a diving expedition get more complex the further away from home you go. Heavy diving equipment cannot always be shipped abroad and so the expedition may involve a certain dependence on others.

Planning an overseas trip uses the same process as any other expedition, but you need to be aware of the differences compared with home; from potentially dangerous marine life to differently organised, or absent, emergency services.

Exotic locations

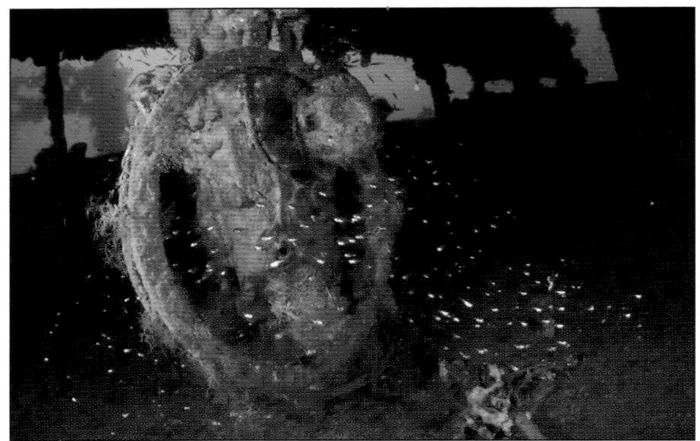

Chuuk lagoon (formerly known as Truk) contains the remains of second world war Japanese ships and aircraft. There are some 70 ships and more than 400 planes sunk within the lagoon

A Galápagos batfish: the Galápagos Islands are the most famous wildlife site in the world. They were made famous by Charles Darwin as the place where he developed his ideas on the theory of evolution

The Red Sea is one of the most accessible coral reef locations for European divers. Although heavily dived, there are still many rarely visited sites

The Great Barrier Reef is the largest coral reef on Earth. It is visited by thousands of divers but still has many unexplored sites

The Mediterranean sea was the birthplace of diving: but many sites remain to be explored such as this Blenheim bomber in 42m off the coast of Malta

Cold-water diving at Silfra fresh-water spring in Iceland rewards divers with crystal clear waters but in water temperatures of 2°

Choosing a destination

Ultimately, as for any expedition, the type of overseas expedition you choose will depend on your team. Your team may be already assembled, for example your dive club, and you will need to tailor the expedition to the experience and organisational abilities of your group. You may wish to join an existing team expedition such as one of the many volunteer coral reef surveys that are undertaken. On the other hand, you may wish to plan an adventurous expedition of your own for which you will need to source your own team, with relevant individual skills, specifically for the purpose.

Key to choosing where to go is also the composition of the team. For a dive club that has not done much recent overseas diving, an ideal first foreign trip might be a dive package to somewhere relatively close to home. The club's overseas diving could develop over several years moving from organised dive packages towards an independently organised expedition - broadening the range of possible sites.

It is impossible to produce a comprehensive list of worldwide diving locations, but a wide selection of places can be found on the BSAC Travel Club website, where you can also find a good deal of information and advice on running overseas expeditions.

You may wish to develop your team or yourself further by encouraging them to undertake a specific project, such as scientific study of a coral reef, producing a dive guide to a wreck diving location or a technical expedition to further the experience levels of your team. If you are able to assemble a bespoke team - the world is your oyster!

Knowing the interests of your team helps you choose an appropriate activity, and there may be the opportunity overseas to do types of diving not available at home. Are your divers interested in wrecks, coral reefs, lagoons, drift dives, wall dives, deep dives, shallow dives, underwater photography, underwater archaeology, inland lakes, ice dives, sharks or other marine species?

Of course, as at home, finance must be considered. Grant funding can be available to help you to develop more challenging expeditions. The BSAC Expedition Grants Scheme (BEGS) sponsors up to five grants a year. The conditions of this scheme are posted on the BSAC website. The BSA Jubilee Trust also provides grants for expeditions that have a specific scientific nature.

The BSAC Travel Club can help you with planning

Various other sources of funding for diving expeditions may be available to individuals, for example, within the military, from the Royal Geographical Society, private companies and charities.

Or there are opportunities to pay to be a volunteer diver within a pre-existing expedition such as those coral reef surveys that are very popular with students. If you have links with global companies, other organisations or the military, you may be able to source facilities, such as boats and accommodation, in other remote places where the organisation operates.

So, before choosing where to go, think about the composition of your team, the interests of your team and the likely financial implications of your chosen destinations.

Making an overseas expedition happen

There are three stages associated with making any expedition happen - the three Ps - planning, preparation and presentation. As we saw in Chapter 3, by far the most important of these are the first two.

As early as possible, a detailed overall plan should be completed to enable the expedition team to start preparing. Be aware that flexibility may be needed, and that the plan may need to be tweaked as preparations progress.

Planning to go overseas

There are some important differences to bear in mind when planning to go overseas.

Having defined broadly where you want to go and what you want to do, the next stage is to conduct research into the potential site or sites. This may be a harder task for overseas locations as you cannot just pop down and see for yourself. It is important that your information is accurate, which means checking several different sources. Also consider the timing of your expedition – make sure that it does not coincide with seasonal bad weather, poor visibility, extremes of temperature or the wrong season for your favourite marine animal.

Research

It is often helpful to begin to research several alternative destinations that will satisfy your criteria. As a picture of each emerges from your research, you will be able to choose which suits the expedition best.

Information is widely available from many sources. A considerable amount of detail is available on the internet, but remember that this may sometimes just be the view of an individual so it's always worth checking other sources. Many books are available – either specialist dive guides, which will help you with the diving aspects, or more general guidebooks that will give you background information about the place, its customs and practicalities.

The BSAC travel website contains much information including reports from other divers who may have been to your proposed location.

Tour operators provide a wealth of information on package expeditions in the form of brochures and advertisements. Dive magazines contain articles and dive guides to a wide range of overseas locations.

An important source of safety information, which should be consulted if you are going anywhere off the well-beaten track, is the government's Foreign and Commonwealth Office website. This will give you information on things such as security warnings and health information.

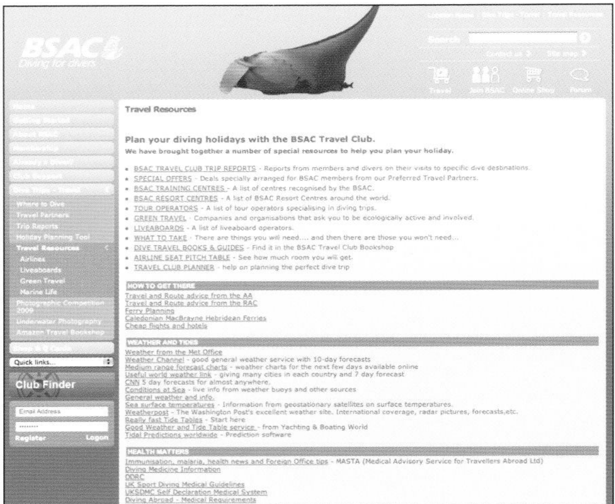

The BSAC travel website contains up-to-date information on many dive locations

Logistics

Having established where you want to go, the next step is to look at the logistics of the trip: ways to get there, where to stay, and what dive or boat facilities you will need. To do this, first consider what it is that you actually need to accomplish your expedition aims. Then look around travel companies, airlines and dive operators to see what combination suits your expedition best. You may choose to go for a package that includes all three or alternatively by putting together travel, accommodation and diving from different sources you may be able to get something more suitable or cheaper.

If your planned expedition is off the beaten track, you will need to do a good deal of planning to ensure that you have suitable support. In an extreme setting, you may need to consider having your own boat, diving equipment, and compressors shipped out to your destination. Care needs to be taken when taking boats abroad as different legal systems will apply. Additional equipment may be required for example. The formal qualifications required of those operating the boat may be different, and extra insurance may well be needed.

The accommodation that you choose must be appropriate for the needs of the expedition. Ensure there is provision for any special needs (such as diet) and that it has appropriate facilities for your team.

If you are on a liveaboard boat, check that the facilities are what you need and that it is equipped (and licensed) to operate in the location, or with the type of diving, you want to do.

Dive planning

Having considered the logistics of the expedition, the next stage is to plan in more detail the key aspects of the diving. This will involve a detailed diving itinerary, a plan of the types of diving, the equipment required and specific risks associated with overseas diving and what responsibilities are expected of the team.

At this point it is important to establish any roles that you expect your team to undertake. These could range from dive managing, through site location and equipment management to catering. This will, of course, depend on your type of expedition; on a package trip many of these activities will be supplied, but need to be planned if your expedition is more reliant on self-organisation. The earlier you allocate responsibilities, the easier it will be for your team members to contribute to the overall plan. It may be helpful to have regular planning meetings to enable the expedition leader to monitor progress and ensure completion of tasks. For a complex overseas expedition, plenty of time will be needed for planning and careful co-ordination by the expedition leader will be necessary to ensure that all pieces in the jigsaw are assembled.

As for home-based expeditions, details of the proposed diving should be communicated to the team members at an early stage. This is important, as members may need to become dive fit, practise techniques, prepare specialist equipment, attend necessary courses and generally achieve a state of preparation appropriate to the expedition.

Safety

Don't forget to plan for the safety of your expedition. Make sure you know the location of local recompression chambers, local hospitals and local doctors. Make sure you know how to contact emergency services and how to evacuate divers to appropriate facilities. If these facilities do not exist, you may need to consider alternatives. You may wish to assemble medically trained personnel on your expedition, or you may consider it necessary to secure a boat with recompression facilities if you are travelling to extreme locations.

Plan an evacuation or emergency strategy (with relevant contact details) and have it available in written form for the team members. Special communications equipment, such as satellite phones or medium frequency radios, may be necessary.

General safety information is available from the BSAC website and Divers Alert Network (DAN). At a well known dive site, safety information may be available from BSAC branches, local dive operators, local skippers and local communities.

In more remote regions you may need to become self reliant, with proper planning and seeking general advice from books like the *Royal Geographical Society Expedition Manual*. The RGS website lists many other specialist expedition manuals including several on expedition medicine (see RGS website).

Health

Don't forget to consider the well-being of your group when not diving. One of the most disruptive aspects can be illness. Although, you can plan and prepare to avoid the major illnesses (see *Disease prevention,* page 150), your team members may be beset by minor, but uncomfortable, illnesses such as stomach problems, as a result of a change of diet or exposure to contaminated food and water.

If your expedition is based in hot, tropical or developing countries, you should take care with what you eat. In general, always eat freshly cooked food and drink boiled or bottled water. Although at home fruit and salad might seem healthy options, in certain parts of the world these are washed in water that may be contaminated or grown in areas where human excrement is used as a fertiliser. In general, avoid fruit and salads that you have not washed yourself.

Shellfish, although often a favourite with divers, should be avoided. These animals are able to concentrate bacteria and toxins that are not always killed by the light cooking usually associated with shellfish. If you must eat shellfish, it should be boiled for a minimum of eight minutes. You should also avoid eating some types of fish that are either toxic in their own right, such as pufferfish, or can ingest toxic micro-organisms during 'red tides', for example. Symptoms of this kind of poisoning include pins and needles and paralysis and may require basic life support.

Because of the differing climates, and differences in temperature encountered in different parts of the world it is often necessary to use different types of protective suit to maintain body temperature. Beware of sunstroke and dehydration, both of which can predispose to decompression illness.

Disease prevention

It is important to consider what vaccinations and prophylactic drugs, such as anti-malarials, might be needed to protect against endemic diseases at your destination. The vaccines you require will depend on where you are going. In general, find out early for some vaccinations as the course may be several months long. Some can also induce uncomfortable side effects, which are best avoided just before an expedition.

There is currently only one disease that requires World Health Organization certified vaccination for entry to some countries and that is yellow fever.

Some vaccinations are routinely given in childhood, but boosters may be required at regular intervals. These general vaccinations should be in date when you travel abroad. Others are only needed if you are travelling to areas of high risk. The main diseases and locations where vaccines are required are summarised in the vaccination requirements table (opposite).

For two of the most serious diseases, Malaria and HIV, there are no vaccines. It is important to understand the mode of transmission of the disease and then to take steps to avoid infection. Malaria is transmitted by mosquito bites while HIV is transmitted by contact with infected blood or sexual intercourse. At sea, both diseases are generally of low risk to divers.

Malaria is found in Africa, South-east Asia, and South and Central America: divers are most likely to encounter it in the Red Sea, some parts of the Carribbean and dives sites in the Far East. Mosquitos feed principally between dusk and dawn. Wearing long sleeves and long trousers during these times is essential to reduce the chances of bites. The use of the insect repellent DEET (Diethyltoluamide) on exposed skin can also reduce chances of bites. At night, insecticide-treated mosquito nets spread over the bed are effective barriers.

Drugs are available for the treatment of malaria – but these do not provide the complete solution. They may not be 100-per-cent effective. Liberal use of these drugs has resulted in drug resistance in most parts of the world. Some can have serious side effects. Mefloquine (brand name Lariam) is effective in most areas of the world and there is little resistance to it. However, it can be associated with unpleasant side effects (nausea, giddiness, insomnia and, rarely, more serious nervous problems such as epilepsy). It is generally not recommended for use by divers because of the similarity of the side effects to the symptoms of decompression illness. Malaria can be a fatal disease: you should consult your GP and a diving doctor for advice on the best drugs to use.

HIV is a worldwide disease, but particularly prevalent in African countries. It can be prevented by avoiding contact with human blood: the use of gloves when conducting first aid or handling blood is the most effective protection.

Most GPs should be able to advise on travel drugs. For specific information on diving, BSAC medical referees should be consulted (see BSAC website). Generic information is available from the Department of Health (UK), the excellent website hosted by the Centre for Diseases Control (CDC) in the USA and the World Health Organization.

Local customs

Consider local regulations such as permission to dive, wreck laws, marine life laws, laws on alcohol consumption, community laws, sensitivities to religion and general behaviour towards local people.

Vaccination requirements			
Vaccination	Primary course of vaccination	Booster required	Region(s) of the world
General			
Tetanus	3 months	Yes	Worldwide. Most people vaccinated in childhood.
Polio	Monthly	Yes	Developing countries. Most people vaccinated in childhood.
Diptheria	3 months	Yes	Worldwide but rare. Most people vaccinated in childhood.
Haemophilus influenzae	4–6 months	Yes	Worldwide. Most people vaccinated in childhood.
Influenza	Single dose	Yes	Worldwide. Given to at-risk groups, such as the elderly.
Pneumococcal infection	Single dose	Yes	Worldwide. Most people vaccinated in childhood.
Travel-specific			
Yellow fever	Single dose	Yes	Mainly sub-saharan Africa and South America.
Typhoid	Up to 2 months	Yes	Common in regions associated with poor hygiene. Waterborne –possible risk to divers.
Hepatitis A	Single dose	Yes	Common in regions associated with poor hygiene.
Hepatitis B	6 months	Yes	Worldwide. Spread by sexual intercourse and by blood transfusion.
Tuberculosis	Single dose	No	Developing countries. Usually covered by a BCG vaccination in childhood.
Japanese B encephalitis	1 month	Yes	Rural Asia. Mosquito transmission – low risk to divers.
Tick-borne encephalitis	Up to 6 months	Yes	Forested areas of Europe – low risk to divers.
Meningococcal infection	Single dose	Yes	Mainly sub-saharan Africa but can occur worldwide. Low risk to divers.
Rabies	1 month	Yes	Worldwide except UK, Scandinavia and Australia. Dog bites – low risk to divers.
Cholera	Since 2004, 'Dukoral' has been available. You are advised to consult your doctor	-	Mainly sub-saharan Africa and South-east Asia. Associated with poor hygiene.

Checklist of paperwork required for an overseas expedition

- ❑ Passports (valid for at least six months before return)
- ❑ Visa, if necessary
- ❑ Extra photographs in case of need for local visas or passes
- ❑ Photocopy of your passport
- ❑ Driving licence (and any special requirements for your destination)
- ❑ Money (travellers cheques or local currency – check in advance)
- ❑ Credit/debit cards (check in advance)
- ❑ Insurance documentation and contacts
- ❑ Important phone numbers/contacts at home
- ❑ Important phone number/contacts at your destination (embassy, hotel, dive operator etc)
- ❑ Vaccination certificates if required
- ❑ Any relevant medical paperwork
- ❑ Diving qualification records and log books
- ❑ Photocopies of diving qualifications and log books
- ❑ Information (eg serial numbers, photographs, description) on any valuable items
- ❑ Luggage contents list (especially diving equipment) in case of loss
- ❑ Paperwork or licenses needed for customs (eg related to importation/dangerous goods)
- ❑ Test certificates for cylinders if transporting

Going overseas

Preparing to go overseas

Make sure team members know the full details of the expedition - for example costs, what they will get, what they need to do and what they need to bring. You can then obtain deposits upfront.

Hopefully your planning stage will have identified helpers within the team to carry out specific tasks. Someone will need to book flights, boats and diving facilities as planned. This will form the basic platform for the expedition. Where possible try to use suppliers who can be trusted - most major travel suppliers are bonded and you will have some security. However, smaller local businesses may not be. Try to obtain references from other users or seek details through a local national tourist office.

Although late bookings and budget airlines may offer the promise of bargains - these may be less flexible options. Luggage allowances can often be very small. The bare minimum of diving equipment (suit, basic equipment, regulators, key accessories, no weights and, of course, no cylinders) is likely to weigh 15-20kg. You may need to arrange a further 10-20kg for normal luggage or pay for excess baggage. Try to ensure that any deals you secure are confirmed in writing.

Visa applications, diving permits and any other necessary paperwork should be completed well in advance of the expedition. Don't forget to encourage your team members to check that their passports are in date. Many countries require a passport that is valid for six months after the expected departure date. It is often worth taking passport photocopies and extra photos in case of the need to apply for local visas or permits.

Find out the currency used at your destination and in any transit countries. Ensure that your team members are briefed on costs so that they take enough money with them. Find out what local sources of money such as cash machines and banks are available.

Each team member should have appropriate travel and dive insurance. Check that the insurance covers the diving and other activities that will be carried out. Make sure that it is valid for the geographical location of your expedition - remember this may include travelling across country boundaries by sea.

A checklist of required paperwork may be useful for your team. Dive operators should check your diving qualifications as a matter of course and they may ask to see your recent logbook. Don't forget specialist qualifications such as nitrox or trimix if appropriate.

It may help to have photocopies of qualifications with you in case a dive operator wishes to keep a record of your qualifications.

Finally, don't forget that there may be language differences - remember to take a phrasebook and dictionary.

When booking your diving activities, make sure you know what you are getting. Obtain information on cylinder sizes, pressures, available breathing gases, connections (A-clamp/DIN fittings), weights and other equipment. Make sure you agree with the operator that they are able to accommodate the number and type of dives you are expecting to do. Make sure the dives you will be doing, if you have no control over them, are suitable for the qualifications and experience of your team.

Before you go, organise a shake-down dive to ensure that everyone is fit and ready. This gives you a last minute opportunity to talk to the team and make sure that everything is on track.

Running an expedition overseas

The day-to-day running of an overseas expedition mirrors that of any expedition (see Chapter 5). It is important that the dives are properly dive managed, that normal diver safety considerations are adhered to.

The management of your overseas expedition may vary. On a bespoke expedition, the expedition leader will manage the diving activities as is the case for any expedition - including liaison with the boat skipper as necessary. On other types of expeditions, such as package trips, the diving may be managed by a local divemaster or by the boat operators. In these cases, make sure that safety is being considered.

You should be briefed on the diving activities - listen to what is said as there might be important safety information given. If you are not given a brief, find out information for yourself, by asking, and ensure that your team are aware of what to expect -for example, depths, times and possible hazards. As always, plan your dive and dive your plan. Try to

Dangerous sea creatures and their effects			
Animal	**Effects**	**First aid**	
Stingrays	Injuries caused by treading on spines are most common	Immerse wound in warm water, but not hot water (45°C) Beware secondary problems, such as tetanus	
Sea snakes	Can cause paralysis and cardiac problems	Medical evacuation important Treatment with anti-venom if available	
Portuguese Man of War	Cause severe systemic effects, such as cardiac arrest	Remove tentacles without touching Apply vinegar or dilute acetic acid Medical evacuation important	
Stone fish	Poisonous toxin in spines	Medical evacuation important Anti-venom may be available in some parts of the world	
Lion fish	Poisonous toxin in spines	Medical evacuation important	
Cone shells	Some of these contain serious neurotoxins	No anti-venom available Medical evacuation important	
Blue-ringed octopus	Has a beak that can penetrate a diving suit Venom can cause death within minutes	No anti-venom available Medical evacuation important	
Sea urchins	Spines embedded in feet when trodden on	Spines can be removed with forceps	

maintain some structure to your diving - such as pairing up with a buddy, conducting buddy checks and briefs - even if this is not promoted by the dive operator. Make sure you plan your own decompression routines and keep relevant dive management records to ensure that you or your team members are not at risk. In general, ensure that the actual diving is appropriate to the experience and qualifications of your team members.

During your diving overseas, you may encounter different diving practices with different diving organisations. This may include different signals, different approaches to rescue techniques and even different approaches to diving. If possible, familiarise yourself with differences before you go, but if you can't then you should try to find out as much as you can before diving.

Potentially dangerous sea creatures

Exposure to potentially dangerous animals is another important difference between diving at home or overseas. These can broadly be grouped into those that are poisonous to touch and those that may attack. The larger marine animals, such as sharks and stingrays, are probably the most high profile, but if your expedition takes you to African lakes do not forget crocodiles and hippopotamus.

Encounters with venomous and poisonous animals are most likely to be accidental rather than a deliberate attack. For example, stingrays will not attack unless they are disturbed or trodden on in shallow water. Most other venomous animals are also encountered accidentally, for example, drifting into jellyfish, treading on sea urchins and coming across sea snakes in rock crevices. However, despite the accidental nature of such encounters, the injuries can be serious and in certain cases can result in cardiac arrest.

For the expedition team, it is important to know which species in your location are poisonous and how to recognise them. Avoidance is far better than cure.

Diving with sharks

Your expedition may be directed at diving with sharks or you may just encounter the sharks as part of the normal diving. In both cases you should be prepared. If you suspect casual encounters with sharks, you should brief your divers and include a risk management protocol to cover encounters. Obviously there are different risks associated with different types of sharks, but in general sharks will not deliberately attack you. Your risk assessment should include research on the species of shark and the likely risk of encounter. If you do encounter sharks there is some general advice on how to dive with them.

Sharks can be watched quietly from 5 to 10m away

- Watch from a distance.
- Keep your breathing steady: relaxed with slow exhalations.
- Avoid movement where possible and particularly rapid movements.
- You should be between 5 and 10m away from a shark, at least.
- Avoid swimming towards the shark or chasing it from behind - these types of movements are threatening and can agitate the shark.
- Do not attempt to feed the shark.
- Do not shine bright lights or strobes into sharks' eyes.
- Take care when entering caves or going under overhangs as these can be refuges for sharks.

If your expedition is deliberately aiming to dive with sharks, you may wish to use specialist equipment such as chain mail or shark cages depending on the species you wish to encounter. These techniques are beyond the scope of this book and you should use dedicated operators or seek specialist advice.

Despite all of the hazards associated with overseas diving - few incidents are reported and, with careful risk management, the experience far outweighs the risks. The expedition leader must be prepared to manage the team just as they would on an expedition at home. This may also include dealing with problems, conflicts or other unexpected occurrences. Remember that the expedition leader should try to make the expedition as enjoyable for everyone as possible.

CASE STUDY 10.1

Science in warm waters

'Exercise Jurassic Shark' to the Cocos Islands was carried out by a 14-person, joint-services group from the British Army, Royal Navy and Royal Air Force.

The aims of the expedition were to use radio and satellite tags to track the movement of hammerhead sharks in the Cocos Islands. The expedition personnel were accompanied by a scientist – the Director of Field Operations, Shark Research Institute – and they were accompanied by the President of PRETOMA, a Costa Rican government organisation.

The following briefly describes their expedition.

The story

Shark populations are top-level predators that are important for maintaining appropriate population levels of other species. They are in significant decline as a result of fishing and other activities.

The aims of this expedition were to monitor the behaviour of these sharks and to track their movements. The sharks feed in deep water by night and then return to specific areas by day to be cleaned by cleaner fish (the Barber fish). At cleaning stations, the sharks were tagged using spear guns with either radio or satellite tags. This tagging method seemed to cause little distress to the sharks – unlike traditional methods involving shark capture.

Divers used rebreathers to enable them to get as close to the sharks as possible. Data was collected from the tagged sharks using hydrophones at specific locations and by the download of information from satellite tags to satellites. The expedition was also able to photograph and report on illegal fishing activity in the area.

How they did it

- The organisation of the expedition started in May 2005.
- The expedition took place on 14 days in July 2006.
- Preparation included submission of grant proposals to obtain funding to cover part of the costs and diver training in Plymouth prior to the expedition.
- The expedition cost £51,000. Of this, £38,000 was raised from grant funding with some 20 different grants ranging from £15,000 to £30. The participants themselves paid 25 per cent of the costs – around £1,000 per head. The major costs were the hire of the research vessel the MV Undersea Hunter and diving activities (£27,000) and flights (£10,000).
- Diving was conducted to depths of 40m on rebreathers and nitrox was used to reduce nitrogen loading.
- A total of 307 dives were conducted by the 14-person team
- The expedition was successful. It has led to the funding for follow-up studies and another expedition.

A diver sets up a hydrophone receiver

CASE STUDY 10.2

Cold unknown waters

An expedition to the Falkland Islands was run by BSAC branch members from Darwen Sub Aqua Club and Ribble Valley Sub Aqua Club in 2007 to explore a new part of the world, but also to celebrate Darwen SAC's 25th anniversary.

The story

The four-week expedition involved 16 divers who ranged from BSAC Sport Diver to First Class Diver.

During the expedition more than 30 different sites were dived including *'awesome pinnacles, undived wrecks, drifts and amazing scenic dives with penguins, sea lions and dolphins' ... 'some of the most spectacular diving I have ever done'* to quote an expedition member. For example, the expedition dived the north side of Kidney Island where they encountered a large number of sea lions and penguins swimming around them underwater – a unique experience! They also dived the Argentinian supply ship Buonos Concardinia, which was sunk during the Falklands conflict. Using the charted information on the wreck, the expedition was able to find it within 20 minutes of arriving at its charted position. The orientation and condition were determined as part of the dive, including missile damage on the port side. Another stunning dive was on Sunk Rock – a pinnacle that descended from 12m to a charted depth of 70m. The team discovered a sheer wall on the north-west side that dropped away presumably to 70m. Visibility was around 15m.

Transportation around the islands was very difficult although the team were fortunate to be able to find a local who was able to help them out. The greatest challenge, however, was to ensure safety due to the very remote locations for diving.

How they did it

- The planning for the expedition started 18 months before departure and initially involved the expedition leader and a small team.
- The financing of the expedition was exclusively from the trip members and worked out at around £2,400 per person – which for a two-week stint on the month-long expedition (including flights and accommodation) to such a remote location is very good value.
- The team researched the dive sites using charts, the internet, sailing guides and war diaries.
- The tidal stream information, it turned out, was not always reliable and currents were often unexpected.
- There were no diving facilities available on the Falklands, so everything had to be taken from the UK. The team packed all of their equipment into a container and this was dispatched to the Falklands. The equipment taken included including J-sized oxygen cylinders, two compressors, two RIBs and all the dive kit.
- All diving was conducted from the RIBs. There were some problems, for example, one of the boat engines developed an electrical fault.
- To enable the team to locate dive sites, they also took along side scan sonar, sounders and magnetometers – although the latter was used with limited success due to technical difficulties.
- Divers used nitrox and were limited to no-stop diving with maximum depths of 30m. This was because there was no recompression chamber on the island, no VHF radio and no search and rescue services.
- The container got stuck at the customs in Montevideo for four weeks on the return leg as the ship broke down. While being repaired at Montevideo, the ship was inspected as the O_2 Js had been declared as dangerous goods. The Uruguayan customs wanted the test certificates for each cylinder. This would have taken some time to get from the cylinder supplier, but customs settled for one certificate plus an administration fee.

Overall, the expedition was a resounding success and the team were able to dive in a very adventurous location. The expedition was organised solely by amateur divers without any professional back up or resources and is a good example of what can be achieved with good planning and preparation.

A nitrox filling station was set up on site

Everything had to be brought from the UK...

...including two complete dive boats

Credits

Photography

ADUS imagery	88, 89
Paul Brown, Darwen Sub Aqua Club	157
Bob Anderson and Grigor Browning, Halton Charters	26, 86, 87
Argyll Shipwrecks by Peter Moir and Ian Crawford	37
Tony Baskeyfield	146, 153
Richard Booth	35, 153
Simon Campbell	157
Christopher Dobbs, Mary Rose Trust	143
Geoff Hide	20, 22
Andy Hunt	35, 82, 88, 107
Gareth Lock	69
Orkney Library	81
Tim Priest	146
Major Andy Reid	155
Sophie Rennie	67
Simon Rogerson	142
© Crown Copyright and/or database rights. Reproduced by permission of the Controller of Her Majesty's Stationery Office and the UK Hydrographic Office (www.ukho.gov)	18, 21, 35, 36, 38, 84

All other photography Charles Hood

Acknowledgments

Alison Allan
Colin Aldridge and Bob Williams, Aquascan International
Bob Anderson, Halton Charters
Richard Booth
Thorsten Brabetz, Queen's University of Belfast
Simon Campbell, Ribble Valley Sub Aqua Club
Brian Cumming, BSAC Incidents Adviser
Darwen Sub Aqua Club
Ian Dearden, Darwen Sub Aqua Club
Hywel Dyer
Malcolm Gauld
Paul Haynes
Geoff Hide
Stephen Hodgkins
Andy Hunt
Mark Lawrence, ADUS Ltd and Lochaline Dive Centre
Jane Maddocks, BSAC Wreck Protection and Underwater Heritage Officer
Paul Morris
Nautical Archaeology Society
Robert Peacock
Andy Proctor, BSAC Safety and Rescue Skills Chief Officer
Major Andy Reid
Alastair Reynolds, BSAC
Alan Riley, Riley Electronics Design Ltd
Jeff Reed, BSAC
Mike Rowley
Dave Sydenham
Alan Thomas
Tyneside 114 Sub Aqua Club
Ian Vine
Jim Watson, BSAC
771 Naval Air Squadron - RNAS Culdrose (HMS Seahawk)

Index